AUTHENTIC RECIPES FROM THE REGIONS OF MEXICO

MÉXICO

THE BEAUTIFUL COOKBOOK

Fruit Punch (left, recipe page 54) and Melon Water (right, recipe page 54)

AUTHENTIC RECIPES FROM THE REGIONS OF MEXICO

MÉXICO
THE BEAUTIFUL COOKBOOK

RECIPES BY
SUSANNA PALAZUELOS

TEXT BY
MARILYN TAUSEND

PHOTOGRAPHS BY
IGNACIO URQUIZA

CollinsPublishersSanFrancisco
A Division of HarperCollinsPublishers

First published in U.S.A. 1991 by
Collins Publishers San Francisco

Conceived and produced by Weldon Owen Pty Limited
43 Victoria Street, McMahons Point,
Sydney, NSW 2060, Australia
Phone (02) 929 5677   Fax (02) 929 8352
A member of the Weldon International
   Group of Companies
Sydney • San Francisco • Chicago • London • Paris

Weldon Owen
President: John Owen
Publishing Manager: Stuart Laurence
Foreign Editions Editor: Derek Barton
Managing Editor: Jane Fraser
Project Coordinator: Laurie Wertz
Editor: Virginia Croft
Recipe Translators: Thomas and Carol Christensen
Production: Stephanie Sherman, Mick Bagnato
Design: John Miller, Big Fish Books
Design Concept: John Bull, The Book Design Co.
Map: Mike Gorman
Illustrations: Neil Shigley
Food Stylists: Laura Caraza, Mónica Patiño,
   Kay Mendieta de Alonso
Prop Stylists: Mariana Hagerman, Constanza Linares
Photography Assistant: René López

Library of Congress Cataloging-in-Publication Data:

Palazuelos, Susanna.
   Mexico the beautiful cookbook :
authentic recipes from the regions of
Mexico / recipes by Susanna Palazuelos ;
text by Marilyn Tausend ; photography by
Ignacio Urquiza ; [translators, Thomas and
Carol Christensen ; illustrations, Neil
Shigley].
      p.   cm.
   Includes index.
   ISBN 0-00-215949-X
   1. Cookery, Mexican. 2. Mexico—
   Description and travel—1981-
   I. Tausend, Marilyn.   II. Title.
TX716.M4P35   1991
641.5972—dc20   90-28890

Production by Mandarin Offset, Hong Kong
Printed in Hong Kong

A Weldon Owen ◆ Production

*Pages 2–3: The fishing village of Río Lagartos, in
northern Yucatán, home to thousands of pink flamingos.*

*Right: Bullfighting, la fiesta brava, was introduced by the
Spanish over four centuries ago and remains one of Mexico's
most popular spectator sports.*

*Pages 8–9: Fish Soup (left, recipe page 72) and Clam Soup
(right, recipe page 72, made with clams in their shells).*

*Page 10: Manila mangoes are a special treat, available in
Mexican markets only for a few months each year.*

*Pages 12–13: The rugged scenery near Zacatecas City,
an important mining region.*

*Endpapers: A candy shop in Puebla, Mexico's favorite town
for sweets.*

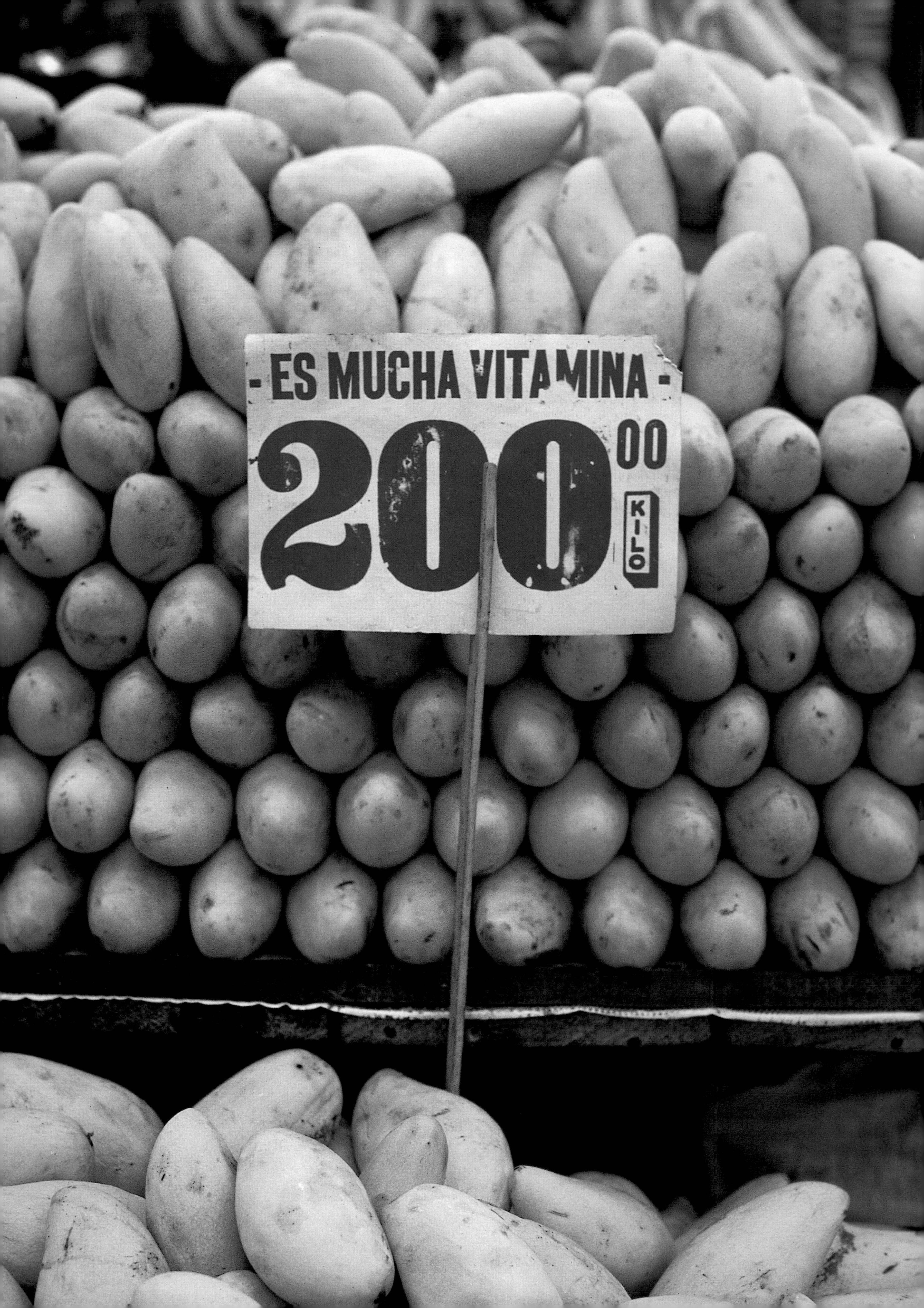

- ES MUCHA VITAMINA -
200 00
KILO

CONTENTS

A Maya woman heads home with her daily supply of masa.

INTRODUCTION

Until recently, most average food lovers thought of Mexican cooking in terms of *tacos, tamales* and tongue-scorching *salsas.* Few were aware of the exquisite *moles* and *pipianes* with their sauces of ground pumpkin seeds and spices, or the naturally "cooked" *ceviche,* a medley of raw seafood marinated in lime juice. Nor did they know that the soul-satisfying cup of hot chocolate they happily sipped on a cold winter day was a gift of the cacao and vanilla of Mexico's first civilizations. Then, in the mid-1970s, British-born Diana Kennedy stirred up the gastronomical world with her cookbooks on the regional cuisines of Mexico, and it was realized that such exotic ingredients as squash blossoms and the fleshy paddles of nopal cactus were being used by Mexican cooks to create subtly flavored dishes very similar to those prepared by the Aztecs. It became obvious that Mexican food was not just another fast food but a distinct and truly great cuisine.

Mexican cooking is more than indigenous dishes journeying untouched through the centuries. It is the grafting of the fruits and vegetables, meats, grains and spices of the Old World onto the root stock of the native foods, resulting in a cuisine that reflects the buffeting and enrichment of its turbulent evolution through the centuries—crêpes of exotic corn fungus, bowls of steaming *menudo,* pit-roasted pork seasoned with the unique flavors of *achiote* and bitter orange, crystallized limes plumped full of grated coconut and,

yes, the uncountable varieties of *tacos, tamales* and *salsas,* shockingly hot to the unprepared palate.

It is thought that ancient ancestors of the early Americans crossed the narrow Bering Sea land bridge and, in a continual search for food, slowly migrated south. Like all primitive people, they lived to eat—and they ate to live. Life revolved around this essential fact. They traveled on foot, carrying their meager possessions, for they did not know of the wheel and had no pack animals. The land was diverse: two lacerating mountain ranges severed the arid highland deserts from the coastal plains. From time to time over the centuries, as they slowly migrated southward, a certain valley would appeal to one clan or a high plateau to another. There they settled, developing their own ways of life around the plants and animals they encountered.

From the beginning, corn has been central to the cuisine of Mexico. Its history began when nomadic hunters discovered that they could obtain a life-sustaining food by poking a hole in the ground with a pointed stick, dropping in a tiny kernel of maize, nurturing it and finally bringing in the harvest, preparing it and eating it. These farmers forged a pattern of culture that would continue for nearly three thousand years. The drama is complicated, involving many different peoples whose plots often overlapped. The Olmecs of Mexico's Gulf coast opened on the stage, followed by the dwellers of Teotihuacán, a metropolis that endured for centuries on the high

In the rugged highlands of Chiapas, Indians preserve the pre-Hispanic way of life, growing the corn and herbs basic to their diet.

15

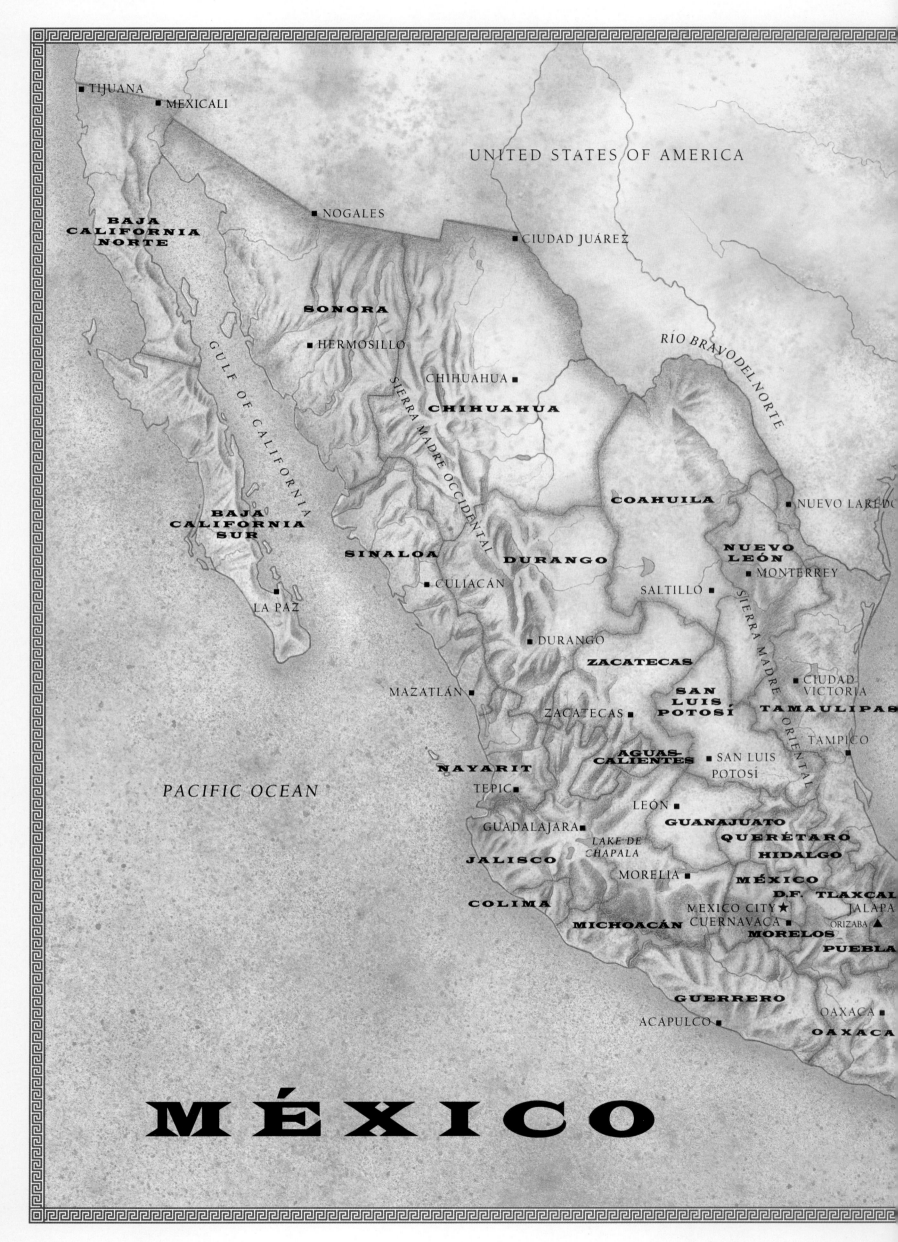

UNITED STATES OF AMERICA

■ TIJUANA
■ MEXICALI

BAJA CALIFORNIA NORTE

■ NOGALES

■ CIUDAD JUÁREZ

RÍO BRAVO DEL NORTE

GULF OF CALIFORNIA

SONORA

■ HERMOSILLO

CHIHUAHUA ■
CHIHUAHUA

SIERRA MADRE OCCIDENTAL

COAHUILA

■ NUEVO LAREDO

BAJA CALIFORNIA SUR

SINALOA

■ CULIACÁN

DURANGO

NUEVO LEÓN
■ MONTERREY

SALTILLO ■

LA PAZ

■ DURANGO

ZACATECAS

SIERRA MADRE ORIENTAL

■ CIUDAD VICTORIA

TAMAULIPAS

MAZATLÁN ■

SAN LUIS POTOSÍ

ZACATECAS ■

■ TAMPICO

AGUAS-CALIENTES

■ SAN LUIS POTOSÍ

PACIFIC OCEAN

NAYARIT

TEPIC ■

LEÓN ■

GUANAJUATO

QUERÉTARO

GUADALAJARA ■

LAKE DE CHAPALA

HIDALGO

JALISCO

MORELIA ■

MÉXICO

COLIMA

MEXICO CITY ★

D.F. TLAXCAL
JALAPA

MICHOACÁN

CUERNAVACA ■
ORIZABA ▲

MORELOS

PUEBLA

GUERRERO

OAXACA ■

ACAPULCO ■

OAXACA

MÉXICO

GULF OF MEXICO

MÉRIDA

YUCATÁN

CAMPECHE

ERACRUZ

VERACRUZ

CAMPECHE

QUINTANA ROO

CHETUMAL

TABASCO

VILLAHERMOSA

ISTMO DE TEHUANTEPEC

CHIAPAS

SAN CRISTÓBAL DE LAS CASAS

TUXTLA GUTIÉRREZ

BELIZE

GUATEMALA

HONDURAS

EL SALVADOR

plateaus outside present-day Mexico City. In the southwest's high valleys there were the Zapotecs, followed closely by the Mixtecs and, far to the south, the Mayas. Tula, capital of the Toltecs, would later replace Teotihuacán in power and set the militaristic pattern of the years to come. And in a grand finale, the Aztecs would follow the Toltecs onto center stage and create the splendor that greeted the soldiers of Hernán Cortés when the curtain went down in the autumn of 1519.

On a set on the other side of the world, the Romans found that eating food became not just a necessity but a pleasure when it was seasoned, and the supreme seasoning was black pepper. After the fall of the Roman Empire in A.D. 395, the value of pepper became so high that a pound was equal to a pound of gold. Over the next thousand years fantastic tales of lands far to the east continued to reach the ears of the rulers of Europe. Then, in the late 1200s, the young adventurer Marco Polo proclaimed that limitless quantities of the fiery black spice could be found in the East, and so began a two-century race among European countries to determine who would control the sea route to what became known as the "spice" islands.

We all know that in 1492 Columbus sailed in search of a western route to India and the spice islands and, thinking he had reached them when he sighted land, named the native people "Indians" and the pungent seasoning they were using "pepper." While he never set foot on the American continent, he nevertheless brought about the gastronomical linking of Europe and the Americas.

Characteristic of ruins in southern Mexico, chac-mool sculptures were placed at the entrances to temples, as recipients of sacrificial offerings to gods.

"I saw neither sheep nor goats nor any other beast—all the trees were as different from ours as day from night and so the fruits, the herbage, the rocks and all things," recorded Columbus of his first landing in the Bahamas on October 12, 1492. This was soon rectified, for on his second voyage he brought pigs, goats, sheep and chickens from his homeland, as well as cattle and horses. He left the animals to multiply, and multiply they did, especially the voracious pig. Twenty-seven years later, when Cortés left Cuba for his conquest of the New World, he had a living commissary to provision his troops. Only several hundred miles apart, the two worlds were about to collide, forever changing the eating habits of the rest of the world.

In the land soon to be known as Mexico, vast agricultural civilizations were flourishing. The vegetarian triad of squash, beans and maize was the main sustenance of the people, though the nobles and priests ate such delicacies as quail and turkeys, small hairless dogs, fish and wild game, and drank *pulque* and chocolate. *Atole,* a corn gruel, was the usual first meal of the day for all, and the main meal was composed of *tamales* and stews flavored with mouth-blistering *chiles* and scooped up with tortillas.

The new settlers came from all the different provinces of Spain, bringing with them the ingredients and memories of a cuisine infused by twenty-eight generations of Moorish control. Not only livestock and poultry but wheat, rice, onions, garlic, citrus fruit and sugar cane found an accepting home in the new land.

A ranch in San Luis Potosí, where sheep is used for Sunday barbacoa. The meat is wrapped in fragrant maguey leaves and cooked underground.

Never before—or after—has there been a culinary merger with such a widespread influence.

The Spaniards came to the New World in search of gold, but it was their discovery of new foods that has had the greatest impact on the world: corn, beans of great variety, peanuts, sweet potatoes, squashes, pumpkins, tomatoes and the little-known but highly nutritional amaranth. The fruits they found—the fragrant pineapple, guava, papaya and avocado—have enriched the diets of many people, and the three major flavorings from Mexico—*chile,* chocolate and vanilla—certainly changed the taste of foods eaten around the world.

Think how dull an Indian curry would be without *chiles* to give it life—or a Hungarian goulash without paprika. It is said that in Hunan, people can live without meat but not without hot pepper. Imagine Italian food without the Mexican contribution. There would be no pizza or spaghetti without tomatoes; no polenta without corn; no minestrone without beans and zucchini. So, too, there would be no Spanish gazpacho, no German chocolate cake, no Swiss candy bars, no American turkey and pumpkin pie.

The true dawn of Mexican cuisine began when the Spanish allowed the subjugated Indians to have a few chickens, a pig, a goat or even occasionally a sheep or cow. Pork in particular was favored, and all parts of the animal were consumed with gusto. At first the Spaniards wanted to eat only dishes from home, but soon the ingenuity of Indian cooks expanded their culinary horizons, and the two food cultures merged into one, with *masa* dishes and *chiles* finding a place on Spanish tables, and eggs, meat, cheeses and citrus fruits eagerly adopted by the Indians and mestizos.

To the Spaniards it was not enough just to subjugate the Indians; it was equally important to save their souls. From the very beginning the Catholic church participated in the conquest of Mexico. With the establishment of convents, nuns began to play a crucial role in developing the cuisine of the country, using their imagination to transform the ingredients they found in the marketplace into complex and exotic dishes like *moles* and many sweets and desserts, which soon found their way into the homes of wealthy and aristocratic Creole and Spanish families.

For nearly three hundred years, Mexico was dominated by the Spanish aristocracy. September 16, the anniversary of the day in 1810 when Mexico proclaimed its independence from Spain, is a holiday passionately celebrated everywhere in the country. Beginning with the "cry for Independence" by the president the night before, the air reverberates with the emotional excitement of the people and the sound of exploding fireworks. Food stalls and vendors line the streets, and restaurants are packed with people enjoying the traditional *tacos, pozole, birria* and *enchiladas.*

Unfortunately, independence did not bring tranquility. During the following half-century, various improvised armies crisscrossed the mountains and valleys of Mexico, breaking the barriers of culinary seclusion. The women not only fought alongside their men but learned to adapt local ingredients to feed the bands of soldiers. Their one constant foodstuff was *masa,* a dough of ground dried corn and water, in its infinite variety of forms.

Weary of war, the people of Mexico finally formed their first civilian government, led by a Zapotec Indian

Abundant along both the Pacific and Gulf coasts, huachinango (red snapper) is the most commonly served fish in Mexico.

named Benito Juárez. Conservatives who opposed reform sought the help of Napoleon III of France, who sent troops to Mexico and in 1864 installed the amiable, well-meaning but inept Viennese prince, Maximilian, as emperor of Mexico.

We owe the next main enrichment of Mexican cuisine to the tastes of the emperor's wife, Carlotta. She appreciated the foods of her new home but craved the more sophisticated European cuisine. To this end she brought to Mexico a Hungarian chef named Tudor, who, with the help of four other cooks, two confectioners and one baker, inspired the aristocracy with dishes of Austro-Hungarian, Italian and French origin. Although Maximilian's reign lasted only three years, it left such an impression on Mexican cooking that many experts consider it one of the five most distinct and creative cuisines in the world, alongside French, Indian, Chinese and Italian.

By 1876 the Mexicans again took control of their own country, with General Porfirio Díaz serving thirty years as president. The Porfirian reign evolved its own aristocracy, characterized by an even more opulent European influence. The excesses of this period and the resulting inequality between the classes triggered another bloody struggle. The Mexican Revolution, under the command of such leaders as Emiliano Zapata and Pancho Villa, continued until 1920, and again the women, known as *soldaderas,* not only fought alongside the men but carried with them their *comals* and *cazuelas.* Although there were sporadic outbursts in the following decade, the 1934 election of President Lázaro Cárdenas and the dominance of a new political party ushered in the present period of political stability.

During the golden age—the 1930s to the early 1950s—artists and intellectuals joined together in an attempt to interpret the values of Mexico's past and increase the people's pride in their heritage. They communicated through music, literature and art, with Diego Rivera, David Alfaro Siqueiros and José Clemente Orozco achieving world-class status for their artistic efforts.

In the kitchens a different creative re-evaluation began. Through long tradition, influential restaurant chefs and cooks in the homes of the upper class had stressed the refined European cuisine, but in 1981 many distinguished women chefs from Mexico joined together to form the Círculo Mexicano de Arte Culinario, a group dedicated to preserving, enhancing and promoting the regional dishes of Mexico. They researched family recipes, asked "what" and "why" of the Indian cooks they knew, and began to adapt what they were learning into dishes that would excite today's taste. Members of this group, as well as other cooks, have contributed recipes to this book, sharing both traditional dishes and new interpretations. The recipes cover the entire spectrum of Mexican cooking, from the ubiquitous *frijoles de la olla*—the pot of beans found simmering in almost every Mexican kitchen—to the elegant lobster and pine nut crêpes served in the sophisticated restaurants of Mexico City.

Enjoy, and *buen provecho!*

The Baroque contours of the Basilica of Our Lady of Guanajuato. The 17th-century church holds a statue of the Virgin of Guanajuato, a gift to the city from King Philip II of Spain in 1557.

THE MAYA WORLD

THE MAYA WORLD

As written in the Popul-Vuh, the sacred writings of the Mayas, the gods four times tried to create man. The first man was made of clay, but because he was without reason he was destroyed. The second was of wood, and the third of a type of yucca and reeds. But because they had no souls, they were also destroyed, in "great floods from the Heart of the Heavens," and then "darkness covered the face of the earth and black rain fell, by day and by night." Some managed to escape to the deep jungles and today are thought to be monkeys—men without souls. Finally the Creator, the Molder, decided to use white and yellow corncobs and was pleased with the results, and "this is how our forefathers and our fathers were created and formed."

Historically, the ancient Mayas are believed to be descendants of a North American tribe of people who first migrated to western Guatemala around 3000 B.C. They later spread out in all directions. One group, known as the Huaxtecs, separated themselves both culturally and linguistically from their former kinsmen and settled around northern Veracruz, Tamaulipas and San Luis Potosí. It was in Chiapas, the Mexican state closest to Guatemala, where the Maya culture reached its zenith in the awe-inspiring centers of Palenque and Yaxchilán. This is a country of high mountain valleys, spectacular waterfalls and sky-lifting extinct volcanoes. Only scattered groups of Maya Indians now remain,

Previous pages: A Maya ruin overlooks the Caribbean Sea. Left: Chichén Itzá, in the northern Yucatán peninsula, was a sacred center for the Mayas and, later, the Toltecs. Beyond the serpent head and the reclining chac-mool lies the famous pyramid, El Castillo.

25

The bright colors on the houses of the Yucatán peninsula are not a new tradition: the Mayas and other ancient civilizations painted their temples with brilliant pigments, now faded through the centuries.

Used for drinks, desserts and main dishes, coconuts color the food traditions throughout coastal Mexico.

settled in isolated valleys, each continuing a unique manner of dress, dialect and customs.

San Cristóbal was the first capital of Chiapas, a state named for the prevalent *chía,* a seed used to make a popular local drink. It is a city seemingly frozen in time. The weekday marketplace remains the hub of Indian life; the vividly dressed Chamula and Zina-canteco Indians still come to town to buy and barter, using old weights and measures from years gone by to judge the cost of a pound of black beans or half a watermelon. Competing with the bright colors and pungent odors of the herbs and produce are stalls with incense and candles in exotic shades, each color representing a special type of prayer.

The foods of Chiapas reflect both the Maya past and the influence of the Spanish conquerors. The region is known for its unusual *tamales:* round ones of pork; long ones stuffed with chicken, cinnamon and saffron; and a special *tamale* that combines olives, hard-boiled eggs, chicken and bananas, all steamed in *masa* wrapped in banana leaves. The soups are unusual too. One *caldo* (broth) thick with corn, fresh cheese and small *masa* balls is flavored with *chipilín,* a delicious herb. The best known is *sopa de pan,* an intriguing layered soup of bread, bananas, vegetables and exotic seasonings.

However, it is the Yucatán peninsula, the enormous, flat thumb of land jutting northward into the warm

A market scene in San Cristóbal de las Casas, Chiapas, where the herbs and bananas will show up in the local soups and tamales.

tide of European adventurers who became rich from the local species of agave plant, whose fibers, or sisal, could be made into binding twine. Having few ways to spend their wealth in this remote part of the world, they designed lush parks and long boulevards lined with flowering trees, and each tried to outdo the others in building the most ornate townhouses. The competition extended into the kitchen, with wealthy families vying to present the most elaborate and abundant dining tables to their guests.

Native cooks combined the ingredients they had been using throughout the years with the new foods furnished by the Spanish and created dishes unique to the Yucatán peninsula. Balls and small oblong blocks of *recados*—sensuous combinations of spices, bitter orange juice and *achiote*—are sold in all the local markets. They are used to flavor and color fish, fowl or meat that is wrapped in fragrant banana leaves and slowly steamed for hours in a stone-lined pit, or *pib*—a technique almost identical to the luau of the Hawaiian Islands. *Cochinita pibil,* a small pig cooked in this manner and traditionally garnished with pickled onions, is probably the best known of all Yucatecan dishes. Another dish from the past eaten today just as it was eaten around 1700 is *papadzules*—*tacos* containing chopped hardboiled eggs, covered first with a sauce of ground pumpkin seeds, then with one of tomatoes and topped with glistening pumpkinseed oil. Sizzling *sopa de lima* is a newer creation from the kitchens of Mérida, combining chicken and vegetables in a broth flavored with the region's bitter lime, which cools the seemingly unending heat of this land.

With more than a thousand miles of coastline surrounding the three states on the peninsula—Quintana Roo, Campeche and Yucatán—seafood is plentiful, and Ciudad del Carmen in the western part of Campeche is the major fishing port. The dawn comes up fast and hot over the water, and the fishermen come in early with their fresh catches—usually of *cazón* (shark), *pulpo* (octopus), *robalo* (snook), *calamares* (squid) and *huachinango* (red snapper). The subtle flavor of the small *cazón* makes it a delicacy that is used in many dishes, the most widely known being *pan de cazón* (shark's bread)—tortillas layered or stuffed with black beans and fish and covered with a sauce of tomatoes and that hottest of hot *chiles,* the *habanero.*

The foods eaten by the people on the remote eastern side of the peninsula are similar. Quintana Roo, until recently locked off from the rest of Mexico by dense jungle, was the last region in the country to become a state. Its Caribbean-looking capital, Chetumal, neighbors Belize, and both sides of the border share such staple dishes as beans and rice sweetened with coconut milk and eaten with fried bananas.

Today this area of the Yucatán peninsula is best known for its resorts—Cozumel, Cancún and its neighbor, the more leisurely Isla Mujeres. The growing presence of tourists in these vacation spots and at the archaeological sites of Tulum, Palenque and Chichén Itzá has had little effect on the Mayas. While the origins of most Mexicans are blurred by time, the Mayas have remained predominantly Indian, and despite the changes in the rest of the world over the last four hundred years, they still live much as their ancestors did—speaking the same language and carrying on the culinary traditions of the past.

turquoise waters between the Gulf of Mexico and the Caribbean, that most people associate with the Maya world. It is a dry land; the majority of its rivers and lakes lie underground, formed by rain seeping through the shallow layer of soil and thirsty underlying limestone. The ancient Mayas built most of their ceremonial cities around *cenotes,* large natural wells, or sink holes, formed wherever the thin surface of limestone collapsed, exposing the fresh subterranean waters.

During the first eight centuries of the Christian era, the Mayas built enormous centers with vast temples, palaces and massive pyramids covered with elaborate murals. To guide the ceremonial year, the Mayas created a calendar and a form of writing so that they could record critical events. By A.D. 900 this group of Indians had reached artistic and intellectual heights that few other civilizations in the world could match at the time.

By 1517, when Hernández de Córdoba, a recent arrival to Cuba, accidentally landed on the shores of the Yucatán peninsula, the Maya civilization was still impressive but already beginning to wane. After a fierce battle at Campeche, the Spaniards were defeated and returned to Cuba, but their descriptions of this different world spurred many an adventurer to try his luck. The quest was on. In 1542 the Spanish finally managed to establish Mérida as their capital in this isolated part of Mexico, building it on the ruins of an abandoned Maya city. The lure of cheap land and labor set off another

Antojitos y Bebidas

Sopes *("crispy masa boats")* and tacos, *stacked for snacking.*

ANTOJITOS Y BEBIDAS

Previous pages: Enchiladas Potosí Style (recipe page 48) and Margaritas (recipe page 56). Above: A walk through any Mexican town reveals vendors serving up antojitos, *the foods of the street—sometimes as simple as fresh corn grilled over hot coals.*

"**S**udden cravings," "hankerings" or "little whims"—all are used to define the collection of foods that the Mexican people eat out of hand during all hours of the day. *Antojitos* are the foods of the street, the foods of the marketplace, and most are made of a centuries-old source of nourishment—*masa,* a dough of ground dried corn and water.

Made of *masa,* the tortilla is the bread, the plate and the spoon of Mexico. Quickly cooked on a *comal,* folded over cheese with a sprig of *epazote,* it becomes a *quesadilla.* Simple but exquisite. *Tacos,* soft or crispy tortillas covered with practically everything edible; layered *tostadas;* stuffed *gorditas* and *panuchos; sopes* and *garnachas,* their edges pinched to hold a filling; the more elaborate *enchiladas*—the choice is endless and each region has its own specialties.

Where *antojitos* are eaten, close by are giant jars of *aguas frescas*—cooling beverages of blended fruit pulp. Vivid green from pungent limes, rosy pink and orange from sweet melons, they sit in colorful rows, ready to quell the surprising heat of a plate of *tacos* and *salsa.* Two of the favorites are also the most unusual: *agua de tamarindo,* made from the sticky pod of the tamarind tree, and the ruby red *agua de jamaica,* made from the hibiscus blossom.

For every special occasion in Mexico, there are *tamales,* the food of fiestas. In pre-Conquest days, a young Aztec couple was considered married only when the old woman who arranged the union tied the bridegroom's cloak to the blouse of the bride and the

In Tabasco, cacao beans are dried out on the street. Since pre-Columbian times, Mexicans have preferred to enjoy their chocolate as a drink, whipped into a froth and sipped from a mug.

couple shared a dish of *tamales*. Unadorned and unaccompanied, filled or unfilled, wrapped in corn husks, fresh leaves of corn or banana or the large, pungent leaves of *hierba santa,* this steamed *masa* offering is served as a gift to the gods.

During the Days of the Dead, the first days in November set aside to welcome back the spirits of family members who have died, all of a dead person's favorite foods are set out amid jars of brilliant saffron-colored *zempasúchil* (marigolds), burning candles and incense. Everything is festive, more like a party, and *tamales* and cups of frothy chocolate are shared with both the living and the dead.

From the beginning there was chocolate. According to legend, Quetzalcóatl, the god of light, came to earth on the beam of the morning star to help the impoverished Toltec Indians. As he came to know and love these people, he taught them how to grow cacao and prepare chocolate, the sacred drink of the gods. When his fellow gods discovered this, they became greatly angered and sent the god of darkness to earth, where he tricked Quetzalcóatl into drinking deeply of the heady *pulque* and becoming drunk in front of his people. Thoroughly ashamed, Quetz-alcóatl ascended to his home, the evening star. As a final gesture to his Indian friends, he scattered the remainder of his cacao seeds upon the shores of Tabasco, where they grew and flourished as an everlasting gift from the god of light.

The cacao beans were roasted and ground, mixed with water, sweetened with honey and flavored with allspice or vanilla to make a drink reserved for the privileged few. Cortés observed the Aztec ruler Moctezuma II drinking chocolate from impressive golden cups, and soon the beverage was transported to Europe, where, with a few additions and changes, it became the drink of the elite.

Pulque, the original Mexican alcoholic beverage, is the naturally fermented sap of the maguey, or century plant, grown on the high plateaus. In pre-Conquest times the priests used it in their rituals to celebrate the deeds of the brave. Its inebriating effects were well known and definitely not condoned—the penalty for drunkenness was death! The mildly intoxicating *pulque* is still found today in the maguey-growing regions of the central highlands, where it is often tempered with blended fruits to balance the spicy foods it usually accompanies.

The hard-drinking Spaniards decided to improve on the Indians' *pulque.* Using a distilling process learned from the Moors, they roasted, crushed and fermented the huge (80–200 pound) pineapple-shaped hearts of smaller species of maguey to produce the potent and popular mescal and tequila. Today tequila is most commonly drunk from small glasses, its taste both muted and intensified by a lick of salt from the side of the hand and a suck of lime. This may be followed by a sip of *sangrita,* originally a blend of pomegranate syrup and bitter orange juice mildly seasoned with *chile.*

One of Mexico's many brands of beer or *agua mineral* usually shares the table with the food. With more than 300 springs in the country, mineral water was a popular beverage in Mexico long before it became the "drink to drink" in the United States. Mexican beer is justly famous, and Mexicans consume great quantities of it—at last count, more than a hundred bottles of beer per person each year. The first license to sell beer was granted in 1544 for a mixture of barley, sugar, tamarind and lemon. However, it was three hundred years before beer making became a major industry in Mexico. The country now produces a variety of beers that are known and prized throughout the world.

Some sophisticated urban restaurants offer Mexican wines, which can be quite good but are inconsistent. Each year in Baja California Norte, Querétaro and Aguascalientes, more than a million cases of red and white wines are produced from vineyards that would have been outlawed before independence. Spain prohibited the growing of grapes in Mexico, even for sacramental purposes, requiring all wine to be imported from the mother country.

A cup of rich, fragrant coffee usually ends the meal. Although not indigenous to Mexico, coffee readily adapted to the slopes of the Sierra Madre in Veracruz and Chiapas. Most people order the dark-roasted bean served *con leche* (with milk), but espresso and plain American-style coffee are also popular. The traditional *café de olla,* brewed in a large earthenware pot (*olla*) and infused with cinnamon bark and dark brown sugar, is harder to find except in homes or family-style restaurants, but it is worth the search.

The *bebidas* and *antojitos*—the drinks and snacks of the country—are all savored and appreciated as a meaningful part of the Mexican cycle of life.

Fresh fruit and vegetables make a cooling snack on a hot day—juicy mangoes, melons and pineapple, or jícama *and cucumber with a dash of* chile piquín. *Giant jars of* aguas frescas *are never far away.*

Melted Cheese with Mushrooms, Chile Poblano Strips and Chorizo

JALISCO

QUESO FUNDIDO CON CHAMPIÑONES Y RAJAS DE POBLANO

Melted Cheese with Mushrooms and Chile Poblano Strips

Queso fundido *is featured along with grilled* cabrito *(baby goat) around Guadalajara and across the northern states of Mexico, where it may be called* queso flameado. *The stringy melted cheese is served in shallow clay or metal dishes and scooped up with floppy flour tortillas. A spicy tomato* salsa *is added right before eating. This recipe uses mushrooms and* chile poblano *strips, but fried and crumbled* chorizo *is another delicious possibility.*

1 *chile poblano,* roasted (see glossary), peeled and cut into strips (about ½ cup)
2 tablespoons (1 oz/30 g) butter
salt and freshly ground pepper
3 oz (60 g) mushrooms, sliced
2 cups (8 oz/250 g) grated mild Cheddar or Monterey Jack cheese
10–12 flour tortillas

✳ Sauté the *chile* strips in 1 tablespoon of the butter, season lightly with salt and pepper and set aside.
✳ Sauté the mushrooms in the other tablespoon of butter until they begin to release their juices. Season with salt and pepper and set aside.
✳ Lightly grease 2 *cazuelitas* or small flameproof casseroles. In one, place half the cheese and half the *chile* strips. In the other, place the remaining cheese and half the mushrooms. Cover the *cazuelitas* with aluminum foil and set over low heat until the cheese begins to melt, about 3 minutes. Uncover and cook another 2 minutes or until the cheese is completely melted. Add the remaining mushrooms and *chile* strips to their respective *cazuelitas.*
✳ Serve hot with flour tortillas, so that the cheese can be used in preparing individual *tacos.* Can also be served with *salsa mexicana* (page 200).

SERVES 6

Tortillas made with Fresh Masa

TORTILLAS DE MASA FRESCA

Tortillas Made with Fresh Masa

Fresh masa is readily available from just about any tortilla factory. It's best to use the dough the same day, but it can be refrigerated for a few days in a bowl covered with a damp cloth. Before using, the dough should be allowed to stand at room temperature for an hour or two; otherwise, the tortillas will tend to break when they are fried. Keep a small glass or cup of water nearby to moisten your hands slightly as you work the dough.

10 oz (315 g) fresh *masa*
warm water as needed
1 or 2 tablespoons all-purpose (plain) flour (optional)

✳ Heat a *comal* or iron skillet (ungreased). Moisten your hands and knead the *masa* for 2–3 minutes. Form into 10 small balls; each should be about the size of a walnut and weigh about 1 oz (30 g).
✳ Knead each ball slightly. The dough should feel somewhat moist and elastic. If it is too moist, dust it with a little flour; if it is too dry, sprinkle it with a little water.
✳ Cover a tortilla press with a sheet of plastic wrap and place a ball of dough in the center. Place another sheet of plastic wrap on top, lower the top lid of the press and push down on the handle. The tortilla formed should be 4½–5 in (10–13 cm) in diameter. If you are

making *picaditas* or *quesadillas,* only press the handle halfway down, to form a tortilla about 3 in (7.5 cm) in diameter.
✳ Open the tortilla press and remove the top sheet of plastic wrap from the tortilla. Lift the tortilla using the bottom sheet and turn it over onto your hand. Peel off the bottom sheet of plastic wrap and place the tortilla on the hot *comal*. Be careful not to "toss" the tortilla onto the *comal* or skillet because that would trap air and prevent it from cooking evenly.
✳ As soon as the edges of the tortilla start to dry out, after about 20 seconds, turn it over. Cook the second side for 15–20 seconds and turn the tortilla again. After about 15 more seconds, remove the tortilla from the heat. Transfer to a cloth so that the tortillas can be kept covered.

MAKES ABOUT 10 TORTILLAS

TORTILLAS DE MASA HARINA

Tortillas Made with Masa Harina

Masa harina (literally, "dough flour"), a unique kind of flour or meal made from corn, can be thought of as dried masa. Although neither corn flour nor cornmeal can be substituted, masa harina is widely available in the United States under the Quaker brand.

2 cups (8 oz/250 g) *masa harina*
1½ cups (12 fl oz/375 ml) lukewarm water
   (approximately)

✳ *Note:* Keep a small bowl of lukewarm water nearby as you work to moisten your hands.
✳ Place the *masa harina* in a large bowl and add the lukewarm water, mixing with your hands to incorporate the flour and form a ball. Cover with a cloth and let stand for 5–10 minutes.
✳ Heat a *comal* or iron skillet (ungreased). Knead the dough for 2–3 minutes, then form into balls about the size of a walnut.
✳ Cover a tortilla press with a sheet of plastic wrap and place a ball of dough in the center. Place another sheet of plastic wrap on top, lower the top lid of the press and push down on the handle. The tortilla formed should be 4½–5 in (10–13 cm) in diameter. If you are making *picaditas* or *quesadillas,* only press the handle halfway down, to form a tortilla about 3 in (7.5 cm) in diameter.
✳ Open the tortilla press and remove the top sheet of plastic wrap from the tortilla. Lift the tortilla using the bottom sheet and turn it over onto your hand. Peel off the bottom sheet of plastic wrap and place the tortilla on the hot *comal*. Be careful not to "toss" the tortilla onto the *comal* or skillet because that would trap air and prevent it from cooking evenly.
✳ As soon as the edges of the tortilla start to dry out, after about 20 seconds, turn it over. Cook the second side for 15–20 seconds and turn the tortilla again. After about 15 more seconds, remove the tortilla from the heat. Transfer to a cloth so that the tortillas can be kept covered.

MAKES ABOUT 10 TORTILLAS

Tortillas made with Masa Harina

Pork and Chicken Taquitos served with Guacamole

GUACAMOLE

Avocado Dip

*In the language of the Aztecs, the combined words for
"avocado" and "mixture" translate into* guacamole—*a
wonderful concoction that is perfect served with tacos or*
botanas *(before-meal snacks). In Mexico,* guacamole *is still
made with the traditional* molcajete *and* tejolote *(mortar
and pestle) or with a fork and bowl. A food processor or
blender should not be used because the mixture should have a
chunky texture. Although hard avocados are best ripened at
room temperature in a paper sack, one should not overlook the
advice of a Mexican adage: "Avocados and girls are ripened
with squeezes."*

2 large avocados
1 tablespoon finely chopped onion
1 or 2 *chiles serranos,* sliced
1 large tomato, peeled and chopped
2 sprigs *cilantro* (coriander), chopped
lime juice
salt

✳ Cut the avocados in half, remove the pits and scoop
out the flesh. Mash with a fork.
✳ In a bowl or *molcajete,* combine the avocado, onion,
chiles, tomato and *cilantro* and mix thoroughly. Add a
few drops of lime juice and salt to taste. Serve immediately.

SERVES 6

TAQUITOS DE PUERCO O POLLO

Small Tacos with Pork or Chicken

*Tacos date from early Indian civilizations, when stews were
eaten rolled up in tortillas. They are now enjoyed everywhere
in Mexico—at any time and with almost any filling
imaginable. It is said that the* taquero, *the man who sells
tacos, is always the first to arrive at any spectacle.*

1 lb (500 g) boneless cubed pork or chicken
3 black peppercorns
1 clove garlic, peeled
salt
4 cups (32 fl oz/1 l) water
3 tablespoons chopped *cilantro* (coriander)
1 onion, chopped
20 corn tortillas
oil for frying

✳ Place the pork, peppercorns, garlic and 1 teaspoon salt
in a saucepan, add the water and bring to a boil. Lower
the heat so that the mixture simmers and cook,
covered, for 35 minutes or until the pork is tender. Let
cool, then shred the meat.
✳ Mix the *cilantro* with the chopped onion and season
with a little salt. Add the shredded pork to this
mixture.
✳ Place a large spoonful of the meat mixture in the
center of each tortilla, roll up and secure with 2 toothpicks. Slice each *taco* in half.
✳ Heat ½ in (1 cm) oil in a skillet, add the *taquitos* and
fry until they are golden brown. Remove the toothpicks and serve the *taquitos* as a snack, accompanied by
guacamole (see previous recipe) and *salsa de tomate verde
con aguacate* (page 198).

SERVES 6–8

SONORA

BURRITAS

Burritas

*Wheat fields and cattle ranches dominate the landscape in
Sonora, so it is not surprising that the everyday* taco *there is
made of wheat-flour tortillas and shredded beef or dried beef
jerky (*machaca*). Chilorio (page 37) also makes a tasty
filling. Burritas are usually served with a fiery* salsa *and
beans, or the beans can be a part of the filling, mixed with
crumbled* chorizo *or cheese. For a* chivichanga, *fry the
burrita in oil until crisp.*

2 tablespoons oil
1 lb (500 g) *machaca* (recipe follows)
½ onion, chopped
salt
12 flour tortillas
salsa mexicana (page 200)

✳ Heat the oil in a skillet, add the *machaca* and onion
and sauté, stirring constantly, until well browned. Add
salt to taste.
✳ Warm the tortillas on a *comal* or iron skillet. Transfer
to a plate and fill each one with several heaping spoon-
fuls of the *machaca.* Roll up. Serve with the *salsa* on the
side.

SERVES 6

MACHACA

2 tablespoons dried oregano
3 cloves garlic
3 tablespoons lime juice

1 teaspoon salt
½ teaspoon freshly ground pepper
2 lb (1 kg) beef brisket, cut into 4 pieces

✱ In a blender, purée the oregano, garlic, lime juice, salt and pepper. Rub the meat well with this mixture, cover and refrigerate for at least 4 hours, preferably overnight.

✱ Heat a heavy skillet and brown the meat on both sides, turning twice, for 3–4 minutes or until the juices are clear. Let cool enough to handle, then shred finely with your fingers, discarding any fat or connective tissue.

✱ Place one-third of the shredded meat on a wooden board and pound with a wooden mallet. Repeat with the remaining meat. Spread the meat on an ungreased baking sheet and let air-dry for 5–6 hours, turning frequently.

✱ You may store the dry meat in plastic freezer bags and freeze for up to 3 months.

MAKES 2 LB (1 KG)

SINALOA

CHILORIO

Chile-Seasoned Pork

This traditional spicy pork dish from inland Sinaloa is customarily served with flour tortillas, white rice, refried black beans and guacamole, *somewhat like a Mexican*

"combination" plate in other countries. It also makes an exciting filling for tacos *and* burritas.

3 lb (1.5 kg) boneless pork, cut into 1-in (2.5-cm) cubes
1½ cups (12 fl oz/375 ml) water
2 teaspoons salt
2 tablespoons lard (optional)
3 *chiles anchos* (1½ oz /45 g), seeds and membranes removed
1 teaspoon dried oregano
½ teaspoon ground cumin
⅓ cup (½ oz/15 g) coarsely chopped parsley
6 cloves garlic

✱ Place the pork, ½ cup (4 fl oz/125 ml) of the water and the salt in a large saucepan. Simmer, covered, for 45 to 50 minutes or until all the liquid has cooked off and the pork fries in its own rendered fat. If there is not enough fat, add the lard so that the pork fries to a golden brown. Set aside.

✱ Place the *chiles* in a small saucepan with the remaining 1 cup (8 fl oz/250 ml) water. Cover and cook over low heat for 10 minutes. Transfer the *chiles* and cooking water to a blender, add the oregano, cumin, parsley and garlic, then purée.

✱ Add the puréed *chiles* to the fried pork, bring to a boil, lower the heat and simmer, covered, for 1 hour or until the pork is tender and can easily be cut with a fork. It may be necessary to add another cup (8 fl oz/250 ml) of water to the pan, depending on the tenderness of the meat.

SERVES 6

Burritas made with Chile-Seasoned Pork (left) and Machaca (right)

Panela Cheese with Oregano

QUESO PANELA CON ORÉGANO

Panela Cheese with Oregano

Panela is a fresh white cheese known for its versatility. It can be eaten alone, as a dessert with slices of ate *(fruit paste) or in this flavorful way combined with oil and oregano. Queso fresco or a fresh mozzarella that is packaged with its whey can be substituted.*

1 lb (500 g) *queso panela* (or *queso fresco* or fresh
   mozzarella cheese)
6 cloves garlic, crushed
⅓ cup (3 fl oz/80 ml) olive oil
½ cup (4 fl oz/125 ml) corn oil
2 tablespoons ground oregano

✱ Place the cheese in an earthenware or ovenproof dish. Pierce the outside of the cheese with a fork.
✱ In a small bowl, combine the garlic, olive oil, corn oil and oregano until they are thoroughly blended. Pour over the cheese. Refrigerate, covered, for at least 4 hours, preferably overnight. During this time, baste the cheese with the oil 3 or 4 times.
✱ Preheat the oven to 350°F (180°C). Bake the cheese for 15 minutes or until slightly soft. Serve warm with crackers or sliced *bolillos* (hard bread rolls).

SERVES 6

MINILLA DE PESCADO

Shredded Fish with Olives and Capers

This botana recipe from Diana Kennedy—made of fish, olives and capers—is very typical of the cooking along the Veracruz coast. In the northern part of the state, it is often made from the fleshy and gelatinous parts picked from the head of the sabalo *(a species of milkfish), while farther south it is more likely to be made from* robalo *(a type of snook). In fact, it is good for using up any leftover fish—shrimp, crabmeat, or even canned tuna or poached chicken. It can be made ahead and refrigerated, but bring to room temperature before serving. Accompany with crisp fried tortillas.*

¼ cup (2 fl oz/60 ml) olive oil
⅓ cup (3 oz/90 g) finely chopped onion
1⅓ cups (7 oz/220 g) chopped poached fish or drained
   flaked tuna
3 pickled *chiles jalapeños* (or to taste), finely chopped
10 pitted green olives, finely chopped
10 large capers, finely chopped
¾ cup (6 oz/185 g) finely chopped tomato
2 tablespoons lime juice
salt

✱ Heat the oil in a skillet or preferably a wok, add the onion and stir-fry for about 2 seconds. Add the fish and continue frying over high heat, stirring constantly, until the fish starts to brown—about 20 seconds.

✱ Add the *chiles,* olives, capers and tomato and continue the frying and stirring until the mixture is almost dry, 8–10 minutes. Sprinkle with the lime juice and add salt to taste. Serve warm or at room temperature.

SERVES 4

Chiles Moritas Rellenos con Salsa de Nuez

Stuffed Chiles Moritas with Nut Sauce

It is not just the fresh chile poblano *that is stuffed in Mexico. This delightful version uses the small dried and smoked* morita *or the similar* chipotle. *While both are difficult to find outside Mexico, they are well worth the search, as there is no substitute for their unique flavor.*

CHILES

5 oz (150 g) *chiles moritas* or *chiles chipotles* (about 20)
2 tablespoons oil
12 cloves garlic
1 onion, sliced
2 cups (16 fl oz/500 ml) red wine vinegar
salt
10 black peppercorns
1½ tablespoons dried oregano
6 oz (185 g) *piloncillo* (raw sugar), grated

FILLING

1 tablespoon oil
½ onion, finely chopped
2 cloves garlic, finely chopped
½ cup (4 oz/125 g) finely chopped tomato
¼ cup (1 oz/30 g) raisins
¼ cup (1 oz/30 g) chopped blanched almonds
1 whole chicken breast, about 12 oz (375 g), cooked
  and finely shredded
1 teaspoon salt
½ teaspoon freshly ground pepper

2 eggs, separated
¾ cup (3 oz/90 g) all-purpose (plain) flour
oil for frying
¾ cup (3 oz/90 g) walnuts
1 cup (8 fl oz/250 ml) thick cream *(crème fraîche)*

✱ Rinse the *chiles* and pat dry. Heat the oil in a large skillet and sauté the *chiles,* garlic and onion.
✱ Add the vinegar, salt, peppercorns, oregano and *piloncillo* and simmer for 10 minutes. Remove the skillet from the heat, let the mixture cool and pour into a glass jar or an earthenware crock. Refrigerate for at least 24 hours.
✱ To prepare the filling, heat the oil in a skillet and sauté the onion until it is softened, about 5 minutes. Add the garlic, tomato, raisins, almonds and 2 tablespoons of the vinegar marinade from the *chiles.* Stir, then add the chicken and the salt and pepper. Cook over low heat, stirring constantly, for 8 minutes. Set aside.
✱ Wearing rubber gloves (to avoid irritating your skin), make a slit the length of each *chile,* being careful not to tear it. Remove and discard the seeds and membranes. Use a small spoon to put a small amount of the filling

in each *chile.* Do not use too much or the filling will spill out when the *chile* is fried.
✱ Beat the egg whites until they form stiff peaks. Add the egg yolks one at a time, being careful not to stir too much (or the egg whites will lose volume).
✱ Place the flour on a large plate. In a large skillet, heat 1 in (2.5 cm) oil until very hot. Turn each *chile* in the flour to coat, then dip in the beaten egg and immediately place in the hot oil. Fry the *chile* on one side until golden brown, then use a fork and a slotted spoon to turn it over and brown on the other side. Do not try to fry more than 2 *chiles* at a time because they need room to brown properly. Drain in a colander, then transfer to a platter.
✱ Blend the walnuts with the cream and add a pinch of salt to taste. Serve the *chiles* with a little of the walnut cream poured over them and pass the rest of the cream in a sauce dish.

MAKES 20 STUFFED CHILES

*Stuffed Chiles Moritas with Nut Sauce (left)
and Shredded Fish with Olives and Capers (right)
served with Sangría (recipe page 56)*

GUERRERO

PICADITAS

Masa Sopes

This version of sopes *is from Puerto Marqués, a small beach community southeast of Acapulco. Whether they are called* picaditas *or* picadas, garnachas *or* gorditas, *these little "masa boats" are characterized by their pinched-up rims, which hold the savory filling.*

10 oz (315 g) *masa*
2 tablespoons oil or melted lard
¾ cup (6 oz/185 g) *frijoles refritos* (page 201)
salsa de molcajete (page 198)
1 cup (8 fl oz/250 ml) thick cream *(crème fraîche)*
1 cup (4 oz/125 g) crumbled *queso fresco* (or feta cheese)
½ cup (4 oz/125 g) chopped onion

✱ Heat a *comal* or iron skillet over medium-high heat. Moisten your hands with lukewarm water and knead the *masa* for 2–3 minutes. Form into 10 small balls about the size of a walnut, each approximately 1 oz (30 g). Place each ball in a tortilla press and push the handle down halfway, to form a 3-in (7.5-cm) round of dough.
✱ Place the *picadita* on the hot *comal*. Turn after 45–50 seconds or when the edges begin to dry out. After another 45 seconds, pinch the center of the *picadita* with your fingers. Turn it another time so that the pinched part is on the bottom. Cook for 45–60 seconds or until the dough looks cooked and its outer edge is a light golden brown.
✱ Remove from the heat and use your fingers to crimp the edge of the *picadita* to form an edge like a pie crust, between ¼ and ½ inch (6 mm and 12 mm) high. Wrap in a clean cloth and set aside. This can be done up to 2 hours before serving.
✱ Just before serving, heat the *comal*. Lightly grease the

Masa Sopes (top) and Bone Marrow Patties (bottom)

pinched surface of the *picaditas* with the oil or lard. Place each *picadita* on the *comal* with the pinched edge up. As soon as the oil begins to bubble, remove from the heat.

✻ Spread each *picadita* with the *frijoles refritos* and cover with the *salsa*. Add a dollop of cream and sprinkle with the cheese. If you wish, you may add the chopped onion or pass it in a separate bowl.

✻*Variation:* The *picaditas* can be fried instead of toasted on the *comal*. Fried bits of *chorizo* can be added and the beans omitted. In short, *picaditas* are very versatile; the filling used depends only on the ingenuity of the cook.

MAKES 10 PICADITAS

Tortitas de Tuétano

Bone Marrow Patties

This century-old recipe for tiny crisp-fried patties of marrow and masa *topped with an avocado sauce is excellent as a first course or as a main dish for a light meal.*

PATTIES

1 lb (500 g) marrow bones, cut into 2–3 in (5–7.5 cm) pieces
1 cup (8 fl oz/250 ml) water
2 *chiles anchos,* seeds and membranes removed
1½ lb (750 g) *masa*
3 tablespoons all-purpose (plain) flour
oil for frying

SALSA

2 tomatoes, peeled and chopped
1 onion, finely chopped
2 avocados, peeled, pitted and finely diced
1 *chile serrano,* chopped
1 tablespoon minced *cilantro* (coriander)
1 tablespoon oil
1 teaspoon red wine vinegar
salt

✻ To make the patties, scoop the marrow out of the bones and set aside. You should have about 1 cup (8 oz/250 g).

✻ Bring the water to a boil in a small saucepan, add the *chiles* and return to a boil. Remove the pan from the heat and let the *chiles* stand in the water for 5 minutes. Drain, reserving 2 tablespoons of the water. Transfer the *chiles* with the water to a blender and purée.

✻ In a large bowl, use your hands to mix the *masa,* bone marrow and flour together. Add the puréed *chiles* and knead until the mixture is smooth.

✻ Shape the *masa* mixture into tiny patties 2–3 in (5–7.5 cm) in diameter and ⅛ in (3 mm) thick. Heat ½ in (1 cm) oil in a skillet and fry the patties in batches, using a slotted spoon to remove them from the skillet. Drain on absorbent paper.

✻ Combine all the *salsa* ingredients in a small bowl. Arrange the patties on a platter and place a dab of *salsa* on each.

SERVES 6

Tortillas Dipped in Beans

Enfrijoladas

Tortillas Dipped in Beans

A typical dish for almuerzo *(a late breakfast),* enfrijoladas *can be livened up by serving pickled* jalapeños *on the side. While the type and color of the bean that is used varies from region to region, it is the ebony-hued* frijol negro *(black bean) that is most typical of this dish.*

2 cups (1 lb/500 g) *frijoles de la olla* (page 208) with their liquid
2 tablespoons oil
¼ onion
salt
oil for frying
12 corn tortillas
½ cup (4 fl oz/125 ml) thick cream *(crème fraîche)*
3 oz (100 g) crumbled *queso fresco* (or feta cheese)
1 onion, thinly sliced (optional)

✻ In a blender, purée the *frijoles de la olla* with their liquid. The mixture should be the consistency of a sauce; if too thick, add up to ½ cup (4 fl oz/125 ml) water.

✻ Heat the oil in a skillet and brown the onion quarter slightly. Add the puréed beans and simmer for 2 minutes. Add salt to taste. Discard the onion.

✻ Heat ½ in (1 cm) oil in a skillet and fry each tortilla briefly (about 10 seconds) on both sides. Immerse the tortilla in the bean purée and fold it in half, then in half again to form a triangle. Transfer to a plate, spoon on a little cream and sprinkle with cheese. Garnish with the onion slices.

SERVES 6

Shark in Tortilla Pockets

CAMPECHE

PANUCHOS DE CAZÓN

Shark in Tortilla Pockets

There are many versions of these panuchos, *or stuffed tortillas, a specialty of the Yucatán peninsula. They are also simply referred to as* pan de cazón *(shark's bread). If small dogfish shark is unobtainable, another meaty white fish such as mackerel can be substituted.*

SHARK

1 lb (500 g) shark steaks or mackerel fillets
3 bay leaves

4 cloves garlic, 2 whole, 2 minced
¼ onion
1 tablespoon oil
½ cup (4 oz/125 g) diced onion
1 lb (500 g) tomatoes, finely chopped, with peel and
   juice
2½ tablespoons chopped *epazote*
1 teaspoon dried oregano
salt and freshly ground pepper

RED ONIONS

2 tablespoons oil
1 lb (500 g) red onions, sliced
2 cloves garlic
½ cup (4 fl oz/125 ml) white vinegar

¾ cup (6 fl oz/180 ml) water
3 bay leaves
1 small sprig thyme
1 small sprig marjoram
1 teaspoon dried oregano
1 teaspoon salt
¼ teaspoon freshly ground pepper

oil for frying
12 corn tortillas
1 cup (8 oz/250 g) *frijoles refritos* (page 201)
pickled *chiles serranos*

✳ Heat 2 cups (16 fl oz/500 ml) water in a saucepan. When it comes to a boil, add the shark, 1 bay leaf, the whole garlic cloves and the onion quarter. Cover and cook over high heat for 20 minutes. Set aside.

✳ In a large skillet, heat the oil and add the diced onion and minced garlic. Sauté for 1 minute, then add the tomatoes. Stir and cook over medium heat for 3 minutes or until the tomato changes color. Add the *epazote,* 2 bay leaves and oregano and season with salt and pepper. Cover and cook over low heat for 2 minutes.

✳ Drain the shark and crumble it (not too finely). Add it to the skillet and cook over high heat for 2 minutes. Lower the heat and cook another 5 minutes, stirring constantly. Set aside.

✳ To prepare the red onions, in a nonreactive (not aluminum) saucepan, heat the oil, add the onions and sauté lightly. Add the garlic and sauté for 1 minute. Add the vinegar, water, bay leaves, thyme, marjoram, oregano, salt and pepper. Cook, uncovered, for 10 minutes or until the onions are soft. Correct the seasonings and set aside.

✳ Place 1 in (2.5 cm) oil in a large skillet. When it is hot, add a tortilla and fry until it puffs up. Remove the tortilla with a skimmer and, while it is still warm, carefully make a small horizontal opening in it, being sure not to pierce the other side. Repeat this procedure with all the tortillas.

✳ Carefully place a spoonful of *frijoles refritos* in the "pocket" you have made in each tortilla. Transfer the tortilla to a platter and arrange some cooked shark and a layer of red onions on top of the *panucho.* Garnish with the pickled *chiles serranos.*

✳*Note:* If you are unable to open a pocket in the tortilla or if the tortilla does not puff up, you can take a lightly fried tortilla, spread it with beans, cover with another tortilla, then arrange the shark and red onions on top.

SERVES 6

TORTAS

Hard-Roll Sandwiches

In every corner of Mexico you will find tiny torta stands selling gargantuan layered sandwiches of beans, chile, *cheese, onions, tomato, cabbage, avocado and, if that is not enough, a fried egg, meat, turkey or chicken. This is all put inside a bobbin-shaped hard bread roll called a* telera. *A hard French roll can be used or even a* baguette, *which can then be sliced crosswise into serving sizes.*

6 *teleras* or other hard bread rolls, each about 3 oz (90 g)
6 tablespoons (3 oz/90 g) *frijoles refritos* (page 201)

shredded cabbage or lettuce
2 cups (12 oz/375 g) shredded chicken, pork or *tinga poblana* (page 149) or 6 fried eggs or filling of your choice
6 slices onion
6 slices tomato
6 slices avocado
6 slices *queso fresco* (or feta cheese)
6 pickled *chiles serranos,* cut into thin strips
salt
6 tablespoons (3 fl oz/90 ml) thick cream *(crème fraîche)* (optional)

✳ Slice each *telera* in half lengthwise. Pick out a little of the center from both halves of the roll.

✳ Spread the bottom half of the roll with *frijoles refritos.* Top with cabbage or lettuce, chicken (or whatever filling you prefer), a slice of onion, tomato, avocado and cheese and 2 strips of *chile.* Sprinkle with salt to taste. If you wish, spread cream on the top half of the roll before placing on the *torta.*

SERVES 6

Hard-Roll Sandwich made with Ham

Green Chilaquiles

and shred the chicken, reserving 2 cups (16 fl oz/500 ml) of the stock.

✳ Place the *chiles* and remaining 3 cloves garlic in boiling water and cook for 5 minutes. Add the *tomates verdes*, cook 5 more minutes and drain. Transfer the *chiles*, garlic and *tomates verdes* to a blender, add the remaining onion, then purée. Add 1 teaspoon salt, the *cilantro* and 1 cup (8 fl oz/250 ml) of the reserved stock, and process briefly. Set aside.

✳ Heat 1 tablespoon oil in a skillet, add the sauce and sauté for 5 minutes. Correct the seasonings, lower the heat, cover and cook for 10 minutes. If the mixture is too thick, dilute with more chicken stock.

✳ Cut the tortillas in half and cut each half into 3 pieces. Place ¼ in (1 cm) oil in a large skillet. When it is very hot, add one-third of the tortilla pieces and fry, stirring constantly, until they are golden and crisp, 3 to 4 minutes. Transfer to a colander. Repeat until all the tortillas are fried. Drain and set aside.

✳ Before serving, heat the sauce and add the epazote. Add the tortillas and stir carefully so as not to break them. Add the shredded chicken and top with cream and cheese. Cook for 2–3 minutes or until the cheese melts.

* Chilaquiles Rojos: *To make red* chilaquiles, *substitute 1½ lb (750 g) ripe tomatoes for the* tomates verdes. *Instead of boiling, roast the tomatoes (see glossary), peel and then purée with the boiled* chiles. *(Photograph page 53)*

SERVES 6 AS MAIN COURSE, 8 AS FIRST COURSE

CHILAQUILES VERDES O ROJOS

Green or Red Chilaquiles*

The Aztecs combined their leftover tortillas with chiles and herbs to create chilaquiles, *which in their Náhuatl language means just that—"chiles and herbs in broth." Every Mexican cook seems to have their own version of this versatile dish, which can be served either for* almuerzo *(brunch) or* cena *(supper).* Chilaquiles *can be prepared ahead up to the point of adding the sauce to the fried tortilla pieces.*

1 whole chicken breast, about 12 oz (375 g)
5 cloves garlic
1 tablespoon plus 1 teaspoon salt
½ onion
7 sprigs parsley
6 *chiles serranos* (or to taste)
1½ lb (750 g) *tomates verdes,* husks removed
¼ onion
½ cup (¾ oz/20 g) chopped *cilantro* (coriander)
1 tablespoon oil
16 corn tortillas, preferably day-old
oil for frying
1 small sprig *epazote*
1 cup (8 fl oz/250 ml) thick cream (*crème fraîche*)
½ cup (2 oz/60 g) crumbled *queso fresco* or *queso añejo* (or feta cheese)

✳ Place the chicken in a large saucepan and add enough water to cover. Add 2 cloves of the garlic, 1 tablespoon of the salt, ½ onion and the parsley. Cover and simmer for 20 minutes or until the chicken is tender. Remove

ESTADO DE MÉXICO

TOSTADAS DE CEVICHE

Tostadas with Ceviche

María Dolores Torres Yzábal's fish version of tostadas *comes from the beautiful mountain resort town of Valle de Bravo.*

¼ cup (2 fl oz/60 ml) lime juice
¼ cup (2 fl oz/60 ml) water
¾ teaspoon salt
8 oz (250 g) mackerel fillets (or any meaty saltwater fish such as striped bass, grouper, halibut or fluke), finely chopped
oil for frying
8 corn tortillas
2 avocados, about 8 oz (250 g) each, peeled and pitted
1 tablespoon cream
1 tablespoon milk
4 *chiles serranos,* thinly sliced
4 green (spring) onions, thinly sliced

✳ Combine the lime juice, water and ½ teaspoon salt in a glass bowl. Soak the fish in this mixture for 5 hours, refrigerated, stirring occasionally.

✳ Heat ½ in (1 cm) oil in a small skillet and fry the tortillas until they are golden brown—about 2 minutes.

✳ Mash the avocados and add the cream, milk and ¼ teaspoon salt. Drain the fish and pat dry.

✳ On each tortilla, spread a little of the avocado, then some of the fish. Garnish with *chile* and green onion.

SERVES 6

Tostadas with Ceviche (front) and Chicken Tostadas (rear)

JALISCO

TOSTADAS DE POLLO

Chicken Tostadas

A simple layering of chicken, refried beans and the makings of a lettuce, avocado, onion and tomato salad, topped off with sour cream and cheese. Served on an edible tortilla plate, it makes a balanced meal that goes well with pozole *(page 88) or vegetable soup.*

oil for frying
12 corn tortillas
1½ cups (12 oz/375 g) *frijoles refritos* (page 201)
3 cups (9 oz/280 g) shredded lettuce
1 whole chicken breast, about 12 oz (375 g), cooked and shredded
1 onion, sliced or chopped
2 tomatoes, sliced

1 avocado, peeled, pitted and cut into strips
salt
1 cup (8 fl oz/250 ml) thick cream *(crème fraîche)* or sour cream
¾ cup (3 oz/90 g) crumbled *queso fresco* (or feta cheese)
salsa de molcajete (page 198) or *salsa mexicana* (page 200) (optional)

✽ Heat ½ in (1 cm) oil in a small skillet and fry the tortillas until they are crisp and golden, 45 seconds to 1 minute on each side. Place in a colander and set aside. They can be prepared up to 1 hour before serving.
✽ Heat the *frijoles refritos*. Spread each *tostada* with *frijoles* and top with lettuce, chicken, 2 slices of onion, 2 slices of tomato and a strip of avocado. Sprinkle lightly with salt. Place a tablespoon of cream on top and sprinkle with the cheese. Pass the *salsa* separately.
✽*Variation: Machaca* (page 36) can be used in place of the chicken.

MAKES 12 TOSTADAS

Quesadillas with Potato and Chorizo Filling, Cheese Filling and Squash Blossom Filling

Quesadillas

Quesadillas

The authentic quesadilla is made with an uncooked tortilla that is stuffed, folded over and cooked on a comal. *Cheese with a sprig of* epazote *is the classic filling, but popular variations include mushrooms, potatoes with* chorizo, *or squash flowers; see following recipes. It is important that these be served the moment they are cooked.*

1 lb (500 g) *masa*
3 tablespoons all-purpose (plain) flour
1 tablespoon melted lard
1 teaspoon baking powder (optional)
½ teaspoon salt
oil for frying

✳ Place the *masa* in a large bowl and add the flour, lard, baking powder and salt. Moisten your hands and knead for 5 minutes. Cover with a damp cloth and let rest for 10 minutes.

46

the *quesadillas,* 2 at a time, for 2 or 3 minutes on each side or until lightly browned. Do not let them stick together as they fry.

✳ Serve with *guacamole* (page 36) and *salsa mexicana* (page 200).

MAKES 12 QUESADILLAS

RELLENO DE QUESO

Cheese Filling

1 cup (4 oz/125 g) grated *queso manchego, queso Oaxaca,* Monterey Jack or Muenster cheese
small sprigs *epazote* (optional)

✳ Place a spoonful of cheese and a sprig of *epazote* in each *quesadilla.*

MAKES 1 CUP (4 OZ/125 G)

RELLENO DE PAPA CON CHORIZO

Potato and Chorizo Filling

2½ cups (13 oz/410 g) peeled and cubed potatoes
1 *chorizo* (5 oz/155 g) or other spicy sausage, casing removed and chopped

✳ Cook the potatoes in boiling salted water. When they are tender, drain and place in a bowl. Mash slightly with a fork.
✳ Heat a skillet, add the *chorizo* and cook over low heat for 8 to 10 minutes.
✳ Add the *chorizo* to the potatoes. Moisten with a tablespoon of the fat rendered from the *chorizo* and mix well.

MAKES ABOUT 2½ CUPS (1¼ LB/625 G)

RELLENO DE FLOR DE CALABAZA

Squash Blossom Filling

2½ cups (5 oz/155 g) squash (zucchini) blossoms or 1 can (7 oz/220 g) squash (zucchini) blossoms, drained
1 tablespoon oil
½ cup (4 oz/125 g) finely chopped onion
1 clove garlic, minced
1 tomato (6 oz/185 g), peeled and finely chopped
¼ cup (3 oz/90 g) diced *chile poblano,* seeds and membranes removed
1 tablespoon chopped *epazote*
1 teaspoon salt

✳ Remove the stems and pistils from the flowers. Rinse with water, drain and chop coarsely.
✳ Heat the oil in a skillet, add the onion and garlic and sauté for 2 minutes. Add the tomato, stir and heat for 3 minutes or until the mixture comes to a boil. Add the flowers, *chile poblano, epazote* and salt. Cook, uncovered, over medium heat until the flowers are soft and the excess liquid has evaporated, about 4 minutes.

MAKES ABOUT 2½ CUPS (1¼ LB/625 G)

✳ Form the *masa* into 12 balls. Line a tortilla press with plastic wrap, place a ball of *masa* in the center and cover with another piece of plastic. Press lightly to form 4-in (10-cm) circles. Peel the plastic from the top of the tortilla and spread a spoonful of filling (recipes follow) on the tortilla in a half circle, leaving a ½-in (1-cm) margin around the edge. Fold the tortilla in half and remove the plastic from the bottom. Press the edges of the *quesadilla* to seal.
✳ In a skillet, heat ½ in (1 cm) oil to 375°F (190°C). Fry

OAXACA

ENCHILADAS ROJAS

Red Enchiladas

Enchiladas were also known as tortillas con chile *in the last century. If one remembers that* enchilar *means to cover, wrap or coat with* chile, *it will be easier to visualize a major step in preparing* enchiladas—*dipping them in a* chile *sauce. These are often served as a breakfast dish.*

6 *chiles guajillos*
3 *chiles pasillas*
3 tomatoes (18 oz/540 g)
¼ onion
2 cloves garlic
2 small sprigs marjoram (optional)
1½ cups (12 fl oz/375 ml) chicken stock (page 72)
2 tablespoons oil
salt
18 corn tortillas
2 whole chicken breasts, about 12 oz (375 g) each,
   cooked and shredded
1 onion, sliced
1 cup (4 oz/125 g) crumbled *queso fresco* (or feta cheese)
½ cup (4 fl oz/120 ml) thick cream *(crème fraîche)*
   (optional)

✱ Toast the *chiles* (see glossary), remove the seeds and membranes and soak in warm water for 20 minutes. Roast the tomatoes (see glossary) and peel them. Roast the onion quarter and garlic.
✱ Drain the *chiles* and transfer to a blender. Add the tomatoes, onion, garlic, marjoram and chicken stock, then purée until smooth. Heat the oil in a skillet, add the purée and simmer for 10 minutes over low heat. Add salt to taste.
✱ Dip a tortilla in the sauce and transfer to a plate. Place a little chicken on the tortilla and roll it up. Place the *enchiladas* on a platter, cover with the remaining sauce, garnish with sliced onion and sprinkle with the cheese. If you wish, you can top with a layer of cream and heat in the oven until it melts and browns.

SERVES 6

SAN LUIS POTOSÍ

ENCHILADAS POTOSINAS

Enchiladas Potosí Style

These unusual enchiladas, *with red chile ground in the* masa, *are sold from small stands in the industrial capital of San Luis Potosí. More like a* quesadilla *in appearance, they are usually served with shredded lettuce and* guacamole *(page 36).*

2½ oz (75 g) *chiles anchos,* seeds and membranes
   removed
1 cup (8 fl oz/250 ml) hot water
1 tablespoon lard
1 tablespoon oil
¼ cup (2 oz/60 g) minced onion
1¼ cups (5 oz/155 g) crumbled *queso fresco*
   (or feta cheese)
1 lb (500 g) *masa*

½ teaspoon salt
oil for frying

✱ Toast the *chiles* (see glossary) and soak in the hot water for 25 minutes, then purée in a blender with ½ cup (4 fl oz/120 ml) of the water in which they soaked. Melt the lard in a small skillet, add the *chile* purée and sauté for 5 minutes. Set aside.
✱ Heat the oil in a small skillet, add the onion and sauté until it is transparent. Remove from the heat and stir in the cheese. Add 1 tablespoon of the *chile* purée and stir well. Set aside.
✱ Place the *masa* in a bowl, add the remaining *chile* purée and the salt and knead for 5 minutes or until all the ingredients are thoroughly combined. Cover with a damp cloth and let rest for 20 minutes.
✱ Form the *masa* into balls about the size of walnuts, place between 2 pieces of plastic wrap in a tortilla press, and flatten to form circles about 3 in (7.5 cm) in diameter. Remove the plastic. Spread a tablespoon of the cheese mixture in the middle of each circle, leaving a narrow margin. Fold the circles in half and press the edges to seal.
✱ Heat a *comal* or iron skillet and toast the *enchiladas* for 2 or 3 minutes on each side or until the *masa* changes color and seems cooked. (The *enchiladas* can be prepared in advance up to this point and refrigerated for up to 3 hours.) Heat ½ in (1 cm) oil in a skillet, add the *enchiladas* 2 or 3 at a time and fry for 3 or 4 minutes on each side. Drain and serve.

MAKES 16 SMALL OR 12 MEDIUM ENCHILADAS

Photograph pages 28–29

AGUASCALIENTES

ENCHILADAS VERDES

Green Enchiladas

According to Renato Luduc, the writer and poet from the state of Aguascalientes, "After the cock fights, after card games, there is no Aguascalientes visitor or family member who doesn't go on to savor a plate of chicken enchiladas or some other regional dish at the stands lined up alongside the beautiful gardens of San Marcos."

1 whole chicken breast, about 12 oz (375 g)
6 cups (48 fl oz/1.5 l) water
5 cloves garlic
1 small onion (4 oz/125 g), ½ cut in half, ½ thinly sliced
3 small sprigs parsley
salt
1 carrot, cut into large pieces
2–4 *chiles serranos*
2 lb (1 kg) *tomates verdes,* husks removed
½ cup (¾ oz/20 g) coarsely chopped *cilantro* (coriander)
1 tablespoon oil
12 corn tortillas
oil for frying
½ cup (4 fl oz/125 ml) thick cream *(crème fraîche)*
   (optional)
½ cup (2 oz/60 g) crumbled *queso fresco* or grated
   Cheddar cheese (optional)

Red Enchiladas

✱ Place the chicken, water, 3 cloves garlic, ¼ onion, parsley, salt to taste and carrot in a large saucepan, cover and simmer until the chicken is tender, about 20 minutes. Remove and shred the chicken, reserving the stock.

✱ Add 2 cloves garlic and the *chiles* to a saucepan of boiling water. After 5 minutes, add the *tomates verdes* and cook another 7 minutes. Drain.

✱ In a blender, purée the *tomates verdes* with the garlic, *chiles* and another onion quarter. Add the *cilantro* and process briefly so that the *cilantro* is not ground too fine. Add 1 cup (8 fl oz/250 ml) of the reserved chicken stock.

✱ Heat the oil in a small skillet and sauté the puréed *tomates verdes* in it. Add 1 teaspoon salt and correct the seasonings. Lower the heat and cook, uncovered, for 10 minutes. If the sauce is too thick, add another ½ cup

(4 fl oz/250 ml) stock.

✱ Heat ½ in (1 cm) oil in a skillet and fry the tortillas in it until they just begin to soften, 10 seconds on each side. Immerse each tortilla in the warm sauce, then transfer to a plate. Place some chicken in the center of each tortilla, roll up and arrange on a platter. Spoon the warm sauce over the *enchiladas,* garnish with the sliced onion and add cream and *queso fresco* if you wish.

✱*Variation:* The *enchiladas* can be placed in an oven-proof dish, covered with sauce, wrapped in aluminum foil and placed in a preheated oven (375°F/190°C) for 10 minutes. Remove from the oven, sprinkle with Cheddar cheese and return to the oven until the cheese browns slightly.

SERVES 6   *Photograph page 50*

Green Enchiladas (recipe page 48) and Fermented Pineapple Drink

NAYARIT

TEPACHE

Fermented Pineapple Drink

A refreshing fermented beverage made from Mexico's native pineapple and popular in many regions of the country.

1 whole ripe pineapple, about 3 lb (1.5 kg)
12 cups (96 fl oz/3 l) water
20 oz (600 g) *piloncillo* (raw sugar) or brown sugar
1 3-in (7.5-cm) stick cinnamon
3 whole cloves

✱ Wash the pineapple thoroughly, remove the stem and cut the pineapple into large pieces, rind and all.
✱ Place the pineapple chunks in a large bowl and add 8 cups (64 fl oz/2 l) of the water and the *piloncillo,* cinnamon stick and cloves. Cover and let stand in a warm place for 48 hours.
✱ Strain the *tepache* and add 4 cups (32 fl oz/1 l) water. Or, if you prefer, add 1 cup (8 fl oz/250 ml) of beer (lager) and let stand an additional 12 hours, then strain and add 3 cups (24 fl oz/750 ml) water.
✱ Serve cold, with ice cubes.

SERVES 6

GUERRERO

TAMALES EN HOJAS DE PLÁTANO

Tamales Wrapped in Banana Leaves

The people in southern Mexico often wrap their tamales in banana leaves instead of corn husks, first wilting the leaves by quickly holding them over a flame or a very hot electric burner. It is said that "the good tamale is known by its wrapper," so try tying the wrapped tamales with narrow strips of the leaf to make a secure and attractive package. Frozen banana leaves from the Philippines can be found in most Asian and Mexican markets.

1 lb (500 g) lean pork
3 cloves garlic
½ onion, cut in half
1 teaspoon salt
6 *chiles anchos,* seeds and membranes removed
8 *chiles guajillos,* seeds and membranes removed
2 tomatoes
1 teaspoon dried marjoram
4 black peppercorns
2 whole cloves
1 lb (500 g) *masa*
5 tablespoons (2½ oz/75 g) lard
1 large banana leaf, plus leaves to line steamer

✱In a large saucepan, cover the pork with water and add 1 garlic clove, 1 onion quarter and ½ teaspoon salt. Bring to a boil, cover and simmer until the pork is tender, 45–60 minutes. Shred the meat, reserving the stock.
✱ Toast the *chiles* (see glossary), place in a bowl, cover with warm water and soak for 20 minutes. Meanwhile, roast the tomatoes (see glossary), peel and purée in a blender. Roast the other onion quarter, 2 cloves garlic, marjoram, peppercorns and cloves.
✱ Drain the *chiles* and transfer to a blender. Add the roasted onion, garlic, marjoram, peppercorns, cloves and 1 cup (8 fl oz/250 ml) of the reserved stock, then purée until smooth.
✱ Melt 1 tablespoon of the lard in a skillet and sauté the *chile* purée in it for 5 minutes. Add the puréed tomatoes and sauté for another 5 minutes; add the pork, stir and cover. Lower the heat and cook for 10 minutes.
✱ Hold the banana leaf directly over the heat for 5 seconds. Cut into 5-in (13-cm) squares.
✱ Knead the *masa* with 2 tablespoons (1 oz/30 g) of the lard for 5 minutes.
✱ Use the remaining lard to grease one side of the banana leaf. Place a 3-in (7.5-cm) square of *masa* on the lard and top with 1½ tablespoons of the pork mixture.
✱ Fold the opposite edges of the leaf toward the center, then do the same with the other edges, to form a closed rectangle. To secure, tie the *tamales* with narrow strips of leaf.
✱ Place 2 cups (16 fl oz/500 ml) water in a pressure cooker, then cover the steamer basket with a layer of flattened banana leaves. Add the *tamales* to the steamer basket and cover with another layer of leaves. Place the lid on the pan and cook for 20 minutes. If you use an ordinary steamer, follow the same procedure but use 4 cups (32 fl oz/1 l) water and cook for 1 hour.
✱ Serve warm, with *frijoles refritos* (page 201).

SERVES 6–8

NAYARIT

ATOLE DE PIÑA

Pineapple Atole

Atole, the ancient Indian gruel of Mexico, is still the traditional accompaniment for tamales. *There are literally dozens of variations, some mixed with* chiles, epazote, *vanilla, strawberry or, as in this common version, pineapple.*

5 oz (155 g) *masa*
water
11 oz (345 g) pineapple pulp
4 oz (125 g) *piloncillo* (raw sugar)
2 cups (1 lb/500 g) cubed pineapple

✻ Stir the *masa* in 4 cups (32 fl oz/1 l) water. Let stand for 15 minutes, then strain the water and set it aside.
✻ In a blender, purée the pineapple in 1½ cups (12 fl oz/375 ml) water. Strain and set the pineapple water aside.
✻ In a saucepan, combine the strained *masa* water, *piloncillo,* 2 cups (16 fl oz/500 ml) fresh water and the pineapple water and set over medium heat. Boil, stirring constantly, for 15 minutes or until thickened.
✻ Remove from the heat, add the pineapple cubes and stir for another 5 minutes. Serve hot.

SERVES 6

DISTRITO FEDERAL

TAMALES VERDES DE POLLO

Chicken Tamales with Green Sauce

Tamales *have been fiesta food since pre-Hispanic times, when they were considered a gift from the gods during the twelfth month of the Maya eighteen-month calendar year. Because this time coincided with the Spanish conquerors' celebration of All Saints Day, the* tamale *became the food displayed and eaten in honor of all those who had died. This version, however, is sold every morning and late afternoon at special* puestos (tamale stands) *in Mexico City.*

4–6 *chiles serranos*
13 oz (410 g) *tomates verdes,* husks removed
1 clove garlic
½ cup (4 fl oz/125 ml) chicken stock (page 72)
½ cup (¾ oz/20 g) *cilantro* (coriander)
1 tablespoon oil
¼ onion
2 chicken breasts, about 12 oz (375 g) each, cooked and shredded
salt
30 dried corn husks, soaked in warm water until pliable
4 cups (20 oz/625 g) *masa*
½ cup (4 oz/125 g) melted lard

✻ Cook the *chiles* in a saucepan of boiling water for 4 minutes. Add the *tomates verdes* and cook 2 more minutes. Drain and transfer the *chiles* and *tomates verdes* to a blender. Add the garlic and chicken stock, then purée. Add the *cilantro* and process briefly.
✻ Heat the oil, add the onion and sauté until transparent. Add the *tomate verde* purée and cook over high heat for 5 minutes. Add the shredded chicken, stir,

cover and cook over low heat for 5 minutes. Add salt to taste. If the mixture is too thick, thin with a little chicken stock. Set aside.
✻ Place the *masa* in a large bowl, add 1 tablespoon salt and knead for 2–3 minutes. Add the melted lard and knead 5 minutes more.
✻ Spread out a corn husk, place 1½ tablespoons of *masa* on it and flatten the *masa* with the palm of your hand so that it covers a 2-by-3-in (5-by-7.5-cm) square, leaving a 1-in (2.5-cm) border on all sides. Place 1½ tablespoons of the cooked chicken on top. Roll the husk lengthwise, then fold up the base and fold down the pointed tip by about one-third. Set aside the prepared *tamales* so that the filling does not leak out.
✻ Put 4 cups (32 fl oz/1 l) of water in the bottom of a steamer and cover the basket with a layer of corn husks (about 8). Set the *tamales* in the basket upright and slightly inclined so that the *masa* does not slip to the bottom. As soon as the water comes to a boil, lower the heat, cover and cook for 1 hour (25 minutes in a pressure cooker) or until the *masa* does not stick to the corn husk when a *tamale* is unrolled.
✻ Serve hot or at room temperature.

MAKES ABOUT 20 TAMALES

Tamales Wrapped in Banana Leaves (front), Chicken Tamales with Green Sauce (center) and Pineapple Atole (rear)

Fresh Corn Tamales and Café de Olla

MICHOACÁN

UCHEPOS

Fresh Corn Tamales

For some reason these delicate fresh corn tamales of Michoacán are never quite the same when prepared else-where, but they still are unique and very good. In Mexico

they would be made with fresh field corn, which has a higher starch content. The best substitute is corn that has been picked for several days and is not too sweet or tender.

8–10 ears (cobs) corn
⅓ cup (3 fl oz/80 ml) milk
2 tablespoons sugar
½ teaspoon salt
2 tablespoons softened butter or lard

✳ Use a sharp knife to slice through the thick end of the corn ears. Remove the husks, being careful not to break them, and set aside. Slice the kernels off the cobs; you should have about 5 cups (20 oz/625 g). Place the kernels in a bowl. Moisten your hands and use them to stir the kernels so that any corn silk sticks to your hands and can be removed.

✳ Place 1 cup of the corn kernels in a blender and process at high speed, adding milk as necessary. Do not process too thoroughly; the mixture should be the consistency of cottage cheese. Repeat until all the corn has been processed.

✳ Stir in the sugar and salt and mix well. Add the softened butter or lard and combine thoroughly.

✳ Place the steamer basket in a steamer and add hot water up to ½ in (1 cm) below the bottom of the basket. Line the basket with the stiffer corn husks.

✳ Take a pliable corn husk, spread it out and place a tablespoon of the filling in it. Roll up the husk loosely and fold the point over the seam. Stack the prepared *tamales* in the steamer basket with their seams and points facing up, being careful not to crush them.

✳ Cover with another layer of corn husks and place the lid on the steamer. When the water comes to a boil, reduce the heat to low and cook for 1 hour or until the filling inside a husk appears curdled.

✳ Let the *tamales* cool for at least 20 minutes so that they dry and the filling does not stick to the husks.

✳ The *tamales* can be served rolled in the husk or unrolled and placed 2 on a plate with a little *salsa de molcajete* (page 198) and a tablespoon of *crème fraîche*. Or they can be served by themselves.

✳*Note:* The *tamales* can also be cooked in a pressure cooker. After the steam escapes, close the valve and cook for 20 minutes.

SERVES 14–16

Café de Olla

Coffee in a Clay Pot

For this popular after-supper drink, coffee, sugar, cinnamon and spices are simmered in a clay pot to produce a most distinctive flavor that is best appreciated when served in small clay mugs. For best results, use a coarsely ground, dark-roasted coffee like a Viennese roast.

5 cups (40 fl oz/1.25 l) water
½ cup (2 oz/60 g) coarsely ground dark-roasted coffee
4 oz (125 g) *piloncillo* (raw sugar)
1½ 4-in (10-cm) sticks cinnamon
5 whole cloves
peel from ¼ orange

✳ Heat 4 cups (32 fl oz/1 l) of the water in an *olla* or small saucepan over moderate heat. When it comes to a boil, lower the heat and add the coffee, *piloncillo*, cinnamon sticks, cloves and orange peel. Simmer for 5 minutes.

✳ Add 1 cup (8 fl oz/250 ml) cold water, remove from the heat and cover. Let stand for 5 minutes. Strain before serving.

SERVES 6

OAXACA

Champurrado

Chocolate Drink

Atole made from the treasured cacao bean was reserved only for the noblemen of Moctezuma's court, who drank it from special gold ceremonial cups. The women were served their atole flavored with chía and a topping of chile. Oaxaca is especially famed for its chocolate, which is sold in all of its markets. It does good to pay heed to the time-proven advice "Ni amor recomenzado ni chocolate recalentado" ("Neither rekindle a love affair nor reheat chocolate").

water
4 oz (125 g) *masa*
2 oz (60 g) *piloncillo* (raw sugar)
1 4-in (10-cm) stick cinnamon
5 oz (155 g) semisweet (cooking) chocolate

✳ Stir the *masa* in 4 cups (32 fl oz/1 l) water. Let stand for 15 minutes, then strain the water and place it in a saucepan with another 4 cups (32 fl oz/1 l) water, the *piloncillo* and cinnamon stick.

✳ Cook over medium heat, stirring constantly, for 10 minutes. Add the chocolate and stir for another 15 minutes or until the chocolate melts. Serve hot.

SERVES 6

Red Chilaquiles (recipe page 44) and Champurrado

Almond Eggnog

PUEBLA

ROMPOPE DE ALMENDRAS

Almond Eggnog

This rich Mexican eggnog is easily prepared and keeps under refrigeration for a long time, but it is also found premixed in bottles. It can be sipped from small glasses or served over berries or gelatin (jelly).

6 whole cloves
1 4-in (10-cm) stick cinnamon
2 cups (16 fl oz/500 ml) rum, or to taste
6 cups (48 fl oz/1.5 l) milk
2½ cups (20 oz/625 g) sugar
½ cup (2 oz/60 g) finely ground blanched almonds
15 egg yolks
¼ teaspoon grated nutmeg

✴ Marinate the cloves and cinnamon stick in the rum for 24 hours.
✴ Boil the milk and sugar in a large saucepan. Add the almonds and cook over low heat for 5 minutes. Set aside.
✴ Beat the egg yolks for 5–10 minutes until they form a ribbon. Mix 1 cup (8 fl oz/250 ml) of the boiled milk into the egg yolks. Add this mixture to the rest of the milk and cook over low heat, stirring constantly with a wooden spoon, for 10 minutes or until thickened.
✴ Remove the cloves and cinnamon and stir the rum into the eggnog. Sprinkle each serving with nutmeg. Serve at room temperature or chilled.

SERVES 8–10

GUERRERO

AGUA DE FRUTAS

Fruit Punch

A light rum could be added to this fruit punch for a more spirited beverage perfect at a festive brunch.

3 cups (1½ lb/750 g) coarsely chopped papaya
   (pawpaw)
3 cups (1½ lb/750 g) coarsely chopped pineapple
1 cup (8 oz/250 g) roughly chopped watermelon
3 cups (24 fl oz/750 ml) freshly squeezed orange juice
4 cups (32 fl oz/1 l) water
⅓ cup (3 oz/90 g) sugar, or to taste

✴ In a blender, purée the papaya, pineapple, watermelon and orange juice. Pour into a pitcher, dilute with the water and add sugar to taste.
✴ Serve with ice and garnish each drink with a small chunk of pineapple.
✴*Note:* You can purée the pineapple first and strain before adding the other ingredients.

SERVES 6–8   *Photograph page 4*

AGUA DE MELON

Melon Water

While licuados *are drinks made with blended milk and fruit,* aguas frescas *are made with water and usually contain the more acidic fruits. Both drinks are good uses for any overripe fruit such as pineapple, watermelon or strawberries. In Mexican markets, vivid and pastel-colored fruit waters like this are served from large beehive-shaped jars to those passing by.*

1 cantaloupe (rock melon)
8 cups (64 fl oz/2 l) water
½ cup (4 oz/125 g) sugar

✴ Cut the cantaloupe in half, scoop out the seeds and place them in a food processor or blender. Add 3 cups (about 20 oz/625 g) roughly chopped cantaloupe and 1 cup (8 fl oz/250 ml) water. Purée.
✴ Strain the puréed mixture into a pitcher, dilute with 7 cups (56 fl oz/1.75 l) water, add the sugar and stir.
✴ If you like, before serving, cut up the rest of the cantaloupe and place a few small chunks in each glass or in the pitcher.

SERVES 6–8   *Photograph page 4*

GUERRERO

AGUA DE TAMARINDO

Tamarind Water

The tamarind tree from India produces a fuzzy, pod-shaped fruit with a sticky, earth-colored pulp that has a tart flavor. When mixed with sugar or chile, the pulp is eaten as a snack, but when combined with sweetened water it becomes one of Mexico's favorite beverages to serve with antojitos or grilled meats. The three- to four-inch pods are available in specialty Mexican markets.

10 oz (315 g) dried tamarinds, peeled (about 29)
10 cups (80 fl oz/2.5 l) water
½–1 cup (2–4 oz/60–125 g) sugar

✳ Wash the tamarinds and soak in 4 cups (32 fl oz/1 l) hot water for 2 hours.
✳ After the tamarinds have soaked, reach into the bowl and rub them against each other for at least 5 minutes, to obtain as much pulp as possible, about 2 cups.
✳ Strain the liquid into a pitcher, dilute with 6 cups (48 fl oz/1.5 l) cold water and sweeten to taste.

SERVES 8

OAXACA

AGUA DE HORCHATA

Ground Rice Drink

Horchata is another culinary adventure, having its roots in the Arab world, where it was first made from the ground tiger nut. Brought to the New World by the Spanish, horchata first appeared as a popular drink on the Yucatán peninsula. This Oaxacan version uses milk instead of water and sometimes includes the fruit of a local cactus for a pink coloring or a few almonds for flavor. It is important that the rice be finely ground, which is best done in a coffee or spice grinder. Horchata is more flavorful if made a day ahead.

2 cups (10 oz/315 g) long-grain white rice
7 cups (56 fl oz/1.75 l) water
2 4-in (10-cm) sticks cinnamon
2 cups (16 fl oz/500 ml) milk
sugar

✳ In a large bowl, soak the rice in 3 cups (24 fl oz/750 ml) of the water for 2 hours.
✳ Crumble the cinnamon and toast it on a small skillet.

✳ Drain the rice and grind it in a blender or coffee grinder with the cinnamon and milk. Strain the mixture into a pitcher and dilute with 4 cups (32 fl oz/1 l) of cold water. Add sugar to taste.

SERVES 6–8

GUERRERO

AGUA DE JAMAICA

Jamaica Flower Water

This scarlet-colored drink made from the dried calyxes of the jamaica flower is perfect to serve with antojitos. For a more spirited drink, a light rum can be added to it, or mix it into a sangría or wine punch. Highly diuretic, this is a favorite drink of dieters who can tolerate it made without sugar. It is acidic, so only store it in a glass or plastic container. The dried jamaica is available in specialty Mexican markets or can easily be brought back from a vacation trip to Mexico.

2 cups (5 oz/155 g) dried *jamaica* flowers
10 cups (80 fl oz/2.5 l) water
¾ cup (6 oz/185 g) sugar

✳ Rinse the flowers briefly to remove any impurities. Drain.
✳ Place the flowers in a saucepan and add 6 cups (48 fl oz/1.5 l) water. Bring the water to a boil, reduce the heat to medium and cook for 10 minutes. Remove the pan from the heat and let stand for 10–20 minutes.
✳ Strain the water into a pitcher, dilute with 4 cups (32 fl oz/1 l) water and add the sugar.
✳ Serve well chilled.

SERVES 6–8

Tamarind Water (left), Ground Rice Drink (center) and Jamaica Flower Water (right)

Jícama con Piña

Jícama with Pineapple

This botana *(snack) is a refreshing variation of the traditional Jaliscan* pico de gallo *("rooster's beak") made with* jícama, *oranges and* chile piquín. *Since* jícamas *are available in the wintertime, they are one of the harbingers of the Christmas season. The smallest, crispest ones are combined with candies, peanuts, tangerines, sugar cane and small toys and stuffed into* piñatas.

3 cups (1½ lb/750 g) peeled and diced *jícama* (yam bean)
3 cups (1½ lb/750 g) diced fresh pineapple
3 tablespoons finely chopped *cilantro* (coriander)
1 teaspoon salt
juice of 1 lime
1 or 2 *chiles serranos,* diced

✳ Place the *jícama,* pineapple, *cilantro,* salt, lime juice and *chile* in a large bowl, mix thoroughly and chill for at least 15 minutes. Serve cold or at room temperature, using cocktail forks or toothpicks to pick up the fruit.

SERVES 6 AS APPETIZER, 4 AS SALAD

Margaritas

Margaritas

The term "cocktail" is said to have originated in Mexico. According to a widely accepted story, British naval crews used to gather to fortify themselves at a favorite tavern in Campeche. While most liquors were drunk straight, at times the English preferred their tot of rum mixed with other ingredients, which were then stirred with a small wooden spoon. One day an enterprising waiter, being out of these spoons, used pieces of the thin, smooth roots of a plant known as "tail of the cock" because of its peculiar shape. The name "cock's tail" caught on, and by the end of World War I these drinks were the rage of England, Europe and the U.S. nightclub set. The best known in Mexico is the margarita, first made in a Chihuahua bar.

4 cups (32 fl oz/1 l) or more crushed ice
½ cup (4 fl oz/125 ml) white tequila
¼ cup (2 fl oz/60 ml) cointreau
juice of 4 limes
1½ teaspoons salt

✳ In a blender, whirl the ice, tequila, cointreau and lime juice for 30 seconds.
✳ Moisten the rim of 6 glasses with lime juice and invert on a saucer of salt to lightly coat the rims with salt. Divide the margarita mixture among the glasses and serve.

SERVES 6 *Photograph pages 28–29*

Sangrita

Sangrita

This is María Dolores Torres Yzábal's version of sangrita, *a spicy-sweet chaser for tequila. Whenever tequila is asked for in Mexico, it will usually be served in small narrow glasses accompanied by* sangrita *in similar glasses. Try to learn the brand names of the better, smoother, aged tequilas, such as Centenario, Herradura, Cuervo or Sauza. For the finest flavor, ask for* reposado, *which has been aged one year, or* añejo, *which has been stored in white oak barrels for two years.*

2 *chiles anchos,* toasted (see glossary), stems and seeds removed
2 tablespoons finely chopped onion
2 cups (16 fl oz/500 ml) orange juice
juice of 1 small lime
salt

✳ Soak the *chiles* in hot water to cover for 20 minutes and drain.
✳ In a blender, purée the *chiles* with the onion, orange juice, lime juice and salt (to taste) until thoroughly blended. If the mixture is too thick, add more lime and orange juice.

MAKES 4 SMALL "SHOTS"

Sangría

Sangría

This refreshing blend of wine and fruit juices was a gift from Spain to the New World long before the now-popular wine coolers became commercialized. While many of Mexico's spicier foods overwhelm a glass of wine, sangría *is right at home. The amount of sugar in the recipe can be varied, depending on taste.*

4 cups (32 fl oz/1 l) dry red wine
4 cups (32 fl oz/1 l) mineral water
¾ cup (6 fl oz/180 ml) grenadine or sugar syrup
¾ cup (6 fl oz/180 ml) fresh lime juice
1 orange, thinly sliced
½ cup (4 oz/125 g) peeled and chopped peach or pineapple

✳ In a glass pitcher, mix the wine, water, grenadine and lime juice. Stir well. Add the orange slices and chopped fruit. Chill well.
✳ Before serving, add ice cubes.

SERVES 6–8 *Photograph page 39*

*Jícama with Pineapple (top)
and Sangrita with Tequila*

Isthmus of Tehuantepec

ISTHMUS OF TEHUANTEPEC

The Isthmus of Tehuantepec is a beautiful and diverse land, belted tight in the middle by the narrowest part of Mexico, only 125 miles from shore to shore. On the Gulf side of the isthmus, in the states of Veracruz and Tabasco, crops grow easily, nurtured in the deep alluvial soil by almost constant moisture. In fact, the rainfall here is measured in feet instead of inches and in some places totals more than ten feet a year. The southern part of the west coast, however, is dry, and only land that is near rivers can support agriculture.

On both coasts, the conflicts of modern civilization are apparent, as oxen carts compete for space on the highways with green John Deere tractors and mammoth tanker trucks. Oil deposits discovered in the last decade have brought needed jobs to the region but also air and water pollution. The dichotomy between modern and ancient worlds is nowhere more apparent than in Salina Cruz on the coast of Oaxaca. Here, less than fifty miles from where tankers wait offshore for their loads of crude oil, and towering smokestacks dampen the sun with black clouds, the Pacific Coast Huave Indians still live in remote coastal villages built of reeds, carrying on their centuries-old pattern of life.

Two distinct cuisines emerge as the region broadens out from the girdling isthmus. In Veracruz, influenced by Caribbean and African roots, the cuisine developed naturally from the area's abundance of cattle, seafood and produce; in the high, dry scrub land of Oaxaca, however, local fare was "invented" by the demands of daily sustenance. The one unifying food is *frijoles negros*,

Previous pages: Spanish settlers built the church at Mitla, Oaxaca, with stones from the archaeological site next door. Left: A banana seller patiently waits for customers near the Río Tecolutla in Veracruz.

the small ebony beans that in one form or another are the mainstay of the isthmus diet.

The salt waters of the Pacific and the Gulf of Mexico, and the fresh waters of the mountain rivers provide an abundance of fish and shellfish. One of the most unusual, the prehistoric-looking *pejelagarto,* is prepared as a stew in Tabasco.

The waterfront city of Veracruz—once a port of call for Spanish conquistadors, French invaders, African slaves, American marines, and English and Dutch pirates—is characterized by sounds, sights and tastes more reminiscent of the Caribbean or New Orleans than of other Mexican cities. Seafood is eaten at any time of day. A bowl of tangy shrimp soup, perhaps followed by steaming-hot crab legs still in their shells, is a common eye-opener in the morning, when it may be consumed at one of the brightly painted seafood bars by the port. To satisfy between-meal hunger, it is easy to stop for a *taco* made with *salpicón de jaiba* (shredded crab, usually mixed with pickled vegetables).

The main meals along this humid coast are long and leisurely—with talk and laughter and lots of food. On a typical Sunday afternoon in Boca del Río, a small fishing town south of Veracruz, a diner can sit in a big noisy restaurant under a slowly turning ceiling fan while chiclet and gee-gaw vendors ply their wares among tables of large families, young couples and groups of businessmen. Outside, great-tailed grackles screech their harsh "clackit, clackit, clackit," varied by smooth clear whistles. Before long, through the cacophony of competing sounds, the traditional refrains of local *huapangeros* emerge as they move among the tables with their unusual guitars and harp. The white-clad musicians are known throughout Mexico for their ability to create on-the-spot appropriate, but sometimes devastating, lyrics. A young lad begins to dance a fast, generations-old rhythmic tap, his eyes unseeing but feet always moving to the rhythm of the music.

The food arrives quickly, but even sooner come large glasses of *toritos,* a thick, sweet, mildly alcoholic drink of ground peanuts. Dishes then fill the table in overwhelming abundance: huge plates of *camarón para pelar* (shrimp to peel), *pámpano en hierba santa* (whole fish wrapped and steamed in the large leaves of an anise-flavored herb) and *arroz a la tumbada,* a local specialty of short-grained rice and mixed seafood, somewhat similar to a *paella* but with a more powerful taste of garlic and *chile. Pulpos enchipotlados,* tender bits of octopus in a wonderfully spicy sauce, is served with black beans fried with banana to diffuse the heat of the sauce. The most famous dish of the region is *pescado a la veracruzana.* The Spaniards studded the Mexican sauce of tomatoes and *chiles* with green olives and plump capers and, cloaking a whole fish with it, created a superb mingling of the food of two worlds.

All meals end with coffee. Drinking coffee—hot, sweet and strong as love, according to Veracruzanos—is a major activity in the cafés throughout the day. The insistent tinkling of spoons being tapped on coffee glasses signals a request for a waiter to pour a stream of hot milk from a metal container held high above the table to dilute the strong, steaming coffee.

In 1858 a Smithsonian archaeologist discovered a massive carved head of basalt, hidden for centuries on a swampy mangrove island in Tabasco. It was the first clue to the existence of the shadowy Olmec

A Zapotec woman at Oaxaca's main market, which overflows on Saturdays with Indians from the surrounding villages.

civilization, which flourished on this coast well over two thousand years ago, before the Mayas and before the builders of the ancient city of Teotihuacán. Today the empty and forgotten cities of the Olmecs have been swallowed up by the ever-encroaching jungle, and their deeds have been preserved by later Indian civilizations only in legends.

The isthmus was not only home to the first civilization in Mexico and Central America but was also the site of the first Spanish settlement. When Cortés left Cuba in February 1519, he came ashore first on the Yucatán peninsula, then in Tabasco. With their firearms, steel swords and supernatural-appearing horses, the Spaniards easily defeated the local people. In tribute, the Indians presented Cortés with twenty female slaves, who were distributed among his leaders to be their cooks and concubines. These women became the first to combine the foods of two worlds into the beginning of today's Mexican cuisine.

One of the slaves, called Marina by the Spaniards, became the mistress of Cortés. Because she spoke Náhuatl, the language of the Aztecs, she was of great value to him when he next went ashore and met the emissaries of Moctezuma. On a riverbank a few miles from the present city of Veracruz, Cortés established Villa Rica de la Vera Cruz (Rich Town of the True Cross). Although Veracruz was subsequently moved to its present harbor location, a roofless brick ruin held together by tangled vines and mosses still marks the site in the riverside village of La Antigua.

Oaxaca was occupied by the Spanish only three years after Cortés landed in Veracruz, but it was many years before they finally subjugated the million and a half Zapotec and Mixtec Indians inhabiting the great high valley set against the dramatic background of mountains. The Zapotecs, a distinct group of people followed by the Mixtecs, had arrived around the time of Christ, and over the course of many centuries had built the impressive capital city of Monte Albán upon the ruins of more fleeting civilizations. In spite of constant fighting between these two Indian groups, they became united in their battles against both the Aztecs and the Spaniards.

Oaxaca is the land of the seven *moles,* which have been favored since they were invented in the Spanish kitchens of the convents. The word *mole* comes from the Náhuatl word meaning "concoction," which is just what they are—wonderful, complex mixtures of roasted *chiles,* tomatoes and squash seeds from the new home of the Spaniards, and nuts, spices, meats and sesame seeds from the land they left behind. The shiny black *mole negro* uses chocolate as a flavoring, as does the lighter *coloradito,* or red, *mole.* Greens, herbs, *chiles* and the small husked *tomate verde* form the basis of *mole verde.* Other *moles* make use of different *chiles* and spices for a special color and taste.

Lacking an abundance of meat and other common sources of protein, the Indians of this region used what was at hand, and insects and their larvae still play a role in the diet of all classes of people. At the entrances to the two great markets of Oaxaca, finely woven baskets hold various sizes of dried *chapulines* or *grillos* (grasshoppers), which are lightly sautéed and seasoned for *tacos.* Mescal continues its close association with the maguey worm, which is dried and added to bottles of mescal—perhaps for flavor or maybe just as a sign of *macho.* When ground and mixed with salt, however, it does impart a complementary taste to certain tequila cocktails.

The oldest of Mexico's ancient civilizations were the Olmecs, who carved colossal twenty-ton basalt heads at their ceremonial center, La Venta, in Tabasco. La Venta reached its zenith between 900 and 400 B.C.

SOPAS

Squash blossoms make a favorite soup in central Mexico.

SOPAS

Red, green and white are the colors of Mexico's flag, and red, green and white are the colors of its *pozoles,* the country's most famous all-in-one-dish meal. All are redolent of the flavor of long-simmered pork and thick with hominy, but there the similarity ends. Each week in Guerrero when the calendar says it is Thursday, the stomach tells everyone it is green *pozole* day. By three in the afternoon, little *pozole* restaurants are filled with people eating the hearty soup from big earthenware bowls. The verdant color and unusual flavor come from fresh *chiles,* greens, ground pumpkin seeds and tangy little *tomates verdes.* Each dish is further embellished with finely chopped onion, crispy *chicharrón* (crisp-fried pork rinds), cubes of avocado, dried oregano and a squeeze of lime. To ward off starvation before the soup appears, people snack on *chiles jalapeños* stuffed with cheese, plates of *manitas de puerco en escabeche* (pickled pigs' feet) and delicious *tacos de sesos* (brains) flavored with *epazote.*

Pozole blanco (white *pozole*) is a favorite in Guerrero, frequently enriched with the addition of a raw egg. It is in Jalisco, however, that this simple, hunger-satisfying dish comes into its own. Pieces of pork, including the head, simmer with the hominy in an earthenware pot throughout the day. At the time of eating, a dose of ground *chile piquín* or an equally pungent *salsa* is added, then a final benediction of chopped radishes, lettuce or cabbage. The result is a delicious layered meal of meat, starch and vegetable.

In Michoacán, the aromas emanating from enormous pots of simmering broth give promise of the rich taste of *chile ancho* and *chile guajillo.* When served, this deep-red soup, *pozole rojo,* is given the characteristic oregano topping of Guerrero. Variations of all three *pozoles* can be found in each of these states as well as in other parts of Mexico.

Caldo de pollo, mole de olla, clemole and *menudo* are other popular soups served as a complete meal. *Menudo,* a comforting soup of tripe, is commonly eaten the morning after a night of alcoholic indulgence. It is said that the high vitamin B content accompanied by the fiery bite of *chiles* gives a person back his zest for living.

Soups are such an integral part of most Mexican meals that it is hard to believe they are relatively new additions to the table. None of the early Spanish chronicles mentions soups; the closest dish would be the thick stews the Indians cooked in large clay *ollas.* It was not until the infusion of French and other European cultures that soup appeared as a first course. This ranged from the simple *sopa de fideo* (noodle soup) and the wonderful, ubiquitous *sopa de tortilla* (tortilla soup) to the more unusual *sopa de médula (*a rich meat broth full of tasty pieces of mouth-melting bone marrow) and the exotic *sopa de cuitlacoche.* The fungus *cuitlacoche,* which grows in dark globular masses on ears of corn, has a flavor fit for royalty. The Aztecs called it "the excrement of the

Around every corner in Puebla is a tiny restaurant with a fanciful street menu. Hearty soups usually lead the line-up for the comida, the main meal of the day.

god of sustenance," but this appellation should not discourage anyone from eating the fungus, which is truly delicious.

In the mid-sixteenth century the galleons that sailed from the Philippines to the Pacific ports of Acapulco and Barra de Navidad brought the first rice to the New World, where it quickly found a new home. The nuns welcomed this beloved ingredient, and in the convents and kitchens of the Spanish aristocracy, native cooks learned to adapt the grain into their own dishes, combining it with tomatoes, *chiles* and herbs, or even with fried bananas. It was served as a *sopa seca,* or "dry soup"—a transitional dish between the starter and the main course.

Sopas secas are not just rice dishes, although they are the most common. They may be crêpes, soufflés, pasta or even a thick vegetable *budín* (pudding). Many of these dishes are filling enough to be served as the main course of a lighter meal and are often used for brunches or late suppers. Whether eaten as part of a multi-course *comida* or as a separate meal, *sopas secas,* with their mild flavors, are a delicious surprise to those new to the varied flavors of Mexican cooking.

Limes make a daily appearance at the marketplace in Mérida, where sizzling sopa de lima *is a specialty. Cooks throughout the Yucatán peninsula use limes as a basic seasoning, in place of salt.*

Sopa de Pasta

Pasta Soup

Pasta arrived in Mexico during the thirty years of Porfirio Díaz's presidency, with its emphasis on grand continental cuisine. This recipe calls for fideos, or vermicelli, but almost

any soup pasta can be used, even stars, wheels or alphabet types. The trick is to have the noodle acquire the proper light-brown color without getting too dark and bitter tasting.

2 tomatoes
¼ onion
2 cloves garlic

＊ In a blender, purée the tomatoes, onion and garlic with the water. Strain and set aside.

＊ Heat the oil in a large saucepan or Dutch oven, add the pasta and stir until it begins to brown. Pour off the excess oil. Add the puréed tomatoes and boil for 3 minutes, stirring constantly. Add the stock and bring to a boil. Cover and cook over medium heat for 10 to 15 minutes or until the pasta is tender. Add salt to taste. If you wish, garnish with the *chiles*.

SERVES 6

Sopa de Tortilla

Tortilla Soup

If just one soup could be labeled the classic Mexican soup, it would probably be this one, combining as it does the traditional flavors and textures of the country's chile, tomato, avocado, epazote and tortilla.

3 cloves garlic
½ onion, cut into chunks
3 ripe tomatoes
6 cups (48 fl oz/1.5 l) chicken stock (page 72)
1 tablespoon oil
2 small sprigs *epazote*
salt and freshly ground pepper
8–10 day-old corn tortillas
oil for frying
2–3 *chiles pasillas*
2 avocados, peeled, pitted and sliced or chopped
5 oz (155 g) *queso fresco* (or feta cheese), crumbled
½ cup (4 fl oz/125 ml) thick cream *(crème fraîche)*
3 limes, halved

＊ Roast the garlic, onion and tomatoes (see glossary). Peel and core the tomatoes and purée in a blender with the garlic and onion, adding ¼ cup (2 fl oz/60 ml) of the chicken stock if necessary.

＊ Heat 1 tablespoon oil in a large saucepan over high heat and sauté the tomato purée. Boil for 2 minutes, lower the heat and cook, stirring constantly, for another 5 minutes or until the purée thickens and changes color.

＊ Add the remaining chicken stock and *epazote*. Return to a boil, add salt and pepper to taste and cook, covered, over medium heat for 15 minutes.

＊ Cut the tortillas in half and cut each half into thin strips. Heat ½ in (1 cm) oil in a small skillet and, when hot, add the tortilla pieces a few at a time and fry, turning at least once, for about 3 minutes or until golden brown. Remove from the oil with a slotted spatula and drain on absorbent paper. (If using fresh tortillas, dry first in a preheated 250°F/120°C oven for an hour.)

＊ Cut the *chiles* into ½-in (1-cm) rings and remove their seeds. Fry in the hot oil for about 1 minute or until crisp. Drain and set aside.

＊ Five minutes before serving, reheat the soup and add the fried tortilla strips. Garnish each bowl of soup with a few *chile* rings and the avocado. Sprinkle with the cheese. Pass the cream, lime halves and remaining *chile* rings and avocado in separate bowls so that each person can add them to taste.

SERVES 6

Pasta Soup (left) and Tortilla Soup (right)

½ cup (4 fl oz/125 ml) water
2 tablespoons oil
1 package (8 oz/250 g) vermicelli or other thin pasta
8 cups (64 fl oz/2 l) chicken stock (page 72)
salt
chiles serranos (optional)

GUERRERO

CHILATOLE

Corn and Masa Soup

A gruel of ground corn—its flavor livened with chile *and* epazote—*was the main sustenance of the first Indian cultures of Mexico. This much more elaborate version is a natural beginning to a meal of* tacos *or* enchiladas.

3 tablespoons butter
½ tablespoon oil
¼ small onion
3 cloves garlic
10 cups (80 fl oz/2.5 l) chicken stock (page 72)
3 sprigs *epazote*
1 lb (500 g) *masa*
1½ cups (12 fl oz/375 ml) cold water
salt and freshly ground pepper
2 cups (8 oz/250 g) corn kernels
2 *chiles serranos,* seeded and finely chopped
2 cups (16 fl oz/500 ml) thick cream *(crème fraîche)*
1 cup (8 oz/250 g) chopped red onion

✳ In a large pot or Dutch oven, heat the butter and oil. Add the onion and garlic and sauté for 3–4 minutes or until transparent. Add the chicken stock and *epazote* and boil for 10 minutes.

✳ Stir the *masa* into the cold water. Add to the boiling chicken stock and cook, stirring constantly, for 8–10 minutes. Lower the heat and cook for 5 minutes. Add salt and pepper to taste. Strain the stock and return to the pot. Add the corn and *chiles* and cook for another 5 minutes.

Corn and Masa Soup

✳ Before serving, heat the soup and stir in the cream. Bring just to a boil, then serve. Pass the onion in a separate bowl.

SERVES 8

CHIAPAS

SOPA DE PAN

Bread Soup

This unusual and filling bread soup, with its colorful layers of fruits and vegetables, is a typical dish from San Cristóbal de las Casas.

6 cups (48 fl oz/1.5 l) chicken stock (page 72)
2 carrots, peeled and coarsely chopped
1 2-in (5-cm) stick cinnamon
1 sprig thyme
1 sprig marjoram
½ teaspoon freshly ground pepper
¼ cup (2 fl oz/60 ml) dry white wine
salt
3 cups (3 oz/90 g) cubed white bread, either a *baguette* or hard roll
⅓ cup (3 oz/90 g) butter
2 tablespoons oil
8 oz (250 g) onion, sliced
3 cloves garlic
1½ lb (750 g) tomatoes, peeled and thickly sliced
3 hard-boiled (hard-cooked) eggs, sliced
3 teaspoons chopped capers
3 tablespoons chopped green olives (optional)
¼ cup (1 oz/30 g) raisins
ground cinnamon
½ cup (2 oz/60 g) crumbled *queso añejo* (or feta cheese) (optional)

✳ Place the chicken stock, carrots, cinnamon, thyme, marjoram, pepper and wine in a saucepan. Bring to a boil, cover and cook over medium heat for 10 minutes or until the carrots are tender. Add salt to taste. Discard the cinnamon, thyme and marjoram and set the stock aside.

✳ Preheat the oven to 400°F (200°C). Place the bread cubes in a baking pan and bake for 10–15 minutes or until lightly browned.

✳ Heat the butter in a skillet. Add half the bread cubes and fry for a few minutes or until they are golden brown. Transfer to a plate covered with absorbent paper. Repeat the procedure with the rest of the bread cubes. Set aside.

✳ Heat the oil in a skillet, add the onion and garlic and sauté for 3 minutes. Add the tomatoes and cook over medium heat, stirring constantly, for 10 minutes. Set aside.

✳ Fifteen minutes before serving, preheat the oven to 425°F (220°C). Bring the chicken stock to a simmer. Divide the bread cubes and stewed tomatoes among 6 ovenproof bowls, garnish with 2 slices of egg and add the hot chicken stock. Sprinkle with capers, olives, raisins and a pinch of cinnamon. Bake until the soup starts to boil. Serve hot, sprinkled with the *queso añejo.*

SERVES 6

Bread Soup

BAJA CALIFORNIA NORTE

SOPA DE ALMEJAS

Clam Soup

This soup would most likely have been made from the sweet pismo clams of Ensenada, but any other fresh clams could be used instead of canned. The recipe is unusual in that it does not contain any chiles.

3 tablespoons olive oil
¾ cup (6 oz/185 g) chopped onion
2 cups (12 oz/375 g) chopped celery
1 clove garlic, minced
3 cups (1 lb/500 g) peeled and cubed potatoes
8 cups (64 fl oz/2 l) chicken stock (recipe follows)
salt
2 cans (15 oz/470 g each) chopped clams, drained, with juice reserved
1½ cups (2 oz/60 g) finely chopped parsley
juice of 1 lime

✷ Heat 1 tablespoon of the oil in a large pot or Dutch oven, add the onion, celery and garlic and cook for 5 minutes or until transparent. Add the potatoes, chicken stock and 1 cup (8 fl oz/250 ml) of the clam juice and simmer, covered, over low heat for 15 minutes or until the potatoes are tender. Add salt to taste.
✷ Ten minutes before serving, bring the broth to a boil and add the chopped clams. Return to a boil and add the chopped parsley, remaining olive oil and lime juice. Serve immediately.

SERVES 6

CALDO DE POLLO

Chicken Stock and Soup

Eaten everywhere in Mexico, this simple, nourishing soup is often served as a main course. The vegetables may vary, but it is almost always served with lime, chopped onions and green chiles. Chicken stock is a major ingredient in many recipes, so it is wise to make it in advance and freeze it. It can be frozen in ice cube trays, and the cubes stored in plastic bags. Chicken parts such as the back and neck can also be used.

STOCK

1 whole chicken, about 3 lb (1.5 kg), cut into serving pieces
10 cups (80 fl oz/2.5 l) water
1 whole carrot
4 cloves garlic
1 tablespoon salt
6 black peppercorns
1 small sprig parsley
1 small onion, quartered

SOUP

¼ cup (2 oz/60 g) canned or cooked chickpeas
1 *chayote* (vegetable pear/choko), peeled and quartered
1 large potato, peeled and cut into chunks
2 ears (cobs) corn, each cut into 3 pieces
2 carrots, thickly sliced
1 cup (3 oz/90 g) sliced cabbage
2 sprigs *cilantro* (coriander)

1 sprig spearmint
1 cup cooked rice (about 2 oz/60 g uncooked) (optional)
3 limes, sliced
4 *chiles serranos,* seeds and membranes removed, and chopped
½ cup (4 oz/125 g) chopped onion

✷ To make the stock, rinse the chicken and giblets and place in a large pot or Dutch oven. Add the water, whole carrot, garlic, salt, peppercorns, parsley and onion. Bring to a boil, skim the surface, cover and cook over medium heat for 1 hour. Let cool, remove the chicken and degrease the stock.
✷ To make the soup, add the chickpeas after the stock has cooked for only 30 minutes. Cook 30 more minutes, then discard the parsley, onion and whole carrot. Add the *chayote,* potato, corn, sliced carrots, cabbage, *cilantro* and spearmint. Cover and cook over medium heat for 30 minutes or until the vegetables are tender.
✷ To serve, put a piece of chicken and some vegetables in each bowl, add some rice if you like and pour the hot broth over. Pass the lime slices and chopped *chiles* and onion separately.

SERVES 6–8

VERACRUZ

CALDO DE PESCADO

Fish Soup

Variations of this soup, all of which can be made with any firm-fleshed fish such as red snapper or sea bass, are coastal favorites. The best known, caldo largo ("lavish soup"), is from the river port of Alvarado in Veracruz. While the crude vocabulary of the local women is Alvarado's most noted characteristic, caldo largo and flaky little fish pastries are also famous and are sold to those waiting to cross over the toll bridge.

3 tablespoons oil
1 onion, coarsely chopped
3 cloves garlic
1 stalk celery, with leaves, chopped
2 lb (1 kg) fleshy heads and bones from firm fish such as sea bass, halibut, rock cod or red snapper, cut into chunks
10–12 cups (80–96 fl oz/2.5–3 ml) cold water
1 small sprig *cilantro* (coriander)
2 bay leaves
salt
1 *chile guajillo,* toasted (see glossary), seeds and membranes removed
3 tomatoes, chopped
1 sprig *epazote*
1½ cups (8 oz/250 g) peeled and diced potatoes
1¼ cups (10 oz/250 g) peeled and diced carrots
2 teaspoons dried oregano
6 fish fillets, about 3 oz (90 g) each
6 pickled *chiles serranos* or *chiles jalapeños* (optional)

✷ Heat 2 tablespoons of the oil in a large saucepan, add the onion, garlic and celery and sauté over medium heat for 3 minutes. Add the fish heads and bones and stir. Add the water, *cilantro,* bay leaves and salt to taste. When the mixture comes to a boil, lower the heat and

Chicken Soup (left) and Clam Soup (right)

simmer, covered, for 30 minutes.

✳ Transfer the fish heads and bones to a plate. When cool enough to handle, discard the heads and remove the flesh from the bones. Set aside.

✳ Strain the fish stock through a sieve and set aside. Grind the *chile guajillo* in a blender with ¼ cup (2 oz/60 ml) of the stock. Strain and set aside.

✳ Heat 1 tablespoon oil in a large saucepan and sauté the strained *chile.* Add the tomatoes and continue to cook, stirring constantly, for 4 minutes. Add the remaining fish stock and the *epazote.* When the mixture

comes to a boil, add the potatoes and carrots. Lower the heat and cook, covered, for 15 minutes or until the vegetables are tender. Correct the seasonings. Add the oregano and fish fillets and cook over medium heat until the fish flakes easily with a fork, about 10 minutes. Remove from the heat and add the bits of fish that were set aside.

✳ Serve hot, placing a fillet of fish in each soup dish and garnishing with a pickled *chile* if desired.

SERVES 6   *Photograph pages 8–9*

Cilantro Soup (left) and Cuitlacoche Soup (right)

DISTRITO FEDERAL

SOPA DE CILANTRO

Cilantro Soup

Cilantro is not native to Mexico but is now considered one of the country's quintessential flavors. This soup by María Dolores Torres Yzábal is a new addition to Mexican gastronomy.

1 lb (500 g) small zucchini (courgettes), cut into chunks
oil for frying
4 day-old corn tortillas, cut into small squares
6 cups (48 fl oz/1.5 l) chicken stock (page 72)
1 cup (1½ oz/45 g) tightly packed *cilantro* (coriander)
¼ cup (2 oz/60 g) butter
½ onion, minced
2 tablespoons cornstarch (cornflour)
2 *chiles serranos* or *chiles jalapeños*
salt
½ cup (4 fl oz/125 ml) thick cream *(crème fraîche)*
    (optional)
8 oz (250 g) *queso panela* (or fresh mozzarella), cubed
chiles serranos or *chiles jalapeños,* chopped

✱ Cook the zucchini in a covered saucepan with a little salted water for 20 minutes or until crisp-tender. Drain.

✱ While the zucchini are cooking, heat ½ in (1 cm) oil in a small skillet. When hot, add the tortilla pieces a few at a time and fry, turning at least once, for about 3 minutes or until golden brown. Remove from the oil with a slotted spatula and drain on absorbent paper. (If using fresh tortillas, dry first in a preheated 250°F/120°C oven for an hour.)

✱ In a blender, purée the zucchini in the chicken stock. When perfectly blended, add the *cilantro* and blend until smooth or leave coarse, as you prefer.

✱ Melt the butter in a large saucepan, add the onion and sauté until transparent. Add the puréed mixture, the cornstarch stirred into a little cold water, the whole *chiles* and salt if needed. Simmer, covered, over low heat for 10 minutes.

✱ Stir the cream in the soup if you wish and heat a few minutes more or until very hot. Serve the fried tortillas, cheese and chopped *chiles* in separate dishes on the side, to be added to the soup as desired.

SERVES 6

DISTRITO FEDERAL

SOPA DE CUITLACOCHE

Corn Fungus Soup

Colored black from cuitlacoche *(corn fungus), this exotic soup was served to ambassadors and heads of state by Feodora de Rosenzweig Díaz, wife of the subsecretary of foreign affairs from 1964–70. While* cuitlacoche *is highly prized in Mexico, farmers in other countries destroy this corn "smut," depriving many of a chance to taste the unusual fungus. Both canned squash blossoms and canned* cuitlacoche *can be found in Mexican grocery stores or brought back from a trip to Mexico.*

3 cups (12 oz/375 g) corn kernels
10 oz (315 g) squash (zucchini) blossoms (optional)
2 tablespoons oil
½ cup (4 oz/125 g) chopped onion
3 tablespoons finely chopped *epazote*
5 oz (155 g) fresh *cuitlacoche* or 1 can (7 oz/220 g) *cuitlacoche*
5 day-old corn tortillas
oil for frying
8 cups (64 fl oz/2 l) chicken stock (page 72)
5 oz (155 g) *queso fresco* (or feta cheese), cubed

✳ Place the corn in a saucepan, cover with water and simmer, covered, for 10 minutes. Drain and set aside.
✳ Remove the stems and pistils from the squash blossoms, chop coarsely and set aside.
✳ Heat the oil in a large saucepan, add the onion and sauté until transparent. Add the *epazote* and sauté for 2 minutes. Add the squash blossoms, *cuitlacoche* and corn. Cook over low heat for 5 minutes and set aside.
✳ Cut the tortillas in half, then cut into ½-in (1.5-cm) strips. Heat ½ in (1 cm) oil in a small skillet and, when hot, add the tortilla strips a few at a time and fry, turning at least once, for about 3 minutes or until golden brown. Remove from the oil with a slotted spatula and drain on absorbent paper. (If using fresh tortillas, dry first in a preheated 250°F/120°C oven for an hour.)
✳ Five minutes before serving, heat the chicken stock and pour into the pan containing the *cuitlacoche*. Stir for 3 minutes.
✳ Place some cubes of cheese in each soup bowl. Add the hot soup, garnish with tortilla strips and serve immediately. Float a small squash blossom in each bowl if available.

SERVES 6

SONORA

SOPA DE QUESO

Cheese Soup

In some parts of Sonora, potato chunks are added to this typical regional soup. If queso Chihuahua *is not available, use Monterey Jack or a medium-sharp Cheddar.*

1 *chile poblano*
1 green bell pepper (capsicum)
3 tablespoons (1½ oz/45 g) butter
½ cup (4 oz/125 g) chopped onion
5 cups (40 fl oz/1.25 l) chicken stock (page 72)
2 tablespoons all-purpose (plain) flour
2 tablespoons cornstarch (cornflour)
¾ cup (6 fl oz/180 ml) water
4 cups (32 fl oz/1 l) evaporated milk
1 teaspoon salt
1 teaspoon freshly ground pepper
4 oz (125 g) *queso Chihuahua* (or Monterey Jack or medium-sharp Cheddar cheese), finely chopped (about 1 cup)
1 cup (8 oz/250 g) chopped tomato

✳ Remove the stems, seeds and membranes from the *chile* and bell pepper and cut into a small dice; there should be about 1¼ cups.
✳ Melt 1 tablespoon of the butter in a skillet, add the onion and sauté for 2 minutes or until transparent. Add the *chile* and bell pepper and cook for 3 minutes. Set aside.
✳ Bring the stock to a boil in a large saucepan. Stir the flour and cornstarch into the water, add to the stock and stir constantly for 2 minutes. Add the milk and lower the heat. When it comes to a boil, add the bell pepper and *chile* and cook over low heat for 5 minutes. Add the salt and pepper and cook 2 minutes more. Add the remaining 2 tablespoons butter (1 oz/30 g) and set aside.
✳ Before serving, heat the soup and place 2 tablespoons of cheese and 2 tablespoons of tomato in the bottom of each bowl.

SERVES 8

Cheese Soup

Zucchini Soup

simmer for 10 minutes. Add the *chile* strips and cook for 5 minutes. Add the milk and simmer for 5 more minutes.

✱ Before serving, divide the cheese among 6 soup bowls. Pour the hot soup over and serve.

SERVES 6

GUERRERO

SOPA DE CALABACITA CON AVENA

Zucchini Soup with Oatmeal

This soup was created by Adelfa Silva, a transplanted Oaxacan who for two decades has cooked for Mexican and international celebrities in Acapulco. It combines squash with oatmeal in order to produce a thicker soup.

2 tablespoons (1 oz/30 g) butter
1 tablespoon minced onion
1¼ lb (625 g) small zucchini (courgettes), chopped
½ cup (2 oz/60 g) quick-cooking oatmeal (instant breakfast oats)
6 cups (48 fl oz/1.5 l) milk
salt and freshly ground pepper

✱ Melt the butter in a large saucepan, add the onion and sauté for 2 minutes or until transparent. Add the zucchini and sauté for 4 minutes. Add the oatmeal and cook, stirring, for 2 minutes. Add the milk a little at a time, stirring constantly. Add salt and pepper to taste. Cook, covered, over low heat for 15 minutes or until the zucchini are tender.

SERVES 6

MICHOACÁN

MINGUICHI

Chile and Cheese Soup

This unusual soup is named for the Purépecha (Tarascan) Indian combination of chiles *and* queso cotija, *the local cheese of the region. Here,* manchego *is substituted, and Muenster also gives a good but different flavor.*

1½ lb (750 g) tomatoes, quartered
1 tablespoon oil
½ tablespoon butter
½ cup (4 oz/125 g) finely chopped onion
1 clove garlic, finely chopped
kernels from 5 ears (cobs) young corn
1½ teaspoons salt
½ teaspoon freshly ground pepper
3 cups (24 fl oz/750 ml) chicken stock (page 72)
2 *chiles poblanos,* roasted (see glossary), peeled, membranes removed and cut into strips
1 cup (8 fl oz/250 ml) milk
5 oz (155 g) *queso manchego* (or Muenster or young pecorino cheese), diced

✱ In a blender, purée the tomatoes, strain and set aside.
✱ Heat the oil and butter in a skillet, add the onion, garlic and corn and sauté for 5 minutes.
✱ Add the puréed tomatoes, salt and pepper and simmer, uncovered, for 5 minutes. Stir in the stock and

GUERRERO

SOPA DE CALABACITAS

Zucchini Soup

Zucchini, a favorite for Mexican creamed soups, is spectacularly served inside a round squash.

3 lb (1.5 kg) zucchini (courgettes), cut into chunks
4 cups (32 fl oz/1 l) milk
2 cups (16 fl oz/500 ml) chicken stock (page 72)
3 tablespoons (1½ oz/45 g) butter
1 tablespoon minced onion
1½ teaspoons salt
½ teaspoon freshly ground pepper
6 acorn or other round squash (optional)

✱ Cook the zucchini in a covered saucepan with a little water for 20 minutes or until they are crisp-tender. Drain.
✱ In a blender, purée the zucchini, milk and stock. Melt the butter in a large saucepan, add the onion and sauté until transparent. Add the zucchini mixture, salt and pepper. Simmer, covered, over low heat for 5 minutes.
✱ If you like, slice the tops off the squash, scoop out the flesh and serve the soup in these shells instead of large bowls.

SERVES 6

Zucchini Soup with Oatmeal (top) and Minguichi (bottom)

Melon Soup (left) and Cream of Avocado Soup (right)

MICHOACÁN

CREMA DE AGUACATE

Cream of Avocado Soup

The beautiful evergreen avocado tree is native to Mexico. Its fruit has long been prized by the Indians, and the early Spaniards savored its buttery texture and rich flavor. The Hass variety, so popular in California, originated in Atlixco in the state of Puebla, but this soup is from Uruapan in the hot country of Michoacán.

3 avocados, pitted and peeled
1 tablespoon lime juice
7 cups (56 fl oz/1.75 l) chicken stock (page 72)
1 tablespoon chopped *cilantro* (coriander)
1 teaspoon salt
⅛ teaspoon freshly ground pepper
½ cup (4 fl oz/125 ml) thick cream *(crème fraîche)*

✳ Place the avocados in a blender along with the lime juice, chicken stock, *cilantro,* salt and pepper, then purée until smooth. If the soup is too thick, add another cup

(8 fl oz/250 ml) of broth. Cover and refrigerate until well chilled.
✳ Just before serving, stir in the cream and correct the seasonings. If you like, sprinkle chopped *cilantro* on each serving.

SERVES 6

MICHOACÁN

SOPA DE MELON

Melon Soup

Starting a meal with a cool fruit soup is an untraditional but highly satisfactory prelude to a spicy main dish such as pollo en pipián verde *(page 117). Using a very ripe melon gives the soup a better flavor.*

3 cantaloupes (rock melons)
2 tablespoons honey

¼ cup (2 fl oz/60 ml) fresh lemon juice
½ cup (4 fl oz/125 ml) fresh orange juice
¼ cup (2 fl oz/60 ml) port

✳ Cut the cantaloupes in half, remove and discard the seeds, then scoop out the pulp, being careful not to tear the peel. Set the 6 cantaloupe shells aside.
✳ Roughly chop the cantaloupe pulp and purée in a blender with the honey, lemon juice, orange juice and port.
✳ Chill well before serving. Use the cantaloupe shells as soup bowls.

SERVES 6

HIDALGO

SOPA DE NUEZ CON CHIPOTLE

Pecan Soup with Chipotle Sauce

Pecans are widely grown on the slopes of the Sierra Madre in northern Mexico and in limited quantities in southeastern Mexico. Although pecans are predominantly used in desserts, this recipe by María Dolores Torres Yzábal is a delicious exception.

2 tablespoons (1 oz/30 g) butter
2 tablespoons grated onion
1 clove garlic, crushed
2–4 tablespoons tomato paste
8 oz (250 g) shelled pecans
8 cups (64 fl oz/2 l) chicken stock (page 72)
1 small can pickled *chiles chipotles*
salt

✳ Melt the butter in a large saucepan, add the onion and sauté over medium-low heat until transparent. Add the garlic and sauté but do not brown. Add the tomato paste and stir well. Set aside.
✳ Place the pecans in a blender and add the chicken stock and 1 tablespoon of the liquid from the can of *chiles*. Purée and add to the tomato sauce, stirring to prevent sticking to the bottom of the pan. Add salt to taste and let the soup come to a slow boil over medium heat. Cook, covered, for 5 minutes.
✳ Serve in individual soup bowls and garnish with pecan halves or with strips of *chiles chipotles* that are arranged in the center of the bowl to look like a flower.

SERVES 6

TLAXCALA

SOPA DE FLOR DE CALABAZA

Squash Blossom Soup

Squash blossoms can be found in the Mexican markets during the early morning and are most abundant during the rainy season from June to October. You can also find them fresh (in season) or canned at specialty stores outside of Mexico. It is advisable to cook them as soon as possible, as they are extremely delicate and stay fresh for a very brief period.

2 lb (1 kg) squash (zucchini) blossoms
9 tablespoons (4½ oz/135 g) butter

3 green (spring) onions, thinly sliced
6 cloves garlic, slivered
6 *chiles serranos,* thinly sliced
¼ teaspoon each dried marjoram, thyme and tarragon
1 tablespoon chopped parsley
salt and freshly ground pepper
8 cups (64 fl oz/2 l) chicken stock (page 72)
1 boneless chicken breast, about 8 oz (250 g), skin removed and cut into ½-in (1-cm) cubes
⅓ cup (1½ oz/45 g) sliced mushrooms
2 cups (16 fl oz/500 ml) thick cream *(crème fraîche)*

✳ Remove the stems and pistils from the blossoms. Rinse gently, shaking off the excess water. Chop coarsely and set aside.
✳ Melt ¼ cup (2 oz/60 g) of the butter in a large skillet. Add the green onions, garlic and *chiles*. Sauté lightly and add the squash blossoms. Stir for 2 minutes and add the marjoram, thyme, tarragon and parsley. Season with salt and pepper and cook, covered, for 3 minutes.
✳ Heat the chicken stock in a large saucepan and add the flower mixture. Cook, covered, over low heat for 5 minutes. Set aside.
✳ Meanwhile, in a skillet over medium heat, sauté the chicken in 3 tablespoons (1½ oz/45 g) of butter until golden. Set aside.
✳ In the remaining 2 tablespoons (1 oz/30 g) butter, sauté the mushrooms and set aside.
✳ Add the chicken and mushrooms to the hot stock. Correct the seasonings and stir in the cream. Serve piping hot.

SERVES 6   *Photograph pages 64–65*

Pecan Soup with Chipotle Sauce

DISTRITO FEDERAL

SOPA DE OSTIONES AL CHIPOTLE

Oyster Soup Flavored with Chile Chipotle

The unusual taste combination of oysters and smoky chile chipotle flavors this soup served at the Guadiana restaurant in Mexico City.

3 tablespoons olive oil
1½ cups (12 oz/375 g) finely chopped onion
4 cloves garlic
½ cup (3 oz/90 g) chopped celery
2½ lb (1.25 kg) tomatoes, roasted (see glossary), peeled and chopped
1 teaspoon dried oregano
1 teaspoon freshly ground pepper
½ teaspoon salt
½ teaspoon dried thyme
½ teaspoon dried marjoram
2 bay leaves
2 jars (10 oz/315 g each) oysters, drained, with juice reserved
1 tablespoon Maggi (or Worcestershire) sauce
1 teaspoon Worcestershire sauce
2 tablespoons liquid from pickled *chiles chipotles*
bolillo (hard bread roll) or *baguette,* sliced and toasted

✻ Heat the oil in a large saucepan or Dutch oven over medium heat, add the onion and sauté for 4 minutes or until transparent. Add the garlic and celery and cook, stirring constantly, for 2 minutes. Add the tomatoes and cook over high heat for 5 minutes. Add the oregano, pepper, salt, thyme, marjoram and bay leaves. Cook, uncovered, over low heat for 40 minutes. Add 1 cup (8 fl oz/250 ml) of the oyster juice and 1 cup (8 fl oz/250 ml) of water. Cook for 10 minutes.
✻ Strain the mixture through a colander, using a wooden spoon to obtain as much of the liquid as possible. Return the strained stock to the pan and add the Maggi and Worcestershire sauces and the *chipotle* liquid. Correct the seasonings.
✻ Ten minutes before serving, heat the stock over medium heat. As soon as it comes to a boil, add the oysters and cook for 3 or 4 minutes or until their edges begin to curl; do not overcook or the oysters will be tough. Serve in *cazuelitas* or ramekins. Serve with slices of toasted bread.

SERVES 6

TAMAULIPAS

CHILPACHOLE DE JAIBA

Crab Stew

A rich, spicy soup made from the lively little blue crabs from the waters of the Gulf of Mexico. Blue crabs from the eastern U.S. coast can be used, or two small to medium-size Dungeness crabs (or blue swimmer or sand crabs). If the crabs are not alive, the shells can still be used to make the stock. Similar versions of this soup are popular in Veracruz.

12 live small crabs, about 4 oz (125 g) each
10 cups (80 fl oz/2.5 l) water
1 onion, cut in half
4 cloves garlic

3 teaspoons salt
1 bay leaf
1 lb (500 g) tomatoes
1 tablespoon oil
2 small sprigs *epazote*
2–3 pickled *chiles chipotles,* seeded and cut into strips
3 limes, halved

✻ Rinse the crabs in a large colander, scouring the shells with a vegetable brush.
✻ Place the water in a large pot or Dutch oven and add ½ onion, 2 garlic cloves, 1 teaspoon of the salt and the bay leaf. Bring the water to a boil over high heat, add the crabs and return to a boil. Let boil, covered, for 5 minutes, then remove the crabs and let them cool. Reserve the stock.
✻ Remove the shells from 6 of the crabs and cut each in half down the middle. Pick out the meat from the shell and set aside. If there is a yellow lump, it is the egg sac; save it to add to the soup. Return the shells to the pot and cook, covered, over medium heat for 15 minutes. Strain the stock and set aside.
✻ While the stock is cooking, remove the upper shell from the other 6 crabs, remove the bronchial filaments, cut the crab in half and set aside.
✻ Roast the tomato and remaining onion and garlic until the skin of the tomato is completely black (see glossary). Peel the tomato, then purée in a blender with the onion and garlic.
✻ Heat the oil in a large pot over high heat and add the tomato purée. When it comes to a boil, cover, lower the heat and cook for 5 minutes. Add the reserved stock, *epazote, chiles* and remaining 2 teaspoons salt. Bring to a boil, lower the heat and cook, covered, for 15 minutes. Correct the seasonings and add 1 cup (8 fl oz/250 ml) water if necessary.
✻ Before serving, add the crabmeat (and egg sac) that was set aside and the 6 crabs cut in half. Simmer for 3 minutes. Serve with lime halves.

SERVES 6–8

PUEBLA

CLEMOLE CON SALSA DE RÁBANOS

Vegetable Soup with Radish Sauce

This is another substantial peasant mole de olla—*a complete and flavorful meal usually cooked in a large clay pot. The addition of a zesty radish sauce makes this version special.*

SOUP

1½ lb (750 g) boneless lean pork, cubed
½ onion
3 cloves garlic
10 cups (80 fl oz/2.5 l) water
2 tablespoons salt
1½ lb (750 g) *tomates verdes,* husks removed
1 cup (1½ oz/45 g) chopped fresh *cilantro* (coriander)
3 *chiles serranos*
3 ears (cobs) corn, each cut into 3 pieces
8 oz (250 g) small zucchini (courgettes), sliced ½ in (1 cm) thick
8 oz (250 g) young green beans, trimmed and cut in half

Crab Stew (left), Oyster Soup Flavored with Chile Chipotle (center)
and Vegetable Soup with Radish Sauce (right)

SAUCE

1 cup (8 fl oz/250 ml) water
1 tablespoon salt
1 tablespoon vinegar
4 *chiles poblanos,* roasted (see glossary), peeled,
   membranes removed, and cut into strips
6 radishes, finely chopped
½ cup (4 oz/125 g) finely chopped onion
¾ cup (6 fl oz/180 ml) orange juice
½ cup (4 fl oz/125 ml) lime juice

✱ Place the pork, onion, garlic, water and salt in a large pot or Dutch oven. Bring to a boil, skim the surface, reduce the heat and simmer, covered, until the pork is tender, about

45 minutes. Correct the seasonings and set aside.
✱ In a blender, purée the *tomates verdes, cilantro* and *chiles serranos.* Set aside.
✱ To make the sauce, combine the water, salt and vinegar in a bowl, add the *chiles poblanos* and soak for 30 minutes. Drain the chiles and combine with the radishes, onion, orange juice and lime juice.
✱ Twenty minutes before serving, bring the pork mixture to a boil, add the corn, zucchini and green beans and simmer until the vegetables are tender, 10–15 minutes. Bring the soup to a boil, add the *tomate verde* purée, stir and remove from the heat.
✱ Pass the sauce separately, to be served over the hot soup.

SERVES 6

YUCATÁN

SOPA DE LIMA

Lime Soup

This fragrant soup is made from the abundant bitter limes that grow on the Yucatán peninsula, which are very similar to the Key lime of Florida. Since these are both difficult to obtain, the juice of two Persian limes can be substituted in cooking, and slices added when serving.

2 whole chicken breasts, about 12 oz (375 g) each
10 cups (80 fl oz/2.5 l) water
3 cloves garlic
½ onion
3 small sprigs *cilantro* (coriander)
1 tablespoon salt
½ teaspoon ground cumin
1 1-in (2.5-cm) stick cinnamon
1 whole clove
1 teaspoon dried oregano
1 teaspoon oil
½ cup (4 oz/125 g) chopped red onion
½ cup (4 oz/125 g) finely chopped green bell pepper
  (capsicum)
2 cups (1 lb/500 g) peeled and chopped tomatoes
6 Key limes, 3 sliced, 3 halved (see note above for
  substitute)
4 chicken livers, cut up
1 avocado, peeled, pitted and sliced
fried tortilla strips (optional)

✳ Place the chicken breasts, water, garlic, onion, *cilantro* and salt in a large pot or Dutch oven. Bring to a boil and cook, covered, over low heat for 35–40 minutes or until the chicken is tender. Strain and reserve the stock. Shred the chicken and set aside.

✳ Toast the cumin, cinnamon, clove and oregano in a small skillet, then transfer to a blender. Add ½ cup (4 fl oz/125 ml) of the reserved chicken stock and purée.

✳ Heat the oil in a skillet, add the onion and sauté for 2 minutes or until transparent. Add the pepper and sauté for 2 minutes. Add the tomatoes and cook over medium heat for 7 minutes, stirring constantly. Add the rest of the chicken stock and the puréed spices. When the broth comes to a boil, add 2 of the sliced limes, the chicken and the chicken livers. Cover and cook over medium heat for 10 minutes. Correct the seasonings.

✳ To serve, place a slice of lime in the bottom of each bowl and cover with the hot soup. Pass a small plate of lime halves and avocado slices separately. If you like, you can fry some tortilla strips (for method, see recipe for *sopa de cuitlacoche,* page 75) and serve them as a garnish.

SERVES 6

DISTRITO FEDERAL

CALDO TLALPEÑO

Soup Tlalpeño Style

This smoky-flavored soup comes from old Tlalpan, once an area of beautiful haciendas and now a bustling Mexico City suburb. As in many Mexican dishes, a squeeze of lime brings out the taste.

Lime Soup

1 whole chicken breast, about 12 oz (375 g)
6 cups (48 fl oz/1.5 l) chicken stock (page 72)
1 cup (8 oz/250 g) cooked or canned chickpeas
2 cloves garlic
1 tablespoon oil
⅔ cup (5 oz/155 g) chopped carrots
½ cup (4 oz/125 g) chopped onion
2 pickled *chiles chipotles,* seeded and cut into strips
1 small sprig *epazote*
salt
1 avocado, peeled, pitted and cubed
2 tablespoons chopped *cilantro* (coriander) (optional)
lime slices
1 ripe tomato, chopped
2 *chiles serranos,* finely chopped
1 cup cooked rice

✳ Place the chicken, stock, chickpeas and garlic in a large saucepan and cook, covered, over medium heat for 20 minutes or until the chicken is tender. Transfer the chicken to a plate and, when cool enough to handle, remove the meat from the bones, shred and set aside.

✳ Heat the oil in a skillet, add the carrots and onion and sauté for 3 minutes. Transfer to the pot of chicken stock and add the *chiles, epazote* and salt to taste. Cook, covered, for 30 minutes over low heat. Correct the seasonings.

✳ Place a few cubes of avocado and some shredded chicken in each soup bowl. Fill with hot soup and sprinkle with *cilantro* if desired. Serve the lime separately. Pass the tomato, *chiles* and rice in small bowls so that everyone can add to their soup as much as they want.

SERVES 6–8

Soup Tlalpeño Style

Chard Soup (top) and Garlic Soup (bottom)

DISTRITO FEDERAL

Sopa de Acelgas

Chard Soup

Swiss chard is a popular and versatile green found year-round throughout Mexico. Other greens such as spinach can be substituted, creating a different yet delightful soup.

10 oz (315 g) chard (silverbeet), rinsed, drained and
    coarsely chopped
3 eggs, lightly beaten
2 tomatoes
2 cloves garlic
1 tablespoon oil
¼ cup (2 oz/60 g) finely chopped onion
6 cups (48 fl oz/1.5 l) chicken stock (page 72)
salt and freshly ground pepper

✱ In a large bowl, mix the chard with the eggs and set aside.
✱ In a blender, purée the tomatoes and garlic. Strain and set aside.
✱ Heat the oil in a large saucepan, add the onion and sauté until transparent. Add the chard and cook, stirring constantly, until the egg is cooked and the chard changes color slightly. Add the puréed tomatoes, cook for 5 minutes and add the stock. When the mixture comes to a boil, lower the heat and cook, covered, for 15 minutes. Add salt and pepper to taste and cook 5 minutes longer.

SERVES 6

GUANAJUATO

Sopa de Ajo

Garlic Soup

A traditional Spanish soup that was readily accepted in the New World. This version comes from the city of Guanajuato, where it was served in the seventeenth century to the owner of the world's largest silver mine, the Count of Valenciana.

2 tablespoons olive oil
3 oz (90 g) garlic, separated into cloves (about 30)
¼ cup (2 fl oz/60 ml) water
¾ cup (3 oz/90 g) dry breadcrumbs
6 cups (48 fl oz/1.5 l) chicken stock (page 72)
2 eggs

✱ Heat the oil in a large saucepan over medium heat, add the garlic and sauté, stirring constantly, until golden brown, about 8 minutes. Transfer the garlic to a blender, reserving the oil.
✱ Purée the garlic with the water and set aside.
✱ Brown the breadcrumbs in the oil in which the garlic was sautéed. Add the chicken stock and the puréed garlic and simmer, covered, for 15 minutes.
✱ Beat the eggs lightly in a small bowl. Bring the broth to a rolling boil and pour in the eggs in a stream, stirring constantly with a fork. Cook for 3 minutes and serve.

SERVES 6

OAXACA

Lentejas con Fruta

Lentils with Fruit

Lentils, long favored in Old World cuisines, are too often neglected by today's cooks. In this dish, the ancient legume's earthy qualities are complemented by the smoky pork and sweet fruit flavors.

2 cups (12 oz/375 g) dried lentils
8 cups (64 fl oz/2 l) water
8 oz (250 g) bacon, chopped
8 oz (250 g) *longaniza, chorizo* or other spicy sausage,
    casings removed and cut into chunks
1 cup (8 oz/250 g) chopped onion
2 cloves garlic, minced
2 slices fresh pineapple, chopped
1 plantain or large firm banana, about 12 oz (375 g),
    peeled and sliced
1 teaspoon salt
½ teaspoon freshly ground pepper
6 small green (spring) onions
2 tablespoons oil
4 smoked pork chops
1 lb (500 g) blood sausage (black pudding), cut into
    chunks (optional)

✱ Place the lentils and water in a large saucepan and bring to a boil. Lower the heat and simmer, covered, for 45 minutes. If you need to add more water, be sure that it is hot. Drain the lentils, reserving the cooking liquid.
✱ In a large saucepan, sauté the bacon over medium

heat for 2 minutes. Add the *longaniza* and cook, covered, for 3 minutes. Add the onion and garlic and sauté for 3 minutes. Add the lentils, pineapple, plantain, salt and pepper and cook, covered, over low heat for 10 minutes. Add 2 cups (16 fl oz/500 ml) of the liquid in which the lentils cooked and the green onions; cover and cook over low heat for 30 minutes.

✳ While they are cooking, heat the oil in a skillet. Add the smoked pork chops and sauté for 3 minutes on each side. Transfer to a plate. In the same oil, sauté the blood sausage for 2 minutes. Add the chops and blood sausage to the pan with the lentils and cook, covered, for 5 minutes.

✳*Note:* This should not be a soup but rather a lentil casserole. If you prefer it less thick, add 1 cup (8 fl oz/ 250 ml) water.

SERVES 6–8

Lentils with Fruit

Black Bean Soup

ESTADO DE MÉXICO

SOPA DE FRIJOL

Black Bean Soup

The ubiquitous bean makes a filling and soothing soup. There is no substitute for the epazote; *while it can be left out, its unique flavor will be missed. This is an easy plant to grow, and it can even be kept in a pot in the kitchen during the winter months or used dried.*

3 cups (24 fl oz/750 ml) *frijoles de la olla* (page 208)
2–3 cups (16–24 fl oz/500–700 ml) water
4 slices bacon, chopped
⅓ cup (2½ oz/75 g) finely chopped onion
1 small sprig *epazote*
1 tablespoon dried oregano
salt
oil for frying
4 day-old corn tortillas, cut into thin strips
6 tablespoons (3 fl oz/80 ml) thick cream *(crème fraîche)*
6 slices lime

✳ In a blender, purée the *frijoles de la olla* with 2 cups (16 fl oz/500 ml) water.
✳ Brown the bacon in a large saucepan without adding any oil. When the fat has cooked off, remove the bacon and set aside. Sauté the onion in the bacon fat until transparent, then add the bean purée. Cook, stirring constantly, until the mixture comes to a boil, then lower the heat and add the *epazote* and oregano. Add salt to taste and cook, covered, for 10 minutes. If the soup is too thick, add the remaining 1 cup (8 fl oz/250 ml) water.
✳ Heat ½ in (1 cm) oil in a small skillet and, when hot, add the tortilla strips a few at a time and fry, turning at least once, for about 3 minutes or until golden brown. Remove from the oil with a slotted spatula and drain on absorbent paper. (If using fresh tortillas, dry first in a preheated 250°F/120°C oven for an hour.)
✳ To serve, place 1 tablespoon of cream in each soup bowl and ladle the soup on top. Garnish with the tortillas strips, bacon and a slice of lime.

SERVES 6

MENUDO

Tripe Soup

Menudo is made of the honeycomb or other flavorful parts of the vitamin-rich lining of the cow's stomach, which is available scraped, soaked and partially precooked in many meat markets. This simple menudo *is served throughout the northern states topped with* chile piquín, *chopped onion and a squeeze of lime. In other regions, ground dried chile is blended directly into the stock, and the hominy may be omitted. María Dolores Torres Yzábal's version makes an unusual and tasty brunch dish, served with fresh fruit and* chilaquiles *(page 44) or* tamal de cazuela *(page 87).*

2 lb (1 kg) beef honeycomb tripe, cut into 2-in (5-cm) lengths
2 lb (1 kg) beef knuckles (calf's feet), cut into 3–4 pieces
12 cups (96 fl oz/3 l) water
2 teaspoons salt
1 head of garlic
1 onion, quartered
3 cups (1½ lb/750 g) cooked or canned hominy
4 sprigs *cilantro* (coriander)
ground *chile piquín*

✳ Place the tripe and beef knuckles in a large pot or Dutch oven with the water, salt, garlic and onion. Cover and cook for 2½–3 hours over medium heat, stirring occasionally. When half the water has boiled off, add more hot water to cover the tripe.
✳ Shred the beef knuckles of meat and return to the pot. Discard the bones. Remove the onion and garlic from the stock, add the hominy and *cilantro* and bring to a boil. Correct the seasonings.
✳ Serve in deep bowls. Sprinkle a little *chile piquín* on each serving and pass the rest. Mop up with flour tortillas if you like.

SERVES 8

Menudo

Sopa Fría de Chile Poblano y Almendras

Chile Poblano and Almond Soup

An unusual Mexican variation of the Spanish gazpacho blanco, mingling the almonds from Spain with the chile poblano, this recipe is from Mexico City chef María Dolores Torres Yzábal.

8 *chiles poblanos,* about 2 lb (1 kg)
¼ cup (2 fl oz/60 ml) olive oil
3 cloves garlic, crushed
6 oz (185 g) blanched almonds
5 cups (40 fl oz/1.25 l) chicken stock (page 72)
pinch ground cumin
salt
whole or diced cooked shrimp (prawns), for garnish
  (optional)

✴ Roast the *chiles* (see glossary), peel and remove the seeds and membranes. In a food processor or by hand, chop the *chiles* fine, being careful not to purée.
✴ Heat the oil in a large saucepan or Dutch oven, add the garlic and, before it browns, add the *chiles.* Cook over medium heat for about 5 minutes, stirring constantly so that the *chiles* do not stick to the bottom of the pan.
✴ Grind the almonds in the chicken stock in a blender until perfectly fine. Add this broth to the *chiles,* add cumin and salt to taste and let simmer over low heat for 10 minutes. Remove from the heat.
✴ Refrigerate until completely cold and add the shrimp if desired. This soup tastes better when prepared a day before serving.

SERVES 6

Chile Poblano and Almond Soup

Tamale Pie

Tamal de Cazuela

Tamale Pie

This unusual dish by Margot Rosenzweig de Palazuelos makes a simple supper when paired with a salad such as chayotes *(page 206) or* mixta con aderezo de aguacate *(page 203).*

10 oz (300 g) boneless lean pork, cut into chunks
6 cups (48 fl oz/1.5 l) cold water
2 cloves garlic
¼ onion
1 teaspoon salt
10 cups (2½ lb/1.25 kg) corn kernels
6 tablespoons (3 oz/90 g) butter, melted
1 cup (8 oz/250 g) lard, melted
1½ teaspoons baking powder
⅓ cup (1½ oz/45 g) all-purpose (plain) flour (optional)
2 cups (16 fl oz/500 ml) sauce from *crepas de mole*
  (page 96)
butter

✴ In a large covered saucepan over medium heat, cook the pork with the water, garlic, onion and half of the salt for about 1 hour or until tender. Drain, reserving the stock, and shred the pork.
✴ Purée the corn in a blender with the butter, lard, baking powder and remaining salt. If the mixture seems very thin because the corn is especially moist, add the flour.
✴ Heat the *mole* sauce and thin with ½ cup (4 fl oz/125 ml) of the reserved pork stock. Add the shredded pork.
✴ Preheat the oven to 400°F (200°C). Butter a large *cazuela* or a 12 x 15-in (30 x 38-cm) baking dish. Spread half the corn purée over the bottom of the dish. Cover with the meat sauce and top with the rest of the corn purée, being careful to cover the meat completely.
✴ Bake for 25–35 minutes or until a toothpick inserted in the center comes out clean.

SERVES 6

White Pozole (top), Green Pozole (center) and Red Pozole (bottom)

GUERRERO

Pozole

Pork and Hominy Soup

The original white pozole *is said to have been created in Chilapa, Guerrero, during the eighteenth century on the occasion of a visit by an important prelate from Puebla. Legend has it that local cooks prepared enormous quantities of nixtamal (softened dried corn kernels) days in advance, but there were not enough people to grind the maize and make tortillas. In desperation, maize was thrown into pots with chicken and herbs, and thus* pozole, *now a revered national dish, was born. In Jalisco and Michoacán is found a* pozole rojo, *rich red with chiles. Chiles anchos can be substituted or combined with the* chiles guajillos. Pozole verde's *green hue and unusual taste and texture comes from ground pumpkin seeds,* tomates verdes *and various greens. All versions of* pozole *are usually served with lime sections.*

1 whole chicken, about 3 lb (1.5 kg), cut up
½ onion
3 cloves garlic
4 teaspoons salt
1 sprig *cilantro* (coriander)
cold water
2 lb (1 kg) boneless lean pork
1 lb (500 g) boneless pork butt (pork leg)
2 lb (1 kg) dried hominy, cooked and drained
3 oz (90 g) dried oregano
1 cup (8 oz/250 g) chopped onions

3 oz (90 g) ground *chile piquín*
5 limes, halved

✳ Place the chicken in a large pot or Dutch oven and add the onion, garlic, 1 teaspoon of the salt and the *cilantro*. Cover with 10 cups (80 fl oz/2.5 l) water, bring to a boil and simmer, covered, over medium heat for 20 minutes or until the chicken is tender. Transfer the chicken to a plate, remove the skin and bones and shred the meat. Reserve the stock. There should be about 8 cups (64 fl oz/2 l).
✳ Place the pork, pork butt and remaining salt in a large pot and cover with 14 cups (112 fl oz/3.5 l) water. When the water comes to a boil, skim the surface and cook over medium heat for 1 hour. Add the hominy and cook another 30 minutes. Remove and shred the meat and return it to the pot.
✳ Add the chicken stock and shredded chicken to the pot, correct the seasonings, cover and cook over medium heat for 20 minutes or until the hominy is tender.
✳ Serve in small earthenware bowls and pass separate dishes containing the oregano, chopped onion, *chile piquín* and lime halves.

SERVES 12

Pozole Rojo

Red Pozole

10–12 *chiles guajillos,* seeds and membranes removed
½ cup (4 fl oz/125 ml) water
¼ onion
4 cloves garlic
7 tablespoons oil

✳ Soak the chiles in hot water to cover for 20 minutes, then drain. In a blender, purée the *chiles* with the water, onion and garlic.
✳ Heat the oil in a skillet over high heat, add the *chile* purée and sauté for 5 minutes. Lower the heat and cook for 10 minutes.
✳ Add this sauce to the *pozole* when you mix in the shredded chicken and pork.

Pozole Verde

Green Pozole

2 cups (8 oz/250 g) hulled raw pumpkin seeds
3 *chiles serranos*
1 lb (500 g) *tomates verdes,* husks removed
2 leaves lettuce
3 small radish leaves
¼ onion
½ cup (4 fl oz/125 ml) chicken stock (page 72)
2 tablespoons oil
1 teaspoon salt

✳ Toast the pumpkin seeds in a skillet until they begin to pop, being careful that they do not burn. Transfer them to a blender and grind to obtain a smooth paste. Set aside.
✳ Bring a large saucepan of water to a boil, add the *chiles* and cook for 5 minutes. Add the *tomates verdes* and

cook for 3 minutes. Drain and set aside.

✳ In a blender, purée the *tomates verdes, chiles,* lettuce, radish leaves and onion with the chicken stock. Set aside.

✳ Heat the oil in a large casserole or skillet. Add the pumpkin seed paste and sauté for 3 minutes, stirring constantly. Add the puréed *tomates verdes* and boil for 2 minutes. Add the salt, lower the heat and cook, stirring constantly, for 7 minutes. Correct the seasonings.

✳ Add this sauce to the *pozole* when adding the shredded chicken and pork.

PUEBLA

MOLE DE OLLA

Mole Soup

Inspired by the Spanish puchero *(stew), this one-dish meal has its roots in the early days of the vice-royalty in Mexico City. It makes a hearty supper dish preceded by* quesadillas. *Serve with hot tortillas, finely chopped onion and lime quarters.*

3 lb (1.5 kg) boneless lean beef, cut into 1½-in (4-cm) cubes
1 beef shank with bone, about 10 oz (315 g)
8 cups (64 fl oz/2 l) cold water (approximately)
1 tablespoon salt
1 sprig *epazote*
5 cloves garlic
3 *chiles anchos*
2 *chiles pasillas*
3 tomatoes
½ onion
2 tablespoons oil
1 *chayote* (vegetable pear/choko), about 10 oz (315 g), peeled and cut into 6 pieces
2 ears (cobs) corn, each cut into 3 pieces
1 lb (500 g) zucchini (courgettes), cut into chunks
4 oz (125 g) tender green beans

✳ Place the beef and beef shank in a large pot or Dutch oven, cover with the water and bring to a boil. Add the salt, epazote and 2 cloves of the garlic. Cover and cook, skimming occasionally, over medium heat for 45 minutes.

✳ While the meat is cooking, toast the *chiles* (see glossary), discard the seeds and membranes and place the *chiles* in a blender.

✳ Roast and peel the tomatoes (see glossary). Add the tomatoes with their juice to the blender along with the onion and remaining 3 cloves of garlic. Purée.

✳ Heat the oil in a skillet over high heat and add the purée. Cook over medium heat, stirring constantly, for 5 minutes.

✳ Add this purée to the pot containing the meat. Correct the seasonings, adding more salt if necessary. Cook, covered, over low heat for 30 minutes.

✳ Add the *chayote* and cook for 10 minutes, then add the corn, zucchini and green beans and cook, covered, over low heat for 10 minutes or until tender. Serve very hot.

SERVES 8–10

Mole Soup

VERACRUZ

ARROZ BLANCO CON PLÁTANOS FRITOS

White Rice with Fried Plantains

This Caribbean-influenced dish uses dark, ripe plantains for a slightly sweet flavor. If not available, use large firm bananas.

2 cups (10 oz/315 g) long-grain white rice
oil
½ onion, cut in half
1 whole clove garlic
5 cups (40 fl oz/1.25 l) hot water
1 sprig parsley
1 teaspoon salt
1 whole *chile serrano*
3 plantains or large firm bananas

✳ Soak the rice for 5 minutes in warm water, rinse well and drain.

✳Heat ½ in (1 cm) oil in a large skillet or casserole, add the rice, onion and garlic and sauté until the rice is trans-lucent and the grains separate. Pour off the excess oil.

✳ Add the hot water, parsley, salt and *chile,* bring to a boil and cover. Cook over low heat for 25 minutes or until the rice is tender.

✳ While the rice is cooking, peel the plantains and cut them lengthwise into strips ¼ in (6 mm) thick and 4 in (10 cm) long.

✳ Heat ½ in (1 cm) oil in a skillet and fry the plantain strips on all sides until they are a dark golden color.

✳ Serve the rice with strips of plantain on top.

SERVES 6

OAXACA

ARROZ NEGRO

Black Rice

Any leftover broth from a pot of black beans is commonly put to good use in this rice dish. A few stranded beans would also be welcomed.

White Rice with Fried Plantains (left), Black Rice (right) and Green Rice with Poblano Strips (rear)

2 cups (10 oz/315 g) long-grain white rice
2 tomatoes
1 tablespoon chopped onion
1 clove garlic
½ cup (4 fl oz/125 ml) oil
3 cups (24 fl oz/750 ml) liquid from *frijoles de la olla*
   (page 208)
1 teaspoon salt
2 whole *chiles serranos*

✳ Soak the rice for 5 minutes in warm water, rinse well and drain. Meanwhile, purée the tomatoes, onion and garlic in a blender and strain. Set aside.
✳ Heat the oil in a skillet, add the rice and sauté, stirring constantly, until it becomes translucent and the grains separate, about 5 minutes. Drain off the excess oil.
✳ Add the puréed tomatoes to the skillet and stir for 3 minutes over medium heat. Add the bean liquid and, as soon as it comes to a boil, add the salt and *chiles*. Cover and cook over low heat until the rice is tender and all the water has been absorbed, about 25 minutes. If the rice dries out before it is cooked, add 1 cup (8 fl oz/250 ml) hot water.

SERVES 6

MORELOS

ARROZ VERDE CON RAJAS

Green Rice with Poblano Strips

Rice is served often in Mexican homes, from plain white rice to more elaborate dishes like this one that can be meals in themselves. The area around Morelos in central Mexico produces a rice that is favored by good cooks, since it has a large, fat grain that gives an excellent result in casseroles. Processed, quick-cooking brands should never be used in Mexican cooking.

2 cups (10 oz/315 g) long-grain white rice
5 oz (155 g) fresh spinach
1 cup (1½ oz/45 g) parsley leaves
1 tablespoon chopped onion
1 clove garlic
½ cup (4 fl oz/125 ml) water
½ cup (4 fl oz/125 ml) oil
3 cups (24 fl oz/750 ml) hot water
salt
2 tablespoons (1 oz/30 g) butter
3 cups (1½ lb/750 g) thinly sliced onions
4 *chiles poblanos,* about 1 lb (500 g), roasted (see
   glossary) and cut into strips
1 cup (4 oz/125 g) grated Monterey Jack or Cheddar cheese
½ cup (4 fl oz/125 ml) thick cream *(crème fraîche)*

✳Soak the rice for 5 minutes in warm water, rinse well and drain.
✳ Rinse the spinach well, place it in a saucepan with no added water, cover and cook over low heat for 5 minutes. Transfer to a blender, add the parsley, onion, garlic and ½ cup (4 fl oz/125 ml) water and purée. Set aside.
✳ Heat the oil in a skillet, add the rice and sauté for 5 minutes, stirring constantly. When the grains begin to separate, remove from the heat and drain off the excess oil. Add the spinach-parsley purée to the skillet and sauté for 2 minutes. Add the hot water and salt to taste. When the mixture comes to a boil, lower the heat and cook, covered, for about 20 minutes or until the rice is tender.

✳ Meanwhile, preheat the oven to 350°F (180°C). Melt the butter in a large skillet, add the onions and *chile* strips and sauté for 5 minutes or until tender. Sprinkle with salt.
✳ Grease a ring mold and arrange a third of the onions and *chiles* in the bottom. Cover with half the rice and add half of the cheese. Cover with the rest of the rice. Cover with foil and bake for 10 minutes.
✳ Turn out the mold onto a platter. Cover with cream and sprinkle with the remaining grated cheese. Place the remaining *chiles* and onions in the center of the mold.

SERVES 6–8

DISTRITO FEDERAL

BUDÍN AZTECA

Aztec Casserole

A layered casserole similar to chilaquiles *(page 44), budín Azteca* makes a perfect main course for today's lighter eaters and is best with a crispy salad such as mixta con aderezo de aguacate *(page 203). The chicken can be omitted for a vegetarian meal, or pork can be substituted. It is often called* budín Cuauhtemoc *or* budín Moctezuma.

2 tablespoons oil
½ cup (4 oz/125 g) chopped onion
2 cloves garlic, finely chopped
3 large tomatoes (1½ lb/750 g), peeled and puréed
1½ teaspoons salt
1 tablespoon butter
3 cups (12 oz/375 g) fresh or frozen corn kernels
20 oz (625 g) zucchini (courgettes) (about 3), chopped
⅓ cup (3 fl oz/80 ml) water
oil for frying
10 corn tortillas
2 *chiles poblanos,* roasted (see glossary), peeled,
   membranes removed and cut into strips
1 cup (8 fl oz/250 ml) thick cream *(crème fraîche)*
1 cup (5½ oz/170 g) cooked and shredded chicken
1 cup (4 oz/125 g) grated *queso manchego* (or Muenster,
   Monterey Jack or white Cheddar cheese)

✳ Heat the oil in a skillet, add the onion and garlic and sauté until transparent. Add the tomatoes and salt and cook over high heat for 5 minutes. Lower the heat, cover and cook for 10 more minutes. Correct the seasonings and set aside.
✳ Preheat the oven to 375°F (190°C). Melt the butter in a saucepan. Add the corn and zucchini and cook for 2 minutes. Add the water, cover and cook over low heat for 8 minutes or until the zucchini is crisp-tender.
✳ Heat ½ in (1 cm) oil in a skillet and fry the tortillas for 30 to 40 seconds on each side, just to soften. Set aside.
✳ Place a thin layer of the vegetables on the bottom of a greased baking dish, top with a layer of 4 or 5 tortillas, then add a layer of the tomato sauce. Add half the remaining vegetables, half the *chiles*, ½ cup (4 fl oz/125 ml) of the cream, half the chicken and ½ cup (2 oz/60 g) of the cheese. Repeat the layers, finishing with the cheese. Bake, uncovered, until the cheese begins to melt, 10–15 minutes. Remove from the oven and serve.

SERVES 6–8   *Photograph pages 64–65*

Arroz a la Mexicana

Mexican-Style Rice

In Mexico, rice dishes are often served as a separate course, as a dry soup (sopa seca) replacing the more usual liquid one. During the years when the wealthy entertained lavishly on their haciendas, both types of soups were presented at the same meal. Whenever the phrase a la mexicana *is used, as in this popular way to fix rice, the dish has been prepared with onions and tomatoes.*

2 cups (10 oz/315 g) long-grain white rice
2 tomatoes
¼ cup (2 fl oz/60 ml) oil
⅓ onion, in chunk
3 whole cloves garlic
4 cups (32 fl oz/1 l) chicken stock (page 72) or water
1 small sprig parsley
3 whole *chiles serranos* (optional)
½ cup (4 oz/125 g) chopped carrot
¼ cup (1 oz/30 g) shelled green peas

✳ Soak the rice for 5 minutes in warm water, rinse well and drain. Meanwhile, purée the tomatoes in a blender and strain.

✳ Heat the oil in a skillet, add the onion and garlic and sauté for 2 minutes. Add the rice and sauté, stirring, until translucent and the grains separate. Pour off excess oil.

✳ Add the puréed tomatoes to the skillet with the rice. Cook for 4 minutes and add the stock, parsley, *chiles,* carrot and peas. When the mixture comes to a boil, cover and cook over medium heat for 20 minutes or until the liquid has been absorbed and the rice is tender.

SERVES 6

Arroz al Estilo Costeño

Rice Cooked Coastal Style

Three kinds of vegetables enhance this rice dish served in Barra Vieja (the Old Sand Bar), south of Acapulco. Here, you sit in sand-floored, palm-thatched palapas on the beach, enjoying huachinango a la talla *(page 173), which usually shares the table with this rice.*

2 cups (10 oz/315 g) long-grain white rice
¼ onion
3 cloves garlic
½ cup (4 fl oz/125 ml) water
oil
1½ cups (12 oz/375 g) chopped carrots
4 cups (32 fl oz/1 l) hot water
2 teaspoons salt
1½ cups (6 oz/185 g) fresh or frozen corn kernels
2 cups (6 oz/185 g) coarsely chopped cabbage

✳ Soak the rice in warm water for 5 minutes, rinse well and drain. Meanwhile, in a blender, purée the onion and garlic in the ½ cup (4 fl oz/125 ml) water and set aside.

✳ Heat ½ in (1 cm) oil in a large skillet, add the rice and sauté, stirring lightly, until the grains separate and become translucent, about 5 minutes. Pour off the excess oil.

✳ Add the carrots and stir for 2 minutes. Add the puréed onion and garlic and stir for 2 minutes. Add the hot water and salt. When the water comes to a boil, add the corn and cabbage, stir, cover the skillet and cook over medium-low heat for 20–30 minutes or until the water is absorbed and the rice is tender.

SERVES 6

Mexican-Style Rice

Noodles with Chorizo (left, garnished with avocado) and Rice Cooked Coastal Style (right)

FIDEOS CON CHORIZO

Noodles with Chorizo

This recipe is very similar to one found in the interior of Catalonia, where, according to food writer Colman Andrews, it is said to be an invention of the Moors, who occupied Spain for almost 400 years.

2 tomatoes
¼ onion
1 clove garlic
1 tablespoon oil
5 oz (155 g) *chorizo* or other spicy sausage, casing removed and cut into chunks
8 oz (250 g) vermicelli
3 cups (24 fl oz/750 ml) chicken stock (page 72)

salt and freshly ground pepper
grated cheese (optional)

✳ In a blender, purée the tomatoes, onion and garlic. Strain and set aside.
✳ Heat the oil in a large skillet, add the *chorizo* and sauté over low heat for 4 minutes, being careful not to let it burn. Transfer the *chorizo* to a plate and set aside. Pour off all but 2 tablespoons of the drippings, add the vermicelli and brown lightly; drain and set aside.
✳ Add the puréed tomatoes to the skillet, cook for 3 minutes, stirring constantly, and add the stock. When it comes to a boil, add the vermicelli and salt and pepper to taste. Cover and cook over medium heat for 5 minutes. Uncover and add the *chorizo*. Continue cooking until the noodles are tender and dry.
✳ Sprinkle with grated cheese if desired and serve hot.

SERVES 6

93

Corn Pudding

TORTA DE ELOTE

Corn Pudding

Corn was the single most important element in the pre-Hispanic diet. This sopa seca *can make use of corn that is not very fresh and thus has a higher starch content. If sugar and cinnamon are added, it can be served for dessert. This recipe is by Margot Rosenzweig de Palazuelos.*

8 cups (2 lb/1 kg) fresh or frozen corn kernels
¾ cup (6 oz/180 g) butter, melted
2 teaspoons baking powder
¼ teaspoon salt
2 tablespoons (1 oz/30 g) butter

✽ Place the corn kernels in a bowl. Moisten your hands and use them to stir the corn to remove any silk adhering to the kernels. Purée the corn in a blender with the melted butter. Transfer to a bowl and add the baking powder and salt.
✽ Preheat the oven to 375°F (190°C). Grease a 9-in (23-cm) square or round baking dish with a tablespoon of the butter, pour the corn into it and dot the surface with the remaining butter. Bake for 30 minutes or until the top is lightly browned and a knife inserted in the center comes out clean.
✽ If you want a sweet pudding, add ¾ cup (6 oz/185 g) sugar and ½ teaspoon cinnamon.

SERVES 6

SOUFFLÉ DE CHICHARRÓN

Fried Pork Skin Soufflé

This is an example of the nouvelle cuisine *being developed in Mexico City by innovative cooks such as Antonio Martinez Camacho. While the packaged pork skins found in grocery stores do not compare with the sheets of freshly fried* chicharrón *in the markets of Mexico, they can be substituted.*

3 tomatoes, peeled
¼ onion
2 cloves garlic
1 tablespoon oil
1 teaspoon salt
4 cups (7 oz/210 g) *chicharrón* or fried pork skins, finely chopped
6 tablespoons (3 oz/90 g) butter
2 tablespoons cornstarch (cornflour)
4 cups (32 fl oz/1 l) heavy (double) cream
6 eggs, separated
¼ teaspoon cream of tartar
butter

✽ In a blender, purée the tomatoes, onion and garlic.
✽ Heat the oil in a skillet, add the tomato purée and sauté for 5 minutes. Add the salt and cook over low heat for 7 minutes.
✽ Place the *chicharrón* in a bowl. Add the sauce, stir and let rest for 10 minutes.

Fried Pork Skin Soufflé

94

Zucchini Pudding

✳ Preheat the oven to 375°F (190°C). Melt the butter in a saucepan, add the cornstarch and stir until smooth. Add the cream and cook over medium heat, stirring constantly, until the sauce thickens, about 8 minutes. Remove from the heat and add the egg yolks one at a time, stirring constantly. Add the *chicharrón* and stir. Set aside.

✳ Beat the egg whites with the cream of tartar until they form stiff peaks, then fold into the mixture. Transfer to a buttered 2-qt (2-l) soufflé dish and bake for 20–25 minutes. Serve hot.

SERVES 6

BUDÍN DE CALABACITA

Zucchini Pudding

Budines, *which are similar to the Jewish kugel or vegetable puddings, are a popular way to serve vegetables in Mexico. This one, made of squash, is most traditional and can be served as a separate course or to accompany a main dish. It* *would nicely complement* lomo de cerdo con salsa de tomate y rajas *(page 136).*

4 cups (1 lb/500 g) chopped zucchini (courgettes)
1 cup (4 oz/125 g) plus 2 tablespoons grated mild white
    Cheddar cheese
1 egg, beaten
1 cup (4 oz/125 g) crushed soda crackers (plain biscuits)
½ cup (4 oz/125 g) butter, melted
¼ teaspoon ground nutmeg
salt and pepper

✳ Preheat the oven to 350°F (180°C). In a covered saucepan, cook the zucchini in boiling water until tender. Drain, then mash them in a large bowl. Add the cup (4 oz/125 g) of cheese and the egg, crackers and butter; mix well with a wooden spoon. Add the nutmeg and salt and pepper to taste.

✳ Transfer the mixture to an ovenproof dish, sprinkle with the remaining cheese and bake until the pudding thickens, 15 to 20 minutes.

SERVES 6

Crêpes with Mole Sauce

OAXACA

CREPAS DE MOLE

Crêpes with Mole Sauce

Mole is usually reserved for fiestas, but there is always some sauce left over, and since its taste improves with time, it is ideal for supper dishes like these crêpes. If you do not have any extra mole on hand, this recipe provides an easy substitute.

CRÊPES

2 cups (16 fl oz/500 ml) milk
1 egg
1 cup (4 oz/125 g) plus 1 tablespoon all-purpose (plain) flour
1 tablespoon oil
butter

SAUCE

3 *chiles anchos,* seeds and membranes removed
10 *chiles guajillos,* seeds and membranes removed
6 cloves garlic
¼ onion
6 whole cloves
1 teaspoon freshly ground pepper
1 small sprig thyme
1 small sprig marjoram
1 cup (8 fl oz/250 ml) chicken stock (page 72)
1 tablespoon oil
2 tomatoes, roasted (see glossary) and peeled
½ cup (4 fl oz/125 ml) water
1 teaspoon salt

FILLING

1 whole chicken breast, about 12 oz (375 g), cooked, boned and shredded
1 cup (4 oz/125 g) grated *queso manchego* (or Muenster or young pecorino cheese)
½ onion, thinly sliced (optional)

❋ To prepare the crêpes, in a mixing bowl, beat together the milk, egg, flour and oil. Let rest for 5 min-

utes. Lightly butter a nonstick crêpe pan and set over medium heat. Pour 1½ tablespoons of the batter into the pan and tilt it to cover the bottom. As soon as the edges of the crêpe begin to dry out, turn it over. When the second side is lightly browned, transfer the crêpe to a plate. Repeat until all the batter has been used. There should be about 22 crêpes. Set aside.

❋ To prepare the sauce, toast the *chiles* (see glossary), soak in hot water for 20 minutes, drain and set aside. Meanwhile, roast the garlic, onion, cloves, pepper, thyme and marjoram. Transfer to a blender, add the *chiles* and stock, then purée.

❋ Heat the oil in a skillet, add the *chile* purée and sauté, stirring constantly, for 8 minutes.

❋ Purée the tomatoes in a blender and add to the skillet. Cook for 5 minutes. Add the water and salt, lower heat, cover and cook for 10 minutes. Correct the seasonings.

❋ To assemble, preheat the oven to 375°F (190°C). Place some chicken in each crêpe, roll up and cut off the uneven edges. Arrange in a single layer in a greased ovenproof dish. Cover with the sauce and bake for 15 minutes. Remove, sprinkle with the cheese and return to the oven for 5 more minutes or until the cheese begins to melt. Garnish with the onion if desired and serve warm.

SERVES 8

DISTRITO FEDERAL

CREPAS DE CUITLACOCHE CON SALSA DE POBLANO

Corn Fungus Crêpes with Poblano Sauce

This intriguing marriage of French crêpes with Mexican corn fungus was first served in the court of Emperor Maximilian and his wife, Carlotta. It is a very distinguished dish for special occasions.

CRÊPES

2 cups (16 fl oz/500 ml) milk
1 small egg
1 cup (4 oz/125 g) plus 1 tablespoon all-purpose (plain) flour
1 tablespoon oil
butter

FILLING

2 tablespoons (1 oz/30 g) butter
⅓ cup (3 oz/90 g) finely chopped onion
1 *chile poblano,* seeds and membranes removed and diced
½ cup (2 oz/60 g) corn kernels
1 tablespoon chopped *epazote*
2 cans (7 oz/220 g each) *cuitlacoche* or 5 oz (155 g) fresh *cuitlacoche*

SAUCE

2 *chiles poblanos,* seeds and membranes removed
⅓ cup (3 fl oz/80 ml) milk
¼ cup (2 oz/60 g) butter
1½ tablespoons all-purpose (plain) flour
2 cups (16 fl oz/500 ml) thick cream (*crème fraîche*)
1 teaspoon salt
1½ cups (6 oz/185 g) grated *queso Chihuahua* (or Monterey Jack or medium-sharp Cheddar cheese)

✳ To prepare the crêpes, in a mixing bowl, beat together the milk, egg, flour and oil. Let rest for 5 minutes. Lightly butter a nonstick crêpe pan and set over medium heat. Pour 1½ tablespoons of the batter into the pan and tilt it to cover the bottom. As soon as the edges of the crêpe begin to dry out, turn it over. When the second side is lightly browned, transfer the crêpe to a plate. Repeat until all the batter has been used. There should be about 22 crêpes. Set aside.

✳ To prepare the filling, melt the butter in a skillet, add the onion and sauté for 2 minutes or until transparent. Add the *chile,* corn, *epazote* and *cuitlacoche* with its juice. Cook over medium heat for 5 minutes, stirring constantly.

✳ To prepare the sauce, purée the *chiles* in a blender with the milk. Melt the butter in a small saucepan. Add the flour and cook, stirring constantly, until it is lightly browned. Remove from the heat and continue to stir while adding the cream, *chile* purée and salt. Return to low heat and stir constantly until the sauce begins to boil. Set aside.

✳ To assemble, place a tablespoon of filling on each crêpe, roll up and cut off the uneven edges. Arrange in a single layer in a greased ovenproof dish. Cover with aluminum foil until 15 minutes before serving.

✳ Before serving, preheat the oven to 500°F (260°C). Pour the sauce over the crêpes and sprinkle with the cheese. Bake for about 10 minutes or until the cheese begins to melt. Or place in the broiler (griller) until the sauce bubbles and the cheese is lightly golden.

SERVES 8

Cuitlacoche Crêpes with Poblano Sauce

CROSSROADS OF MEXICO

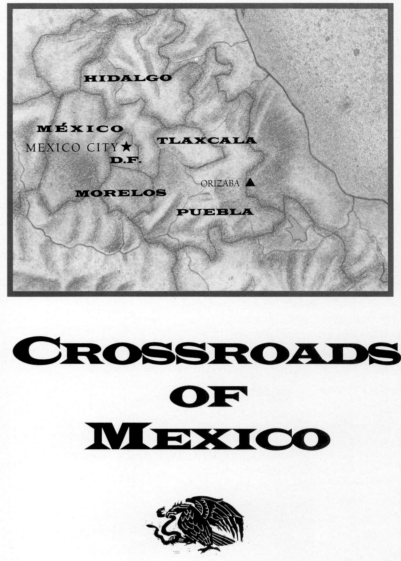

CROSSROADS
OF
MEXICO

In the center of the Mexican highlands is a vast natural coliseum, a dramatic sun-drenched setting where stirring historic events have been staged. None, however, can compare to the fateful day in the autumn of 1519 when the curtain fell on the final act of the Aztec civilization, and the first act of the Spanish Conquest began, forever changing the course of the continuing drama of Mexico.

Before 1000 B.C. semi-nomads moved about the highlands in small bands, hunting and fishing, gathering plants and fruits and occasionally cultivating small fields of maize, squash and beans. The first corncobs were tiny, hardly more than an inch long, but with spring water for irrigation, corn eventually grew larger and more plentiful. The Indians ate their corn in many different ways, even raw, or roasted it on a flat stone pulled white-hot from a fire. When they learned the technique of soaking the dry kernels in water with pieces of *cal* (pure lime) until the skins were soft, they were then able to use this *nixtamal,* as it was called, to make *masa,* grinding the corn on stone *metates.* Shaped into flat pancakes, baked and filled with chopped game, fish or mashed beans—and even then laced with *chiles*—these concoctions became the forerunners of Mexico's *masa* delicacies.

The first real city of the New World, Teotihuacán, was based around the cultivation of a single crop—corn. Built to the north of today's Mexico City, it became a major trade capital, covering over seven

Previous pages: The gray-green spires of maguey plants dominate the haciendas of Tlaxcala. Left: The Palacio Nacional in Mexico City overlooks the city's main square, or Zócalo, where Moctezuma's palace once stood in the Aztec capital of Tenochtitlán.

square miles, and by A.D. 500 had a population of more than 100,000. In about A.D. 600, however, Teotihuacán was looted and burned by tribes from the north and its people were killed or ran away. By the time Moctezuma II became ruler of the Aztecs, about a thousand years later, the city was a holy ruin known simply as the place where the gods had assembled to create the sun. For centuries a group of barbarians known as Aztecs had wandered throughout the north, finally arriving in this temperate valley, where they served as mercenaries for the other tribes. Finally they were allowed to settle on two small, uninhabited islands in the middle of a large shallow lake—a home that was their destiny, as their tribal god had instructed them to settle where they found an eagle perched on a nopal cactus, devouring a snake. This they saw when they settled there in 1325.

Ingredients for mole poblano *in the 17th-century kitchen of the Convent of Santa Rosa in Puebla. The only thing missing is the turkey. The story of how the convent's sister superior invented the renowned Mexican recipe has become legendary.*

By 1519 Tenochtitlán had become a magnificent city of great size, five times larger than London at the time. To feed its many people, farmers encircled the island with *chinampas,* small gardens that seemed to float but were made by building narrow canals through the surrounding marsh lands and piling the tangled masses of rotting swamp vegetation and fertile mud behind retaining walls. On these they grew year-round crops of fresh vegetables and *chiles.*

From the time of the Aztecs, the city was the hub into which all roads led, bringing goods and different types of food from distant parts of the country and later from around the world. And the focal point of its activity were the great markets, from which the medley of tribes and races living in the city were able to find the foods of their childhood tables among the cornucopia of ingredients the markets provided.

Although there is no cuisine unique to Mexico City, two contrasting types of food do stand apart—the enormous variety of the centuries-old *masa* snacks found in the city's markets and streets, and the exciting dishes that have been and continue to be developed by creative chefs using traditional Mexican ingredients in new ways.

Groves of tall pine trees enclose the 9,000-foot-high dry land where Toluca, the capital of the state of Mexico, is located. The best known of its pork products, made from pigs fattened on the abundant corn growing in this high valley, are its red and green *chorizos,* which are strung like rustic Christmas decorations in front of food stands. In Toluca's famous busy Friday market, tasty *carnitas* wrapped in tortillas are sold to hungry passersby.

If one place in Mexico could be considered the birthplace of Mexican cooking, it would be Puebla, a city founded by the Spanish in the sixteenth century as an important crossroads for travelers and armies coming and going between Veracruz and Mexico City. In the convent kitchens of Puebla, nuns created many of the dishes that still serve as the nucleus of Mexico's cuisine, *mole poblano* and *chiles en nogada* being the most famous. The spectacular *chiles en nogada* are *chiles poblanos* filled with a *picadillo* of chopped meats, fruits and nuts, blanketed with an ivory sauce of fresh walnuts and cream and crowned with the jewellike seeds of the pomegranate for delightful contrast in tastes, colors and textures.

Several popular legends tell of the birth of *mole poblano,* a festive dish that epitomizes the culinary marriage between the Spanish and Mexican worlds. While not as fanciful as the one that would have it created when a gust of wind blew just the right amount of spices and condiments into *cazuelas* of simmering turkeys, a more likely story is that it originated when the sister superior of the convent of Santa Rosa was faced with preparing a special meal for a visit from the archbishop and Spanish viceroy. Known for her culinary inventiveness, she probably took note of her helpers' stories about the Indian royal use of chocolate and with their help devised this superb dish, an adaptation of an earlier Maya one.

According to legend, seven tribes of barbarians came to the central valley of Mexico from the north. Six settled beside the lakes in the valley, the seventh going farther east to Tlaxcala, the "land of corn," where it remained independent, one of the few tribes unconquered by the Aztecs. Cortés, after leaving Veracruz, climbed with his troops over a high mountain pass beside the snow-capped peak of Orizaba and eventually came to the fertile lands of Tlaxcala, thickly planted with corn and maguey. After initial fierce resistance, the Tlaxcalans made an alliance with the Spaniards against the hated Aztecs and were instrumental in bringing about their defeat. As a reward, the Tlaxcalans were never subjugated nor even made to pay tributes.

The food of this smallest state in Mexico reflects its individualistic and, some would say, warlike nature. In Tlaxcala and Hidalgo, its neighbor, maguey dominates

The red-tiled roofs of Valle de Bravo, a resort town near Toluca. Its surrounding mountains and lakeside perch make Valle a popular getaway spot for Mexico City residents. Trout from the lake is served in the town's floating restaurants.

both the scenery and the cuisine. In this area immense haciendas were once devoted to the cultivation of maguey and the making of *pulque*. Roadside stands sell *barbacoa en mixiote—chile*-seasoned meat, rabbit or chicken that is wrapped in the tough transparent skin of the maguey and then steam-roasted in pits lined with maguey leaves. *Pulque* usually provides the steam and adds to the flavor, as well as being served as a drink to accompany it. A much-prized delicacy during the rainy season are *tacos* made of *gusanos de maguey,* little worms or larvae that live in the flesh of the maguey. In Hidalgo *escamoles,* the sautéed eggs of a local species of black ant, are used to fill the *tacos* of aficionados.

Morelos, the other small state in this historic valley, is best known for its capital, Cuernavaca, a subtropical weekend vacationing spot. It was a major getaway place for the Aztec rulers as well as Cortés, who built a sumptuous palace atop the ruins of the defeated Tlahuica Indian temples. As could be expected in a place for indulgence throughout the centuries, cooks in Cuernavaca vie to improve on the dishes from Mexico City, using the finest ingredients supplemented by abundant local fruits and vegetables, especially the prized mushrooms of the rainy season.

In the highland valley of Mexico, the Aztecs founded their highly developed society, later to be conquered by Cortés. The land has been briefly ruled by both France and the United States and now boasts the largest city in the world—all of the events in its turbulent life having played a role in its cuisine.

CARNES, AVES Y HUEVOS

Beef served northern-style: plain and simple, with chiles.

CARNES, AVES Y HUEVOS

Previous pages: Stuffed Pork Loin with Tomato Sauce and Green Peppers (left, recipe page 136), Chicken with Mountain Herbs (center, recipe page 112) and Pork Roast Stuffed with Chiles Chipotles and Prunes (right, recipe page 150). Above: Every evening on the plazas of Morelia, cooks prepare pollo de plaza, *a savory concoction of chicken and enchiladas served with carrots and potatoes.*

Ironically, the pre-Columbian Indians of Mexico ate the kind of high-fiber, low-cholesterol, low-fat diet espoused today by doctors—mainly fish and vegetables. Those of the ruling class also ate meat. Rabbit, iguana or armadillo might be trapped, or a small brocket deer or wild pig stalked and killed by the lucky thrust of a javelin, but only turkey, Muscovy duck and a small hairless dog were domesticated for food.

The diet of the Indians was quickly and profoundly changed when the Spaniards introduced livestock to the New World. While the conquerors were reluctant to share the larger animals with their captives, they permitted them to raise chickens, goats and pigs, which soon became important food sources for the Indians.

The self-sufficient and prolific pig became the dowry in the forced culinary union between Spain and Mexico. A visit to the meat stalls of any Mexican market will reveal just how completely the pig is utilized. The head is split and used in the earthy *pozole* (hominy soup) or made into *queso de puerco* (head cheese). The tubelike intestines are stuffed with flavorful ground meat fillings and made into *chorizo* and *longaniza* (sausages), or filled with herb-seasoned blood and transformed into *moronga,* a sausage similar to the Spanish *morcilla* or the tasty *boudin* of France. Nothing is wasted—neither the feet, which are pickled, nor the neck, back and tail bones, which are used to enrich soups and stews. The innards are usually fried for the day's *tacos.*

Even all the fat of the pig is used. The sheets of fat next to the skin are scored in a diamond pattern, hung to dry and the next day twice cooked in huge pots of boiling lard, in which it puffs up into a favorite *botana* (snack)—the crackly *chicharrón.* The soft fat lining the innards is also rendered out to make the savory but

Most of the chickens used in Mexican cooking are free-range. This regal fowl unabashedly takes advantage of his wandering privileges.

While the Spanish brought cattle, pigs and chickens to the New World, the turkey is native to Mexico. Considered a festival food, the big bird shows up at weddings and holiday feasts, usually in the form of mole poblano de guajolote.

often maligned lard. Although today's Mexican cook frequently uses vegetable oil in preparing dishes, lard is still considered indispensable in preparing *tamales*. And *frijoles* without the flavor of lard would be as unthinkable as Italian spaghetti *aglio e olio* without garlic.

In the northern border states, beef is king. As Bernabé Cobo wrote in his work *Obras,* "When faced with the immense grasslands of America, the Englishman paused, called them deserts and tried to find a way around them. The Spaniard embraced the plains, the llanos, the pampas, drove his cattle onto them, and let the multiplying beef make a good life for him. As a result, there were probably more cattle in the New World in the 17th Century than any other type of vertebrate immigrant."

Nowadays, particularly in the north, beef cattle are raised and butchered to produce the same quality of product that is found in the United States. However, in much of Mexico range-fed cattle, often Brahmas, are still raised, which are tough by any standard. To minimize this hazard, steak is sliced with the grain into large thin sheets, tenderized by lime juice and quickly seared.

A law promulgated by the Spanish six months after the opening of the first inn serving food in Mexico City stated:

> For every good hen, not a chick,
> four gold reals must be taxed.
> For every large double chin cock
> the tax shall be six gold reals.

This "double chin cock," or wild turkey, which was domesticated by the Mayas, greatly impressed the more culinary-minded among Cortés' followers, who sent some of the great birds back to Spain on returning boats. The big, meaty birds were an instant sensation in the courts of Europe, soon replacing the peacock on the tables of the nobility and clergy. In Mexico today, even in the poorest households, the noble turkey can be seen strutting in dirt yards, and each market day finds them tethered among seated vendors or carried upside down by their feet, passive and unregal, on display for buyers anticipating the next fiesta, for turkey is the food of celebrations.

The chickens used in Mexican cooking are almost always free-range chickens and can be seen scratching along the sides of roads eating whatever their pecking procures. The result is a chicken that has a great deal more flavor than its northern cousin but is also tougher and needs to be simmered or slowly braised to bring out its best. Every region has its own style of combining shredded chicken with other ingredients to make *tacos, tamales* or *enchiladas,* and there are countless versions of *moles* and *pipianes* using chicken.

Eggs are eaten everywhere, at any time and in many guises. Just a plain plate of scrambled eggs is hard to find in Mexico. Eggs may be prepared as *huevos a la mexicana* and laced with the colorful green *chiles serranos,* tomatoes and slices of onion, or scrambled with spicy *chorizo* or cooked pieces of *nopales* (cactus paddles).

The classic Mexican egg dish is *huevos rancheros,* fried eggs centered on soft-cooked tortillas, slathered with a coarse *picante* tomato sauce and paired with refried beans. Cooks on the Yucatán peninsula carry this robust dish a bit further: for *huevos motuleños* they virtually make a sandwich, putting the egg and beans between two tortillas and then topping the whole structure with chopped ham, cooked peas, cheese and a warm, spicy tomato sauce.

Eggs also are fried and layered for *tortas* (sandwiches) or used as a topping for a rice course. They may be scrambled in a soupy bowl of black beans, as in the *huevos tirados* of Veracruz, or mixed with broken tortillas in a version of *chilaquiles*. And on every restaurant cart of *postres,* the rich convent dessert *huevos reales* (royal eggs) from Puebla is a classic offering.

Butterfly Quail

GUERRERO

CODORNIZ A LA TALLA

Butterfly Quail

Quail was a bird prized by the Aztecs for eating and as a sacrifice to the goddess Chicomecóatl. In this method of cooking, a Guerrero specialty, the meat or fish is first coated with mayonnaise, then basted with a tongue-tingling sauce during grilling.

¼ cup (2 fl oz/60 ml) mayonnaise
1 tablespoon oil
1 teaspoon salt
½ teaspoon freshly ground pepper
12 quail or squabs, about 4 oz (125 g) each

SAUCE

10 *chiles guajillos,* seeds and membranes removed
5 *chiles anchos,* seeds and membranes removed
5 large ripe tomatoes
1 cup (8 fl oz/250 ml) water
4 cloves garlic
3 whole cloves
¼ large onion
1 tablespoon red wine vinegar
½ teaspoon each dried thyme, oregano and marjoram
½ teaspoon ground cumin
¼ cup (2 oz/60 g) butter

2 tablespoons oil
salt and freshly ground pepper

❋ Combine the mayonnaise, oil, salt and pepper in a small bowl.
❋ With a sharp knife, cut through each quail breast and press the bird open in a butterfly shape. Coat both sides of each quail liberally with the mayonnaise mixture and marinate at room temperature for at least 1 hour.
❋ To prepare the sauce, cover the *chiles* with hot water and let soak for 20 minutes. Meanwhile, in a blender, purée the tomatoes, strain and set aside. Drain the *chiles,* then purée with the water, garlic, cloves, onion, vinegar, thyme, oregano, marjoram and cumin until smooth.
❋Heat the butter and oil in a small saucepan. Add the puréed *chiles,* bring to a boil and add the tomatoes. When the sauce comes to a boil, lower the heat and simmer, covered, for 45 minutes to an hour or until the sauce thickens, stirring occasionally. Add salt and pepper to taste. Let cool to room temperature. Baste the quail with half the sauce and marinate, refrigerated, for at least 4 hours.
❋ Preheat an outdoor grill and grease the rack lightly with oil. Coat the quail with half of the remaining sauce. Cook for 4–5 minutes on the breast side and 1–2 minutes on the bone side, basting constantly with the rest of the sauce, until the quail are cooked to the desired doneness.

SERVES 6

Plaza de Morelia Chicken

MICHOACÁN

POLLO PLAZA DE MORELIA

Plaza de Morelia Chicken

While this complete chicken dinner can be found in the restaurants of Morelia, the colonial capital of Michoacán, it is usually bought from vendors in a small plaza several blocks from the main plaza.

1 chicken, about 3½ lb (1.75 kg), cut into serving pieces
4 cups (32 fl oz/1 l) water
2 sprigs parsley
4 cloves garlic
1 onion, halved
1 tablespoon salt
3 (1 lb/500 g) potatoes, peeled and cut into chunks
3 (12 oz/375 g) large carrots, peeled and cut into chunks
3 *chiles anchos*
5 *chiles guajillos*
2 cloves garlic
1 tablespoon lard or oil
oil or lard for frying
12 corn tortillas
5 oz (155 g) *queso fresco* (or feta cheese), crumbled
shredded lettuce
½ onion, thinly sliced

✳ In a large covered saucepan, simmer the chicken in the water with the parsley, garlic, ½ onion and salt for 35 minutes or until tender. Drain, reserving the stock, and set aside. Meanwhile, in another large saucepan, cook the potatoes and carrots in boiling salted water until tender. Drain and set aside.
✳ Remove the stems and seeds from the *chiles*. Toast (see glossary) on a *comal* or iron skillet, then soak in hot water to cover for 20 minutes. Drain and transfer to a blender.
✳ Roast the garlic and remaining ½ onion (see glossary). Add to the blender and purée with the *chiles* and ½ cup (4 fl oz/125 ml) of the reserved stock.
✳ Melt the lard in a skillet until very hot. Add the *chile* purée and cook, stirring constantly, for 2 minutes. Add 1½ cups (12 fl oz/375 ml) of the reserved stock and cook over medium heat for 5 minutes. If the sauce becomes too thick, thin it with a little more stock.
✳ Before serving, heat 1 tablespoon oil in a skillet. Dip both sides of a tortilla in the *chile* sauce, transfer to the hot oil, fry briefly on both sides and transfer to a plate. Place some *queso fresco* in the center of the tortilla and roll up. Repeat for the remaining tortillas. In the same skillet, sauté the chicken pieces on all sides with the carrots and potatoes.
✳On each plate arrange a bed of shredded lettuce. Place 2 *enchiladas* and a piece of chicken on top of the lettuce. Arrange the vegetables on the side. Garnish with onion slices and sprinkle with the remaining *queso fresco*.

SERVES 6

MICHOACÁN

POLLO EN CUÑETE

Chicken in a Clay Pot

The traditional way to prepare this chicken dish is in a clay casserole dish covered with a sealing layer of masa. Small bits of the corn mixture break off and add a thickening texture to the sauce. This modern version is much simpler to prepare.

1 whole chicken, about 3 lb (1.5 kg), cut into serving pieces
11 cloves garlic, crushed
1 tablespoon coarse salt
1 teaspoon freshly ground pepper
2 tablespoons corn or vegetable oil
20 small new potatoes, peeled
¾ cup (6 fl oz/180 ml) red wine vinegar
⅓ cup (3 fl oz/80 ml) olive oil
2 teaspoons salt
6 bay leaves
2 tablespoons each dried thyme and marjoram
2 *chiles serranos* (optional)

✳ Rub the chicken with the garlic, salt and pepper and refrigerate for 2–4 hours.
✳ In a large skillet, heat the corn oil, sauté the chicken briefly and transfer to a *cazuela* or large pot. In the same oil, lightly brown the potatoes, remove and set aside. Add the vinegar to the skillet and bring to a boil, scraping up browned bits from the bottom of the skillet. Pour the vinegar through a strainer over the chicken.
✳ Add the olive oil, salt, bay leaves, thyme and marjoram to the chicken *cazuela*. Bring to a boil over high heat, cover and lower the heat. Every 10 minutes, uncover and stir. After 35 minutes, uncover, correct the seasonings and add the *chiles* and potatoes. Cover and cook over low heat until the potatoes are tender, about 15 minutes.

SERVES 6

OAXACA

Pollo a las Hierbas de la Sierra

Chicken with Mountain Herbs

Tiny potatoes with garlic go well with this aromatic chicken dish by Oaxacan restaurateur Socorrito Zorrilla. If you live in a temperate climate, ask your friends from warmer regions to send you avocado leaves, which can be used dried.

1 large chicken, about 4 lb (2 kg), quartered
salt and freshly ground pepper
3 *chiles anchos*
2 *chiles guajillos*
1 cup (8 oz/250 g) chopped tomato
4 cloves garlic
½ small onion
¼ cup (2 fl oz/60 ml) white vinegar
2 cups (16 fl oz/500 ml) water
12 avocado leaves with stems
1 sprig rosemary
½ cup (¾ oz/20 g) fresh oregano

✳ Season the chicken with salt and pepper and set aside.
✳ Toast the *chiles* (see glossary) and remove their seeds and membranes. In a small saucepan, cook the *chiles* with the tomato over medium heat until softened. Transfer to a blender, add the garlic, onion and vinegar and purée. Coat the pieces of chicken with this purée and let marinate at room temperature for 20 minutes.
✳ Bring the water to a boil. In a deep *cazuela* or pot, prepare an infusion by pouring the water over half of the herbs. Add the chicken and cover with the other half of the herbs. Cook over low heat, covered, for 40 minutes. When the chicken is tender, serve it on the leaves with which it cooked.

SERVES 4   *Photograph pages 104–105*

ESTADO DE MÉXICO

Clemole Castellano

Castillian Duck

Clemoles can be substantial soups, or dishes with sauces lighter than moles. Alicia Gironella De' Angeli, a highly regarded Mexican cookbook author, has harmoniously combined duck in her clemole.

2 tablespoons (1 oz/30 g) butter
1 tablespoon oil
4 whole duck breasts, about 8 oz (250 g) each, cut in half
¾ cup (3 oz/90 g) pine nuts
¾ cup (3 oz/90 g) chopped walnuts
¾ cup (3 oz/90 g) chopped hazelnuts
3 *chiles anchos*, seeds and membranes removed
3 *chiles pasillas*, seeds and membranes removed
1 tablespoon *chile* seeds
¾ cup (3 oz/90 g) toasted breadcrumbs
6 cups (48 fl oz/1.5 l) duck or chicken stock (page 72)
3 tablespoons brown sugar or honey
4 avocado leaves, toasted and crumbled, or ½ teaspoon aniseed, lightly toasted (see glossary)

salt and freshly ground pepper
¼ cup (1 oz/30 g) pine nuts for garnish (optional)

✳ Heat the butter and oil in a large heavy skillet over medium heat, add the duck breasts and sauté until half of their fat has been rendered, about 3–4 minutes on each side. Set aside.
✳ In the duck fat, sauté the nuts, whole *chiles*, seeds and breadcrumbs over medium heat until lightly browned. Cool, then purée with enough stock to form a smooth sauce. Add the sugar and avocado leaves and simmer until the sauce thickens. Add salt and pepper to taste. Set aside.
✳ Finish cooking the duck breasts in a lightly oiled heavy skillet over medium-high heat. Cook the skin side first until golden brown, then turn the breasts over and cook for another 3 or 4 minutes.
✳ To serve, place each breast on top of a small amount of sauce, cover with more sauce and garnish with pine nuts if you like.

SERVES 8

Salsa de Jalapeños y Aceitunas Para Pato

Olive and Jalapeño Sauce for Duck

The first Spaniards planted grapevines and olive trees in Baja California. Sherry and olives make an appearance in this delicate recipe by Alicia Gironella De' Angeli. The sauce is an excellent accompaniment for sautéed duck breasts or for any recipe using duck.

2 tablespoons chopped onion
4 cloves garlic, chopped
1½ cups (12 fl oz/375 ml) dry sherry or dry white wine
¼ cup (2 fl oz/60 ml) olive oil
2 pickled *chiles jalapeños*, seeds and membranes removed
¾ cup (4 oz/125 g) pitted green olives
4 tablespoons minced parsley
white pepper
1½ cups (12 fl oz/375 ml) duck or chicken stock (page 72)

✳ In a small saucepan, cook the onion and half the garlic in the sherry over low heat until the mixture has the consistency of marmalade.
✳ Heat 1 tablespoon of the oil in a skillet, add the *chiles*, olives and most of the parsley and sauté for 1–2 minutes. Stir in the onion and garlic mixture. Cook for 4 minutes over low heat. Remove and stir in a little white pepper. Let cool.
✳ Purée this mixture in a blender, adding stock as needed. Strain.
✳ Pour the sauce over duck. Serve with corn kernels and mushrooms sautéed in oil with garlic and minced parsley.

SERVES 4

Duck with Olive and Jalapeño Sauce (top) and Castillian Duck (bottom)

Turkey with Poblano Mole Sauce

Mole Poblano de Guajolote

Turkey with Poblano Mole Sauce

This legendary dish is said to have been created in seventeenth-century Puebla by Sister Andrea de la Asunción, a Dominican nun from the Santa Rosa convent, with the original recipe including more than one hundred ingredients. Today, mole *remains the classic dish for festive occasions such as weddings and baptisms. It is better to prepare the sauce in advance, adding the turkey when it is reheated—not only because of the work involved in preparing the* mole *but because it tastes better when the various flavors have time to mingle and mellow.*

1 young turkey, about 8 lb (4 kg), cut into serving
 pieces
16 cups (128 fl oz/4 l) water
4 cloves garlic
½ onion
1 tablespoon salt

SAUCE

½ cup (4 fl oz/125 ml) plus 2 tablespoons oil
7 oz (220 g) *chiles anchos,* seeds and membranes removed
3 oz (90 g) *chiles pasillas,* seeds and membranes removed
10 oz (315 g) *chiles mulatos,* seeds and membranes removed
4 *chiles chipotles*
1½ lb (750 g) tomatoes
1 onion, coarsely chopped
10 cloves garlic
5 oz (155 g) blanched almonds
3½ oz (105 g) shelled peanuts
8 whole cloves
4 black peppercorns
1 1½-in (4-cm) stick cinnamon
½ teaspoon aniseed
3 oz (90 g) raisins
3 oz (90 g) unsweetened (cooking) chocolate

1 tablespoon sugar
2 tablespoons salt, or to taste
½ cup (2 oz/60 g) sesame seeds

✴ Place the turkey, water, garlic, onion and salt in a large pot or Dutch oven, bring to a boil, cover and simmer over medium heat for 1 hour or until the turkey is tender. Drain, reserving the stock, and set aside.
✴ To make the sauce, heat 2 tablespoons of the oil in a skillet, add the *chiles anchos, pasillas* and *mulatos* and sauté for 1–2 minutes. Transfer to a bowl, cover with hot water and soak for 30 minutes. Drain, transfer to a blender and purée. Set aside.
✴ Toast the *chiles chipotles* and roast the tomatoes (see glossary). Peel the tomatoes, transfer to a blender, add *chiles chipotles* and purée. Set aside.
✴ In the same oil in which you sautéed the *chiles,* sauté the onion and garlic for 2–3 minutes. Transfer to a blender. In the same oil, sauté the almonds for 5 minutes. Add the peanuts, cloves, peppercorns, cinnamon and aniseed and sauté for 3 more minutes. Transfer to the blender, add the raisins and purée.
✴ Heat the cup of oil in a large pot or Dutch oven. Stir all of the purées together, add to the pot and boil for 5 minutes, stirring constantly. Add the chocolate and sugar, stirring constantly. When the mixture comes to a boil, add 4 cups (32 fl oz/1 l) of the turkey stock. Cover and cook over low heat for 20 minutes. Add the salt and correct the seasonings. If the sauce is too thick, add more stock.
✴ Add the pieces of turkey, cover and cook over medium heat for 10 minutes. Meanwhile, toast the sesame seeds in a small skillet over medium heat until they are golden. Serve the turkey *mole* hot, sprinkled with the sesame seeds.

SERVES 10–12

Pollo en Cacahuate

Chicken in Peanut Sauce

Traditional cook María Dolores Torres Yzábal has nationalized a Spanish almond chicken dish by substituting the New World's peanut. Other Mexican versions are made more picante *by the inclusion of chiles instead of the more subtle Spanish sherry. This dish can be accompanied by very small plain boiled potatoes.*

¼ cup (2 fl oz/60 ml) oil
1 chicken, about 3 lb (1.5 kg), cut into serving pieces
2 cups (16 fl oz/500 ml) chicken stock (page 72)
1 onion, cut into chunks
1 clove garlic, chopped
1 1-in (2.5-cm) stick cinnamon
2 whole allspice
3 tomatoes, peeled, seeded and quartered
½ cup (3 oz/90 g) shelled peanuts
½ cup (4 fl oz/125 ml) dry sherry
salt

✴ Heat the oil in a skillet, add the chicken and sauté until golden brown. Transfer the chicken to a large pot, add the stock and cook until the chicken is tender, about 30 minutes. Drain and reserve the stock.
✴ In the drippings remaining in the skillet, sauté the onion, garlic, cinnamon and allspice. Remove with a

slotted spoon and transfer to a blender. Add the tomatoes, peanuts and ½ cup (4 fl oz/125 ml) or more of the reserved stock. Blend until the sauce is very smooth, add the sherry and pour into the pot containing the chicken. Cook, covered, over low heat until the sauce thickens slightly. Add salt if necessary.

SERVES 6

VERACRUZ

POLLO EN AJILLO

Chicken in Garlic

Garlic lovers will delight in this robust and colorful dish from Xalapa, the capital of Veracruz. According to Mexican cooking authority Diana Kennedy, who contributed this recipe, if at all possible a firm roasting or stewing chicken should be used—one that will not easily fall apart. Alternatively, pork and fish can be used, with the cooking times adjusted.

salt
1 chicken, about 3 lb (1.5 kg), cut into serving pieces
water
4 *chiles anchos,* seeds and membranes removed

14 whole cloves garlic
⅓ cup (3 fl oz/80 ml) olive oil
6 *chiles guajillos*

✱ Lightly salt the chicken and place in large pot or Dutch oven. Cover with 4 cups (32 fl oz/2 l) water and bring to a boil over medium heat. Cover and simmer until the chicken is almost tender, about 20 minutes, turning the pieces once. Drain, reserving 2 cups (16 fl oz/500 ml) of the stock. Set aside.
✱ Meanwhile, soak the *chiles anchos* in hot water to cover for 15 minutes and drain. In a blender, purée the *chiles* with 1 cup (8 fl oz/250 ml) fresh water. Purée the garlic with ⅓ cup (3 fl oz/80 ml) water. Set aside.
✱ Slice the *chiles guajillos* into rings about ¼ in (6 mm) thick and remove the seeds and membranes.
✱ Heat the oil in a skillet, add the rings of *chiles guajillos* and fry for a few seconds or until they are crisp. Add the puréed garlic and sauté for 10 seconds. Add the *chile ancho* purée, stirring and scraping the bottom of the skillet for 5 minutes or until the sauce is somewhat reduced. Add the reserved stock, correct the seasonings and heat through.
✱ Return the chicken to its pot, pour the sauce over, cover and cook over low heat for 25 minutes, stirring frequently.

SERVES 6

Chicken in Garlic (top) and Chicken in Peanut Sauce (bottom)

*Ingredients for Chicken Guadalajara Style (left)
and Chicken in Pumpkin Seed Sauce (right)*

JALISCO

Pollo Guadalajara

Chicken Guadalajara Style

*Guadalajara is a modern city, but its cuisine maintains the
flavor of days gone by. This cold chicken dish is a nineteenth-
century specialty.*

1 roasting chicken, about 5 lb (2.5 kg)
½ onion
4 cloves garlic
2 tablespoons salt
¼ teaspoon freshly ground pepper
7 small sprigs parsley
3 lb (1.5 kg) ripe tomatoes
1 cup (8 oz/250 g) finely chopped onion
3 tablespoons red wine vinegar
2 teaspoons oil
1 tablespoon dried oregano

✳ Place the chicken in a large pot or Dutch oven and
cover with cold water. Add the onion, garlic, 1
tablespoon of the salt and the pepper and parsley. As
soon as the water comes to a boil, lower the heat and
cook, covered, for 35 minutes or until the chicken is
tender. Let cool, then drain and cut into serving pieces.
✳ Meanwhile, roast and peel the tomatoes (see
glossary). Purée in a blender and strain into a large
bowl. Add the chopped onion, vinegar, oil, oregano
and remaining tablespoon of salt. Correct the seasonings.
✳ Place the chicken in the bowl of tomato sauce, turning
to coat well. Cover and refrigerate for at least 3 hours.
Serve cold.

SERVES 6

PUEBLA

POLLO EN PIPIÁN VERDE

Chicken in Pumpkin Seed Sauce

The original pipián was a simple sauce for fish and wild game made of ground pumpkin seeds and fresh green or dried red chiles and has been a part of the Aztec and Purépecha (Tarascan) Indian diets since pre-Columbian times. The convent nuns of Puebla embellished the pipián with spices and herbs and used it to sauce chicken and pork, but when it found its way to some other parts of Mexico, it became known as mole verde.

3 large chicken breasts, about 2 lb (1 kg)
4 cups (32 fl oz/1 l) water
3 cloves garlic
½ onion, cut into chunks
3 sprigs parsley
1 tablespoon salt

PUMPKIN SEED SAUCE

12 *chiles serranos*
2 lb (1 kg) *tomates verdes,* husks removed
¼ onion
2 cloves garlic
1 leaf of romaine (cos) lettuce
1 cup (1½ oz/45 g) coarsely chopped *cilantro* (coriander)
⅓ cup (½ oz/15 g) coarsely chopped radish leaves
1½ cups (6 oz/185 g) unsalted pumpkin seeds
¼ cup (2 oz/60 g) unsalted peanuts
2 tablespoons oil

Chicken Breasts in Poblano Sauce au Gratin

✳ In a large covered saucepan, simmer the chicken breasts in the water with the garlic, onion, parsley and salt for 20 minutes. Drain, reserving the stock. Remove the skin and cut each breast in half. Set aside.
✳ To make the sauce, add the *chiles* to a saucepan of boiling water. Boil, uncovered, for 8 minutes, then add the *tomates verdes* and boil until they change color, 4–5 minutes. Drain and transfer the *chiles* and *tomates verdes* to a blender. Add the onion, garlic, lettuce, *cilantro* and radish leaves, then purée and set aside.
✳ Heat a *comal* or iron skillet, add the pumpkin seeds and toast, stirring constantly, until they pop, about 3 minutes. Transfer to a nut grinder or blender and grind with the peanuts without adding any liquid.
✳ Heat the oil in a skillet, add the ground pumpkin seeds and peanuts and cook, stirring constantly, for 2 minutes. Gradually add the puréed *tomates verdes,* stirring well to eliminate any lumps. Add 2 cups (16 fl oz/500 ml) of the reserved stock, correct the seasonings, bring to a boil then simmer, uncovered, for 10 minutes. Add the chicken breasts and simmer over medium heat for 15 minutes. Stir gently to avoid causing the sauce to separate. If it becomes too thick, add more stock.

SERVES 6

SAN LUIS POTOSÍ

PECHUGAS EN SALSA DE POBLANO GRATINADAS

Chicken Breasts in Poblano Sauce au Gratin

An abundance of chiles *grow throughout this state. They are often combined with excellent local cheeses of cow's and goat's milk in rich creamy dishes like this one.*

3 whole chicken breasts, about 12 oz (375 g) each
salt and freshly ground pepper
1 large *chile poblano*
¼ cup (2 fl oz/60 ml) milk
¼ cup (2 oz/60 g) butter
1 tablespoon all-purpose (plain) flour
1 cup (8 fl oz/250 ml) thick cream *(crème fraîche)*
6 tablespoons (1½ oz/45 g) grated Cheddar cheese

✳ Remove the bones and skin and cut each chicken breast in half. Flatten each half slightly and sprinkle with salt and pepper. Refrigerate for 20 minutes.
✳ Remove the stem, seeds and membranes from the *chile,* then purée in a blender with the milk.
✳ Melt 2 tablespoons (1 oz/30 g) of the butter in a small saucepan. Add the flour and stir until smooth. Add the *chile* purée and stir. Add the cream and stir constantly over low heat until the mixture boils and thickens. Remove from the heat and add salt to taste. (This sauce can be made up to 6 hours in advance and reheated over low heat before using.)
✳ Preheat the oven to 350°F (180°C). Melt the remaining 2 tablespoons butter in a skillet, add the chicken breasts and sauté for 2 minutes on each side. Transfer to a lightly greased small baking dish, cover with the *poblano* sauce, sprinkle with the cheese and bake for 10 minutes.

SERVES 4–6

PUEBLA

Pollo en Orégano

Oregano Chicken

Tehuacán in eastern Puebla is best known for its bottled mineral water, but it is the plentiful oregano that grows on the hillsides surrounding the town and the cones of raw sugar produced by its sugar refineries that make this chicken dish by María Dolores Torres Yzábal unique.

1 large chicken, about 4 lb (2 kg), cut into serving pieces
salt and freshly ground pepper
6 tablespoons (3 fl oz/90 ml) oil
1 lb (500 g) *tomates verdes,* husks removed and coarsely
  chopped
½ onion, chopped
2 pickled *chiles chipotles,* coarsely chopped
2 cloves garlic, crushed
5 tablespoons (2½ oz/75 g) *piloncillo* (raw sugar) or
  brown sugar
1½ tablespoons fresh or 2 teaspoons dried oregano
1 cup (8 fl oz/250 ml) chicken stock (page 72)

✳ Season the chicken with salt and pepper. Heat the oil in a large skillet, add the chicken and sauté but do not brown. Remove the chicken and pour off the oil, leaving only 1 tablespoon in the skillet.
✳ Add the *tomates verdes,* onion, *chiles* and garlic to the skillet and sauté over low heat, stirring constantly, until the onion is transparent. Add the *piloncillo,* oregano and stock and simmer until the mixture thickens slightly. Correct the seasonings. Add the chicken, cover and cook for 30 minutes or until tender.

SERVES 6

Ingredients for Oregano Chicken

NAYARIT

GALLINA DE GUINEA AL MANGO

Cornish Hens with Mango Sauce

The luscious ripe mangoes that grow throughout Mexico's tropical regions sweeten the small birds in this unusual recipe.

6 small Cornish game hens, about 1½ lb (750 g) each
1 teaspoon freshly ground pepper
1 clove garlic
2 teaspoons salt
¼ cup (2 fl oz/60 ml) water
6 tablespoons (3 oz/90 g) butter, melted

SAUCE

1½ cups (12 fl oz/375 ml) syrup from canned mangoes
¾ cup (6 oz/185 g) drained canned mangoes
1 tablespoon butter
1 tablespoon brown sugar

✳ Remove the giblets and sprinkle the Cornish game hens with the pepper.
✳ In a blender, purée the garlic, salt and water. Pour over the hens and marinate, refrigerated, for 2 hours.
✳ To make the sauce, purée the syrup and mangoes. In a small skillet, melt the butter, add the purée and brown sugar and stir. When the mixture begins to boil, remove from the heat and set aside.
✳ About 1 hour before serving, preheat the oven to 500°F (260°C) and place the hens, breast side down, in a greased large baking pan. Baste with the melted butter and bake for 15 minutes. Turn the hens breast side up and bake another 15 minutes, basting frequently. Lower the heat to 375°F (190°C), turn the hens again and bake for 10 minutes. Remove from the oven, drain the juices from the pan and stir in the mango sauce.
✳ Turn the hens breast side up and baste with the mango sauce. Bake for another 5–7 minutes or until they are golden brown. Serve immediately, garnished with extra pieces of mango.

SERVES 6

GUERRERO

PECHUGAS DE PATO EN SALSA DE CIRUELA

Duck Breasts in Plum Sauce

To hunt wild ducks, the Indians covered their heads with hollowed pumpkins, submerged themselves in the shallow waters of the lagoons and patiently waited for the ducks to investigate, grabbing the most curious with their hands. For this recipe by Acapulco cook Kay Mendieta de Alonso, wild duck is used, but it also works well with domestic duck.

5 whole wild duck breasts, about 8 oz (250 g) each, bone removed and cut in half
½ cup (4 fl oz/125 ml) dry red wine
3 cloves garlic, crushed
12 ripe red plums, cut in half and pitted
¾ cup (6 fl oz/180 ml) water
1 tablespoon brown sugar

Duck Breasts in Plum Sauce (left) and Cornish Hens with Mango Sauce (right)

1 tablespoon butter
4 slices bacon
⅓ cup (3 oz/90 g) finely chopped onion
¾ cup (6 fl oz/180 ml) orange juice
¼ teaspoon freshly ground pepper
1 teaspoon salt
1 tablespoon white tequila

OPTIONAL GARNISH

6 plums, cut in half and pitted
2 teaspoons butter
2 teaspoons brown sugar
¼ teaspoon salt

✳ Marinate the duck breasts in the wine and garlic, refrigerated, for at least 4 hours, preferably overnight. Drain and set aside.
✳ Place the plums, ¼ cup (2 fl oz/60 ml) of the water and the sugar in a saucepan. Cook over low heat, stirring constantly, for 6–8 minutes or until the plums soften. Use a spoon to press the pulp through a sieve. Add the remaining water to the pan, swirl around, strain, add to the plum purée and set aside.
✳ Melt the butter in a large skillet, add the bacon and fry until crisp and brown. Remove the bacon, crumble and set aside. Add the duck breasts to the skillet and lightly sauté for 2 minutes on each side. Remove and set aside.
✳ In the same skillet, sauté the onion for 2 minutes or until transparent. Add the orange juice, scrape the bottom of the pan and add the pepper, salt and tequila. When the mixture comes to a boil, strain and transfer to another large pan. Add the plum purée and stir. Add the duck, cover and cook over low heat for 40 minutes or until the breasts are tender. If the sauce becomes too thick, thin with chicken stock or water. Correct the seasonings.
✳ Transfer the duck to a platter, baste with plum sauce and sprinkle with bacon.
✳ To make the garnish, lightly sauté the plum halves in the butter and sprinkle with the brown sugar and salt. Arrange around the platter of duck breasts.

SERVES 4–6

CAMPECHE

Pavo en Frío

Cold Turkey

While the scrub and rain forests are still inhabited by wild turkeys, it is the descendants of the bird that the Maya Indians domesticated centuries ago that are used today for this cold buffet dish.

1 young turkey, about 7 lb (3.5 kg)
3 oz (90 g) cured ham, cut into strips
5 cloves garlic, slivered
2 avocado leaves, central vein removed and cut into strips
12 black peppercorns
1 tablespoon each ground cinnamon and nutmeg
1 teaspoon ground cloves
9 qt (9 l) water
½ head garlic
½ onion
1 tablespoon salt
1 cup (8 fl oz/250 ml) olive oil
4 cups (32 fl oz/1 l) white wine
1 large onion, quartered
2 oranges, sliced
½ cup (4 fl oz/125 ml) lime juice

DRESSING

¾ cup (6 fl oz/180 ml) red wine vinegar
1½ cups (12 fl oz/375 ml) olive oil
salt

✳ Make small slits with a knife all over the turkey and insert the ham, garlic, avocado leaves and peppercorns in them. Rub the turkey with the cinnamon, nutmeg and cloves and wrap it in a double thickness of cheesecloth or a piece of thin white cloth. Transfer to a large pot or Dutch oven and add the water, garlic, ½ onion and salt. Cover and simmer for 1½ hours. Drain, reserving the stock.
✳ Return the turkey and 8 cups (64 fl oz/2 l) of the stock to the pot and add the oil, wine, onion, orange slices and lime juice. Cover and cook over medium heat for 1 hour or until the turkey is tender, basting occasionally. Remove the turkey from the pot and let cool for 30 minutes. Remove the cheesecloth.
✳ To prepare the dressing, measure out 3 cups (24 fl oz/750 ml) of the liquid from the pot. Add the vinegar, oil and salt to taste and mix well.
✳ Remove the skin from the turkey. Slice the breast and the meat from the legs and thighs and arrange on a large platter. Cover with the dressing and refrigerate, covered, for at least 2 hours.

SERVES 12–14

YUCATÁN

Pollo en Escabeche

Marinated Chicken

The word escabeche *comes from the Arabic* sikiube, *which means "acid," and is a method for light pickling. In Mexico,* escabeches *combine wine or vinegar with citrus juices, bay leaves and other herbs. This Maya recipe also includes the*

traditional achiote *paste, or* recado rojo, *which is available in some Hispanic markets or can be made.*

1 whole chicken, about 3 lb (1.5 kg), cut up
10 cups (80 fl oz/2.5 l) water
½ onion, roasted (see glossary)
4 cloves garlic, roasted (see glossary)
salt
3 sprigs *cilantro* (coriander)
2 teaspoons dried oregano
2 teaspoons ground cumin
4 cloves garlic, unpeeled
1 cup (8 fl oz/250 ml) orange juice
½ cup (4 fl oz/125 ml) lime juice or 1½ cups bitter (Seville) orange juice
1 lb (500 g) red onions, thinly sliced
1 teaspoon salt
6 *chiles cristal* or *chiles habaneros*, roasted (see glossary)

MARINADE

3 oz (90 g) *achiote* paste (recipe follows)
½ cup (4 fl oz/125 ml) orange juice
¼ cup (2 fl oz/60 ml) lime juice
1 tablespoon lard, melted and cooled

Cold Turkey (left) and Marinated Chicken (right)

✳ Place the chicken, water, roasted onion and garlic, 1 tablespoon salt and the *cilantro* in a large pot or Dutch oven and cook, covered, over medium heat for about 30 minutes or until the chicken is tender. Drain and set aside.

✳ Meanwhile, toast the oregano, cumin and garlic (see glossary). Peel the garlic and purée in a blender with the oregano, cumin, orange juice and lime juice.

✳ Place the red onions in an earthenware or enamel container and add the purée. Stir, add 1 teaspoon salt and bring to a boil over medium heat. Remove from the heat, add the *chiles* and set aside for at least 2 hours.

✳ To make the marinade, dissolve the *achiote* paste in the orange and lime juices in a small bowl. Baste each piece of chicken with this mixture and marinate at room temperature for 30 minutes to 1 hour. Baste all the chicken pieces thoroughly with the melted lard.

✳ Preheat an outdoor grill and lightly grease the rack. Grill the chicken for 5 minutes on each side, let cool 5 minutes and shred the chicken. (This can also be done in an oven broiler.) To serve, arrange the shredded chicken on a large platter and cover with the red onions and *chiles*.

SERVES 6–8

Recado Rojo

Achiote Paste

1 tablespoon *achiote (annatto)* seeds
½ teaspoon ground cumin
¼ teaspoon dried oregano
8 black peppercorns
½ teaspoon ground allspice
1 whole clove
¼ teaspoon ground *chile piquín*
½ teaspoon salt
2 cloves garlic
3 tablespoons bitter (Seville) orange juice or 2 tablespoons orange juice mixed with 1 tablespoon white vinegar

✳In a nut or coffee grinder, grind the *achiote* seeds, cumin, oregano, peppercorns, allspice, clove, *chile piquín* and salt.

✳ Grind the garlic in a mortar or *molcajete,* add the ground spices and stir in the orange juice to make a paste. Place in a small glass jar, cover and refrigerate until ready to use.

MAKES ABOUT ⅓ CUP (3 OZ/90 G)

Manchamanteles (top) and Pistachio Mole (bottom)

MOLE DE PISTACHE

Pistachio Mole

Martha Chapa puts together the unusual and delicate combination of pistachios and avocado leaves in this new version of mole.

8 chicken legs with thighs
3 cups (24 fl oz/750 ml) white wine
3 cups (24 fl oz/750 ml) water
2 onions, sliced
4 cloves garlic
4 avocado leaves, fresh or dried
salt
6 tablespoons (3 oz/90 g) butter
2 tablespoons oil
1 *chile poblano,* roasted (see glossary), peeled and
   membranes removed
10 oz (315 g) shelled pistachios, skins removed
freshly ground pepper

GARNISH

½ onion, sliced
1 tablespoon butter
fresh avocado leaves (optional)

✳ In a large covered saucepan over medium heat, simmer the chicken in the wine and water along with 1 onion and the garlic, avocado leaves and salt until tender, about 30 minutes. Drain the chicken, reserving the stock, and return to the saucepan.

✳ While the chicken is cooking, heat the butter and oil in a skillet. Add the *chile,* remaining onion and the pistachios and sauté until lightly browned. In a blender or food processor, grind this mixture with a little of the reserved stock, then simmer in a covered saucepan over very low heat for 30 minutes. Pour over the chicken and simmer, covered, for 5 minutes. Before serving, add pepper and more salt if needed.

✳ In a small skillet, sauté the onion in the butter for 5 minutes or until translucent. Garnish with the onions and, if you like, fresh avocado leaves.

SERVES 4–6

OAXACA

MANCHAMANTELES

Sloppy Chicken

The name for this sprightly dish, one of the seven moles *of Oaxaca, is a Spanish translation for "tablecloth stainer," a title that well describes what happens if you spill any of the chile ancho sauce. Tortillas are essential to sop up the sauce and keep spilling to a minimum.*

5 *chiles anchos,* seeds and membranes removed
½ onion
3 cloves garlic
1 3-in (7.5-cm) stick cinnamon
4 whole cloves
4 black peppercorns
5 blanched almonds
½ teaspoon each dried oregano and thyme
3 tablespoons oil
3 large ripe tomatoes
1 chicken, about 3 lb (1.5 kg), cut into serving pieces
1½–2 cups (12–16 fl oz/375–500 ml) water
1 teaspoon salt
1 small sprig parsley
1 sweet potato, about 8 oz (250 g), peeled and cubed
1 tablespoon butter
2 cups (11 oz/345 g) sliced plantain or large firm banana
2 slices pineapple (10 oz/315 g), cubed

✳ Toast the *chiles* (see glossary) on a *comal* or iron skillet, then soak in hot water to cover for 20 minutes. Drain.
✳ Roast the onion, garlic, cinnamon, cloves, peppercorns, almonds, oregano and thyme (see glossary). Transfer to a blender, add the *chiles* and purée.
✳ Heat 1 tablespoon of the oil in a large saucepan. Add the purée and boil vigorously, stirring constantly, for 5 minutes.
✳ Roast the tomatoes (see glossary), peel and purée in a blender. Add to the *chile* purée, lower the heat and cook for 7 minutes, stirring constantly. Set aside.
✳ Heat the remaining 2 tablespoons oil in a large skillet, add the chicken and sauté until lightly browned. Add the

water, salt and parsley. When the water comes to a boil, lower the heat and cook, covered, for 10 minutes. Add the *chile* sauce and continue cooking for 10 minutes. Add the sweet potato and cook an additional 10 minutes.
✳ Melt the butter in a small skillet, add the plantains and pineapple and sauté until lightly browned. Add to the chicken, correct the seasonings and cook, covered, over low heat for 15 minutes or until the chicken is tender.

SERVES 6

TLAXCALA

CAZUELITAS CON HUEVOS Y CHILES POBLANOS

Eggs and Poblano Chiles in Cazuelitas

Although this rich egg dish has traditional ingredients, María Dolores Torres Yzábal prepares them in an untraditional way to create a dish suitable for a first course or a light meal.

4 eggs
1½ cups (12 fl oz/375 ml) thick cream *(crème fraîche)*
¾ teaspoon salt
1½ cups (6 oz/185 g) grated *queso Chihuahua* (or Monterey Jack or medium-sharp Cheddar cheese)
2 large *chiles poblanos,* roasted (see glossary), seeds and membranes removed, and diced

✳ Preheat the oven to 350°F (180°C). In a mixing bowl, beat the eggs with a fork, adding the cream and salt a little at a time.
✳ Divide the cheese evenly among 6 *cazuelitas* or ramekins, top with the *chiles* and fill with the egg mixture.
✳ Place the *cazuelitas* in a hot-water bath and bake for 40 minutes or until set.

SERVES 6

Eggs and Poblano Chiles in Cazuelitas

GUERRERO

POLLO AL CHIPOTLE

Chicken with Chipotle Chiles

Chile chipotle *adds its distinctive smoky flavor to this very spicy chicken. The number of chiles can be reduced to just one if you want flavor without the heat. Cumin is frequently added to dishes of the Pacific coast.*

1 chicken, about 3 lb (1.5 kg), cut into serving pieces
salt and freshly ground pepper
3 cloves garlic
4 black peppercorns
2 whole cloves
½ teaspoon ground cumin
¼ small onion
½ cup (4 fl oz/125 ml) water
2 tablespoons oil
2 onions (13 oz/400 g), sliced
5 small tomatoes (1½ lb/750 g), thinly sliced
3 pickled *chiles chipotles*

✱ Season the chicken lightly with salt and pepper. Set aside.
✱ In a blender, purée the garlic, peppercorns, cloves, cumin and onion quarter with half of the water and set aside.
✱ Heat the oil in a large skillet. Add the sliced onions and cook for 3 minutes or until transparent. Add the purée, stir and cook over medium-high heat for 10 minutes. Add the tomatoes and, when the mixture comes to a boil, lower the heat and cook, covered, for 5 minutes.
✱ In a blender, purée the *chiles* with the remaining water and add to the skillet. Boil for 2 minutes and correct the seasonings. Add the chicken, cover and cook over low heat for 25 minutes or until the chicken is tender.

SERVES 4

VERACRUZ

POLLO A LA NARANJA

Chicken with Orange Sauce

Martinez de la Torre, a small town in Veracruz, is famous for its sweet and juicy oranges, which are ideal for this easy dish.

1 chicken, about 3½ lb (1.75 kg), cut into serving pieces
2½ teaspoons salt
½ teaspoon freshly ground pepper
½ cup (2 oz/60 g) all-purpose (plain) flour
6 tablespoons (3 oz/90 g) butter
2 cups (16 fl oz/500 ml) orange juice

✱ Two hours in advance or the day before, season the chicken with 1 teaspoon of the salt and the pepper. Set aside.
✱ Preheat the oven to 400°F (200°C). Spread the flour on a plate and gently dredge the chicken in it. Melt the butter in a large skillet, add the chicken and sauté over medium heat for 8 minutes, turning once. Arrange the chicken in a single layer in a rectangular baking dish.
✱ Add the orange juice to the skillet, swirl around, strain and pour over the chicken. Sprinkle with the remaining 1½ teaspoons salt and cover the dish with aluminum foil.
✱ Bake the chicken for 20 minutes. Remove from the oven, uncover the dish and turn the chicken over. Cover and return to the oven for 20 minutes. Uncover and bake another 15 minutes or until the chicken is tender.

SERVES 4

DISTRITO FEDERAL

POLLO AL PEREJIL

Chicken with Parsley Sauce

An adventurous combination of flavors that typifies the new style of Mexican cuisine.

2 chiles poblanos, seeds and membranes removed
4 cups (32 fl oz/1 l) water
2 cloves garlic
3 cups (4 oz/125 g) parsley
2 tablespoons (1 oz/30 g) butter
1 tablespoon oil
1 chicken, about 3 lb (1.5 g), cut into serving pieces
½ small onion, finely chopped
1½ tablespoon all-purpose (plain) flour
3 potatoes (22 oz/650 g), peeled and cut into chunks
1 13-oz (400-g) can pickled mushrooms
1½ teaspoons salt
¼ teaspoon freshly ground pepper

✱ In a blender, purée the *chiles* with the water, garlic and parsley. Set aside.
✱ Heat the butter and oil in a skillet, add the chicken and sauté for 3–4 minutes on each side. Add the onion and sauté for 2 minutes. Add the flour and stir into the drippings until smooth. Add the *chile* purée and cook over high heat, stirring constantly, for 5 minutes. Add the potatoes, pickled mushrooms, salt and pepper. Correct the seasonings, lower the heat, cover and cook for 25–35 minutes or until the potatoes are tender.

SERVES 6

OAXACA

HUEVOS OAXAQUEÑOS

Eggs Oaxaca Style

Variations of this egg dish—this one by Socorrito Zorrilla—are popular throughout the Isthmus of Tehuantepec. In Oaxaca, a handful of cooked nopales *(cactus paddles) is often added.*

2 lb (1 kg) tomatoes
6 cloves garlic
1 onion
3 *chiles de agua* or small *chiles poblanos*
10 eggs
½ cup (4 fl oz/125 ml) milk
salt
butter or oil
½ cup (¾ oz/20 g) chopped *epazote*

✱ Roast the tomatoes, garlic and onion (see glossary). Chop very fine. Roast the *chiles* separately (see glossary), remove the membranes and cut into strips.
✱ Beat the eggs with the milk and sprinkle with salt. Scramble the eggs in a lightly greased skillet until just set, stirring constantly.
✱ Place a little butter or oil in a *cazuela* or deep skillet and fry the tomato sauce for 5 minutes. Stir in the *chile* strips and *epazote,* then add the eggs. Correct the seasonings.
✱ This egg dish is usually served very hot, accompanied by *frijoles de la olla* (page 208) and hot corn tortillas.

SERVES 6 *Photograph page 126*

Chicken with Parsley Sauce (top left), Chicken with Chipotle Chiles (top right) and Chicken with Orange Sauce (bottom)

OAXACA

HIGADITOS DE FANDANGO

Festive Chicken

The name of this traditional fiesta recipe contributed by Socorrito Zorrilla literally means "little livers" but is confusingly composed of chicken (usually without livers) and eggs. Cooking in Mexico is not just a matter of taste and smell. In the simple Zapotec Indian kitchens of Oaxaca, the women rely mainly on their ears when preparing this dish. The secret comes from beating the eggs with a large sharp knife until the sound changes from "tlacawhup tlacawhup" to a thicker "whalcawhump."

1 chicken, about 3 lb (1.5 kg)
4 cups (32 fl oz/1 l) water
1 tablespoon salt

½ onion
2 cloves garlic
2 leaves *hierba santa* (optional)
8 eggs
6 tablespoons (3 oz/90 g) lard or oil
1 small onion, chopped
3 cloves garlic, minced
2 large tomatoes, seeded and chopped
4 small *tomates verdes,* husks removed and chopped
1½ teaspoons ground cumin
2 peppercorns, ground
1 whole clove, ground
1 pinch saffron

✳ Place the chicken in a large pot or Dutch oven with the water, salt, onion, garlic and *hierba santa.* Bring to a boil, then cover and simmer for 35 minutes or until the chicken is tender. Drain, reserving the stock. When the chicken is

Festive Chicken (left, served with Pasilla Chile Sauce), Eggs Oaxaca Style (rear, recipe page 124) and Mexican-Style Scrambled Eggs (front)

cool enough to handle, shred the meat. You should have about 2½ cups (14 oz/440 g). Beat the eggs thoroughly in a large bowl and gently stir in the shredded chicken.

✳ Melt the lard in a deep *cazuela* or large skillet. When it is hot, add the onion and garlic and sauté until transparent. Add the tomatoes and *tomates verdes* and sauté until tender—about 5 minutes—then add 2 cups (16 fl oz/500 ml) of the reserved stock and the ground spices. Bring to a boil, lower to a simmer and gradually pour in the chicken-egg mixture. Without stirring, cook the mixture over low heat until the eggs are set.

✳ With a spatula, loosen the sides so that the eggs do not stick to the pan and some of the sauce comes to the top. (There will be a solid egg mass sitting in the sauce.)

✳ Serve with a sauce made from *chiles pasillas* (below).

SERVES 8

Pasilla Chile Sauce

1 tablespoon oil
4 *chiles pasillas,* seeds and membranes removed
1 clove garlic
1 teaspoon salt
⅔ cup (5 fl oz/160 ml) water
1 tablespoon white vinegar
½ teaspoon dried oregano

✳ In a skillet, heat the oil, add the *chiles* and sauté for 40 seconds, stirring constantly. Rinse. Transfer the *chiles* to a blender, add the garlic, salt and water and purée briefly. There should be pieces of roughly chopped *chile.* Transfer to a bowl, stir in the vinegar and oregano and serve with the *higaditos de fandango.*

MAKES ABOUT 1½ CUPS (12 FL OZ/375 ML)

Huevos Rancheros

Huevos a la Mexicana

Mexican-Style Scrambled Eggs

The two favorite egg dishes of Mexico, huevos rancheros *and* huevos a la mexicana, *are both imbued with the* chiles, *onions and tomatoes that give Mexican food its characteristic taste. The seeds and membranes of the* chile *can be removed for a less* picante *dish, or a* salsa de tomate verde cocida *(page 201) added for those who need a fiery breakfast to bring them awake.*

1 tablespoon oil
1 tablespoon chopped onion
¾ cup (6 oz/185 g) chopped tomato
1 *chile serrano,* chopped
⅛ teaspoon salt
2 eggs

✳ Heat the oil in a skillet. Add the onion and sauté until transparent. Add the tomato, *chile* and salt and sauté over medium heat for 5 minutes.

✳ Lightly beat the eggs, add to the tomato sauce and stir gently. Cover and cook over medium heat for 2–3 minutes or until the eggs are set. Serve with hot corn tortillas.

SERVES 1

Huevos Rancheros

Ranch-Style Eggs

In preindustrial times, two breakfasts were served—coffee and pan dulce *in the early hours and a more substantial protein-based meal called* almuerzo *at midmorning. These popular ranch-style eggs were commonly eaten for the late breakfast, but now you find them on menus at all hours of the day, served with* frijoles refritos *(page 201) and extra tortillas.*

¼ cup (2 fl oz/60 ml) oil
1 tablespoon finely chopped onion
½ clove garlic, finely chopped
¾ cup (6 oz/185 g) finely chopped tomato
1 *chile serrano,* finely chopped
⅛ teaspoon each salt and freshly ground pepper
1 corn tortilla
2 eggs

✳ Heat 1 tablespoon of the oil in a small saucepan, add the onion and garlic and sauté until transparent. Add the tomato and cook for 2 minutes. Add the *chile,* salt and pepper and cook another 3 minutes. Correct the seasonings.

✳ Heat the remaining oil in a skillet, add the tortilla, fry for 30 seconds and drain. Pour off most of the oil, add the eggs and fry until set.

✳ Place the tortilla on a plate, top with the fried eggs and cover with the sauce. Serve hot.

SERVES 1

Motul-Style Eggs

Huevos con Chorizo

Eggs with Chorizo

Onions, potatoes or strips of chile *are often added to enhance this rustic mix of scrambled eggs and spicy Mexican sausage, which can be topped with crumbled* queso fresco *and served with a* salsa verde *and tortillas.*

2 tablespoons oil
1 oz (30 g) *chorizo* or other spicy sausage, casing
   removed
2 eggs
pinch of salt

✱ Heat the oil in a skillet, add the *chorizo* and sauté for 4 minutes.
✱ In a bowl, beat the eggs lightly and add the salt. Pour into the skillet and mix with the *chorizo*. Cook for 3 minutes or until the eggs are set, stirring occasionally.

SERVES 1

Huevos Motuleños

Motul-Style Eggs

The elaborate ham-and-egg tortilla sandwich with peas and salsa *gets its name from the small town of Motul, which lies east of Mérida.*

1 tablespoon chopped onion
1 clove garlic
¼ teaspoon ground cumin
2 whole cloves
⅛ teaspoon dried thyme
2 tablespoons water
½ cup (4 fl oz/125 ml) oil
¾ cup (6 oz/185 g) chopped tomato
½ teaspoon salt
2 corn tortillas
2 eggs
1 tablespoon *frijoles refritos* (page 201)
2 tablespoons chopped ham
1 tablespoon cooked green peas
1 slice (½ oz/15 g) mild Cheddar cheese, cut into thin
   strips (optional)

✱ In a blender, purée the onion, garlic, cumin, cloves and thyme with the water. Strain.
✱ Heat 1 tablespoon of the oil in a small saucepan, add the purée and stir for 1 minute. Add the tomato and salt and cook for 5 minutes.
✱ Heat the remaining oil in a skillet. Fry each tortilla in the oil for 30 seconds and drain. Pour off most of the oil, add the eggs and fry until set.
✱ Place a tortilla on a plate. Spread with the *frijoles refritos* and place the fried eggs on top. Cover with the other tortilla, spoon the tomato sauce on top and garnish with the ham, peas and cheese.

SERVES 1

Huevos con Frijoles

Eggs with Beans

In the highlands of Veracruz and in neighboring Oaxaca, soupy black beans and eggs are served up in bowls for a late breakfast. They are sometimes called huevos tirados.

¾ cup (6 oz/185 g) *frijoles de la olla* (page 208) in their
   liquid
2 eggs
⅛ teaspoon salt
⅛ teaspoon freshly ground pepper
1½ teaspoons oil

✱ Heat the beans and set aside.
✱ Mix the eggs, salt and pepper in a bowl. Heat the oil in a skillet, add the eggs and scramble, stirring, until they are soft-cooked.
✱ Add the beans and heat until bubbling. Serve with pickled *chiles* and hot corn tortillas.

SERVES 1

Huevos de Albañil

Bricklayer's Eggs

These "eggs of the bricklayer" are always served with plenty of salsa *to mop up with tortillas. Bricklayers are held in high regard in Mexico; May 3 is a special holiday in their honor and it is customary for construction-site bosses to give workers a celebration* barbacoa *(page 142) on this day.*

1 ripe tomato
2 *chiles serranos*
½ clove garlic

2 eggs
⅛ teaspoon salt
1½ tablespoons oil
¼ onion

✳In a small saucepan, simmer the tomato and *chiles* in water to cover for 5 minutes and drain. Peel the tomato and transfer to a blender. Add the *chiles* and garlic and purée.
✳ In a bowl, lightly beat the eggs with the salt.

✱ Heat the oil in a small skillet, add the onion and sauté for 2 minutes. Add the eggs and scramble for 40 seconds or until soft-cooked. Add the tomato purée and cook over medium heat for 1–2 minutes or until the sauce bubbles.
✱*Note:* This recipe can be doubled or quadrupled.

SERVES 1

---

*Eggs with Beans (top left), Bricklayer's Eggs (bottom left)
and Eggs with Chorizo (right)*

Cheese Omelet with Poblano Sauce

MORELOS

OMELETTE CON QUESO Y SALSA DE POBLANO

Cheese Omelet with Poblano Sauce

The French-style omelet is popular in such weekend getaway spots as Cuernavaca, near Mexico City.

⅓ cup (3 oz/90 g) chopped *chile poblano*
⅓ cup (3 fl oz/80 ml) thick cream *(crème fraîche)*
salt
⅛ teaspoon freshly ground pepper
2 eggs
1 tablespoon butter
¼ cup (1 oz/30 g) grated *queso manchego* (or Monterey Jack or
   medium-sharp Cheddar cheese)

✳ In a blender, purée the *chile* with the cream. Add salt to taste and heat the sauce in a small pan over medium heat; set aside.

✳ Add ½ teaspoon salt and the pepper to the eggs and beat lightly.

✳ Melt the butter in a small skillet. When it is hot, add the eggs. When the edge of the eggs can be lifted easily, place the cheese on one side, roll up and cook until the cheese begins to melt. If the egg starts to brown, lower the heat. Place on a plate and cover with the hot *chile* cream.

✳*Note:* This recipe is easily tripled or quadrupled. The omelets can be made in advance, covered with the *poblano* sauce and baked in a preheated (375°F/190°C) oven for 10 minutes.

SERVES 1–2

Huevos "Rabo de Mestiza"

"Rabo de Mestiza" Eggs

No one seems to know how it got its name, but "in the rags and tatters of the daughter of a Spaniard and an Indian" is the very loose, unliteral meaning given to this hearty dish of poached eggs that dates back to the early days of the Spanish conquest.

½ large tomato
1½ teaspoons chopped onion
⅛ clove garlic
1½ tablespoons oil
½ teaspoon salt
⅛ teaspoon freshly ground pepper
2 eggs
½ *chile poblano,* roasted (see glossary), membranes removed and cut into strips
1 tablespoon grated *queso manchego* (or Monterey Jack or medium-sharp Cheddar cheese)
1 tablespoon thick cream *(crème fraîche)*

✳ In a blender, purée the tomato, onion and garlic. Strain.
✳ Heat the oil in a skillet, add the tomato purée and cook for 5 minutes. Add the salt and pepper, cook another 5 minutes and correct the seasonings. Lower the heat and add the eggs without breaking the yolks. Bring the sauce to a boil and add the *chile* strips and cheese. Lower the heat and continue cooking until the eggs are set.
✳ Before serving, garnish with the cream. Accompany with hot corn tortillas.

SERVES 1

Huevos Ahogados

Drowned Eggs

Many of the larger hotels in Mexico serve these eggs, which are poached floating in a light tomato sauce.

1 small tomato (2 oz/60 g)
1 tablespoon chopped onion
1 clove garlic
2 tablespoons oil
1½ tablespoons chopped *cilantro* (coriander)
1 *chile cuaresmeño* or *chile jalapeño*
⅛ teaspoon salt
½ cup (4 fl oz/125 ml) water
2 eggs

✳ Roast the tomato (see glossary), then peel. Purée in a blender with the onion and garlic.
✳ Heat the oil in a small skillet, add the tomato purée and cook for 3 minutes. Add the *cilantro, chile,* salt and water and boil for 5 minutes. Lower the heat and add the eggs without breaking the yolks. Cover and cook until the whites set, basting occasionally with the sauce.
✳ Serve in an individual *cazuelita* or ramekin. Accompany with hot corn tortillas.
✳*Variation:* Stir 2 tablespoons cooked rice into the sauce before adding the eggs.

SERVES 1

Huevos en Salsa de Tomate Verde

Eggs in Tomate Verde Sauce

Eggs made with salsa and served with beans and tortillas are a quick, tasty, filling and economical breakfast or supper—qualities that make this dish popular throughout the country.

6 oz (180 g) *tomates verdes,* husks removed
2 *chiles serranos*
½ clove garlic
⅓ cup (½ oz/15 g) chopped *cilantro* (coriander)
2 eggs
⅛ teaspoon salt
2 tablespoons oil
2 tablespoons chopped onion

✳ In a small saucepan, simmer the *tomates verdes* and *chiles* in water to cover for 8 minutes and drain. Transfer to a blender, add the garlic and purée. Add the *cilantro* and pulse once to roughly purée.
✳ In a bowl, lightly beat the eggs with the salt. Heat the oil in a small skillet, add the onion and sauté until transparent. Add the eggs and scramble, stirring, for 1 minute or until soft-cooked. Add the sauce, stir and cook for 1 more minute. Serve with hot corn tortillas.
✳*Note:* If the *tomates verdes* are dry, add ¼ cup (2 fl oz/ 60 ml) water to the blender.

SERVES 1

Eggs in Tomate Verde Sauce (top), "Rabo de Mestiza" Eggs (center), Drowned Eggs (bottom)

Queso de Bola Relleno

Stuffed Cheese Round

Quintana Roo, the newest of Mexico's states, is best known for its resorts of Cancún and Cozumel. But for bargain hunters, Chetumal is the place to go, as it is a duty-free port city. It is here that innovative Yucatán cooks purchase the round Edam cheese from Holland to make this substantial and dramatic dish. It makes a perfect, if messy, appetizer, with everyone using tortillas to scoop up the cheese and fillings.

1 round of Edam cheese, about 4 lb (2 kg)

MEAT FILLING

¼ cup (2 oz/ 60 g) lard or oil
½ cup (4 oz/125 g) chopped onion
1 lb (500 g) ground (minced) pork
1 lb (500 g) ground (minced) beef
3 tomatoes, about 22 oz (660 g), peeled and finely chopped
⅓ cup (3 oz/90 g) finely chopped red bell pepper
   (capsicum)
3 tablespoons capers
⅓ cup (2 oz/60 g) pitted and chopped green olives
⅓ cup (2 oz/60 g) raisins
½ teaspoon saffron
¼ cup (2 fl oz/ 60 ml) chicken stock (page 72)
salt
1 tablespoon *achiote* paste (page 121)
¾ cup (6 fl oz/180 ml) bitter (Seville) orange juice or ¼
   cup (2 fl oz/60 ml) lime juice plus ½ cup (4 fl oz/
   125 ml) orange juice
2 hard-boiled (hard-cooked) eggs

RED SAUCE

1 tablespoon lard or oil
½ cup (4 oz/125 g) chopped onion
1 small green bell pepper (capsicum), roasted (see
   glossary) and chopped
3½ cups (28 oz/840 g) peeled and chopped tomatoes
⅓ cup (2 oz/60 g) pitted and coarsely chopped green olives
⅓ cup (2 oz/60 g) capers
1 teaspoon salt

WHITE SAUCE

1 tablespoon lard or butter
2½ tablespoons all-purpose (plain) flour
1¼ cups (10 fl oz/310 ml) water
pinch of saffron
salt

✳ Peel the wax rind from the cheese. Cut a circle 2 in (5 cm) in diameter and ½ in (1 cm) thick from the top of the cheese; this will be the "lid" for the filled cheese. Remove the center of the cheese until you have a hollow shell about ½ in (1.25 cm) thick.
✳ To prepare the meat filling, melt the lard in a large skillet or Dutch oven, add the onion and sauté until transparent. Add the pork and beef and brown for 5 minutes. Add the tomatoes and pepper, stir and bring to a boil over high heat. Lower the heat and add the capers, olives and raisins. Dissolve the saffron in the chicken stock and add to the pan. Add salt to taste. Dissolve the *achiote* paste in the juice and add to the pan. Cook, covered, over medium heat for 15 minutes.

Uncover and pour off ¾ cup (6 fl oz/180 ml) of liquid and set aside. If more liquid remains, cook, uncovered, until almost dry. Finely chop the egg whites and add them to the pan. Stir well and set aside.
✳ To prepare the red sauce, melt the lard in a large skillet, add the onion and sauté for 2 minutes. Add the pepper and sauté for 2 minutes. Add the tomatoes and cook, stirring constantly, for 10 minutes. Add the olives, capers and salt and cook for 5 more minutes. Correct the seasonings and set aside.
✳ To prepare the white sauce, melt the lard in a small saucepan and blend in the flour. Add the reserved liquid from the meat filling, stirring constantly so that no lumps form. Add the water and saffron and cook over a low heat, stirring constantly, until the sauce thickens. Add salt to taste and set aside.
✳ Preheat the oven to 325°F (165°C). Fill the cheese half full of the ground meat mixture. Add the whole egg yolks and fill with the rest of the meat mixture. Place the "lid" on the cheese.
✳ Place the cheese in a 9-in (23-cm) square baking dish and bake until it is slightly softened, about 10 minutes. Remove from the oven and pour the red sauce around half of the cheese and the white sauce around the other half. Bake for 5 minutes or until the sauces are hot and the cheese is soft but still keeps its shape. Serve hot with hot corn tortillas.

SERVES 8–10

Picadillo

Picadillo Filling

Coming from the word picar *(to mince), this recipe of chopped meats, fruits and spices is used as a filling for tacos, chiles or empanadas.*

¼ teaspoon ground cinnamon
¼ teaspoon each dried thyme and marjoram
3 large cloves garlic
3 whole cloves
10 black peppercorns
2 lb (1 kg) lean ground (minced) meat (beef or pork and
   beef mixture)
⅓ cup (3 fl oz/80 ml) oil
¾ cup (6 oz/185 g) finely chopped onion
1½ lb (750 g) tomatoes, roasted (see glossary), peeled
   and chopped
salt
1 2-in (5-cm) stick cinnamon
2 bay leaves
1 large potato, peeled and diced
1 plantain or large firm banana, peeled and chopped
½ cup (3 oz/90 g) raisins
½ cup (3 oz/90 g) blanched almonds, halved and
   toasted (optional)

✳ In a mortar or *molcajete,* grind the cinnamon, thyme, marjoram, garlic, cloves and peppercorns. Transfer to a large bowl, add the meat and use your hands to combine thoroughly.
✳ Heat the oil in a large skillet and add the meat a little

Stuffed Cheese Round (left) and Picadillo Filling (right)

at a time to brown lightly. As the meat browns, remove it from the skillet, transfer to a bowl and set aside. When all the meat has been browned, add the onion to the skillet and cook for 2 minutes. Add the tomatoes and cook over high heat for 4 minutes, stirring constantly. Return the meat to the skillet, stir well and add salt to taste. Add the cinnamon stick, bay leaves, potato and plantain and cook, covered, over low heat for 15 minutes or until the potato is tender.

✳ Uncover, add the raisins and cook another 5 minutes. Correct the seasonings. Sprinkle with toasted almonds before serving if you like.

SERVES 6–8

133

Fried Pork Skins in Green Sauce (top) and
Pork with Chile Sauce (bottom)

CHICHARRÓN EN SALSA VERDE

Fried Pork Skins in Green Sauce

This national favorite for almuerzo *(brunch) is always served in wide clay pots called* cazuelitas, *accompanied by tortillas and usually* frijoles refritos *(page 201) or* huevos a la mexicana *(page 127) and made into* tacos.

3 or more *chiles serranos*
3 cloves garlic
2 lb (1 kg) *tomates verdes,* husks removed
1 teaspoon salt
¼ teaspoon freshly ground pepper
1 cup (8 fl oz/250 ml) water
1 cup (1½ oz/45 g) coarsely chopped *cilantro* (coriander)
1 tablespoon oil
1 large onion, about 8 oz (250 g), sliced
¼ teaspoon ground cumin
8 oz (250 g) *chicharrón* or fried thin pork skins, cut into chunks

✻ In a blender, purée the *chiles,* garlic, tomates verdes, salt and pepper with the water for only 3 or 4 pulses so that the mixture does not become too smooth. Add the *cilantro* and blend for 2 more pulses. Set aside.
✻ Heat the oil in a skillet, add the onion and sauté for 4 minutes. Add the *tomate verde* sauce and cumin and cook over medium heat for 10 minutes. Correct the seasonings.
✻ Add the fried pork skins, cover and cook over low heat for 10 minutes or until they are soft.

✻ If this dish is not going to be served immediately, prepare the sauce in advance; 20 minutes before serving, heat the sauce, add the fried pork skins to it, cover and cook over low heat for 10 minutes.

SERVES 6

SONORA

CARNE CON CHILE

Pork with Chile Sauce

This family recipe from María Dolores Torres Yzábal uses a technique that is unique to northern Mexico: thickening the chile *sauce with flour.*

2 tablespoons (1 oz/30 g) lard
2 lb (1 kg) boneless pork, cut into large cubes
salt
3 cloves garlic, minced
2 *chiles anchos*
3 cups (24 fl oz/750 ml) hot water
1 tablespoon all-purpose (plain) flour
1 teaspoon dried oregano
1 tablespoon white vinegar
½ teaspoon ground cumin

✻ Melt the lard in a skillet over medium heat. When it is hot, add the pork, a little salt and the garlic. Sauté until the pork is cooked, about 20 minutes.
✻ Toast the *chiles* (see glossary) and remove the seeds and membranes. Soak in the water for 5 minutes, then transfer the *chiles* and water to a blender and purée with the flour, but not too smooth. Pour the sauce over the meat and add the oregano, vinegar, cumin and 1½ teaspoons salt. Cook over low heat for 10 minutes, stirring to prevent sticking.
✻ Serve with hot flour tortillas.

SERVES 6

OAXACA

PIERNA DE CERDO ADOBADA

Roast Leg of Pork in Adobo Sauce

This makes a festive buffet dish served with calabacitas picadas *(page 210) and* ensalada rosaura *(page 204). Any leftover pork is ideal as a meat filling for Mexican sandwiches* (tortas) *(page 43).*

2 cups (16 fl oz/500 ml) freshly squeezed orange juice
6 *chiles anchos,* seeds and membranes removed
8 *chiles pasillas,* seeds and membranes removed
¼ onion
⅓ cup (3 fl oz/80 ml) cider vinegar
10 cloves garlic
1 teaspoon dried thyme
3 whole cloves
1 teaspoon ground cumin
1 tablespoon dried oregano
1 2-in (5-cm) stick cinnamon
3 whole allspice

Roast Leg of Pork in Adobo Sauce

2 tablespoons coarse salt
1 leg of pork, about 9 lb (4.5 kg)
2 tablespoons (1 oz/30 g) lard

✳ In a small saucepan, heat 1 cup (8 fl oz/250 ml) of the orange juice until warm. Toast the *chiles* (see glossary) on a *comal* or iron skillet, then let them soak in the orange juice for 20 minutes. Transfer the *chiles* and orange juice to a blender, add the onion and vinegar and purée. Set aside.

✳ In a mortar or a *molcajete,* grind the garlic, thyme, cloves, cumin, oregano, cinnamon, allspice and salt. Add the puréed *chiles* and stir well. Add enough orange juice to dilute the mixture until it has the consistency of yogurt.

✳ Use a fork to pierce the leg of pork all over. Transfer to a baking pan or dish, cover with the *chile*-orange sauce and refrigerate, covered, for at least 6 hours,

preferably overnight. Turn occasionally.

✳ Two hours before roasting, remove the leg of pork from the refrigerator and smear the meat lightly with the lard. Let stand in the sauce at room temperature.

✳ Preheat the oven to 350°F (180°C). Cover the leg of pork with aluminum foil and roast for 2 hours, basting periodically with the pan juices. Turn the meat over, cover and roast about 1 more hour. When the meat can easily be pierced with a fork, in 2–3 hours, turn the oven temperature up to 450°F (230°C), uncover the meat and roast for 5–10 minutes or until browned, being careful not to let it burn. Let stand for 15 minutes before slicing.

✳ If you wish, you can double the quantity of the sauce and serve the extra to accompany the sliced pork.

SERVES 12–16

Pork with Beans (left) and Meatballs (right)

PUEBLA

LOMO DE CERDO CON SALSA DE TOMATE Y RAJAS DE PIMIENTO MORRÓN

Stuffed Pork Loin with Tomato Sauce and Green Peppers

Spinach and cheese make an unusual filling in this old family recipe of Carlota Rosas, a native of Atlixco, Puebla. It is very unusual in that it uses the green bell pepper instead of the more traditional chile poblano.

1 pork loin, about 3 lb (1.5 kg)
1 lb (500 g) spinach, stems removed
1 cup (4 oz/125 g) grated *queso Chihuahua* (or Monterey Jack or medium-sharp Cheddar cheese)
2 tablespoons oil
¼ teaspoon freshly ground pepper
¼ onion
4 cloves garlic
2 cups (16 fl oz/500 ml) water
1½ teaspoons salt
1 bay leaf
1 small sprig thyme
1 small sprig marjoram

SAUCE

2 lb (1 kg) ripe tomatoes
1 tablespoon coarsely chopped onion
1 clove garlic
1 tablespoon oil
salt and freshly ground pepper
1 lb (500 g) green bell peppers (capsicums), cut into
  julienne strips

✱ Preheat the oven to 350°F (180°C). Run a long thin knife through the center of the pork loin from one end to the other, as if you were going to lard the meat.

✱ Rinse the spinach leaves, place in a covered saucepan and steam briefly in just the water that clings to the leaves. Transfer to a colander to drain off the excess water. Chop coarsely and transfer to a large bowl. Add the cheese and mix with the spinach. Spoon this mixture into the center of the pork loin, using your fingers to help stuff it in. Close the ends with toothpicks so that the stuffing will not fall out.

✱ Heat the oil in a skillet, add the pork loin and brown lightly on all sides, about 8 minutes. Sprinkle with the pepper and add the onion and garlic. Sauté briefly, then add the water and bring to a boil, basting the pork with the water and adding the salt.

✱ Transfer the contents of the skillet to a large baking dish and lay the bay leaf, thyme and marjoram on top. Cover with aluminum foil and bake for about 40 minutes.

✱ Meanwhile, prepare the sauce. Core the tomatoes, cut in half and purée in a blender with the onion and garlic. Strain. Heat the oil in a saucepan and add the tomato purée. When it comes to a boil, season with salt and pepper and cook over medium heat for 20 minutes. Lower the heat, add the pepper strips and cook until tender, about 10 minutes.

✱ After 40 minutes, uncover the pork loin and baste with 6 tablespoons of the sauce. Roast, uncovered, for 10 more minutes. Transfer the pork to a platter. Strain the pan juices and add to the tomato sauce. Correct the seasonings.

✱ Let the pork cool for 10 minutes, then slice and serve covered with the sauce.

SERVES 6   *Photograph pages 104–105*

OAXACA

ALBÓNDIGAS

Meatballs

While every state in Mexico seems to have its own meatball specialty, none are browned, instead only being poached in a light sauce. Some are stuffed with hard-boiled eggs; in other regions, chiles become part of the sauce. Chiles y verduras en escabeche (page 212) could be served along with this mild meat dish.

3 small cloves garlic
1 tablespoon chopped onion
2 teaspoons ground cumin
3 whole cloves
¾ teaspoon salt
¼ teaspoon freshly ground pepper
1½ lb (750 g) ground (minced) beef

8 oz (250 g) ground (minced) pork
1 egg
1 tablespoon dry breadcrumbs
1½ tablespoons finely chopped *hierba buena*
2 hard-boiled (hard-cooked) eggs

SAUCE

2 lb (1 kg) tomatoes
1 clove garlic
¼ onion
1 tablespoon oil
2 cups (16 fl oz/500 ml) water
1 teaspoon salt

✱ In a food processor or molcajete, grind the garlic, onion, cumin, cloves, salt and pepper. Transfer to a bowl and add the beef, pork, raw egg, breadcrumbs and *hierba buena*. Use your hands to combine thoroughly.

✱ Cut the eggs in half and cut each half into 9 pieces. Around each piece of egg, form meatballs, using about 1½ oz (45 g) meat for each. Set aside.

✱ To make the sauce, purée the tomatoes, garlic and onion in a blender and strain. Heat the oil in a skillet, add the puréed tomatoes and bring to a boil. Add the water and salt and cook, covered, for 6 minutes. Uncover and add the meatballs. Cook, covered, over low heat for 30 minutes. Correct the seasonings.

✱*Variation:* Add chopped carrot and zucchini (courgette) to the sauce.

SERVES 6–8

QUINTANA ROO

CERDO CON FRIJOLES

Pork with Beans

Wild boar is still hunted in the interior of Quintana Roo, but it is the domesticated pig that is now used for this Maya version of pork and beans, flavored with the aromatic herb epazote.

2 cups (12 oz/375 g) dried black beans, sorted and rinsed
14 cups (112 fl oz/3.5 l) water
1 teaspoon lard or oil
½ onion
2 lb (1 kg) boneless pork, cut into chunks
2 sprigs *epazote*
3–5 *chiles serranos*
1 tablespoon salt
salsa de tomate verde cocida (page 201) (optional)
8 radishes, finely chopped (optional)

✱ Place the beans in a large pot, add 10 cups (80 fl oz/2.5 l) of the water and the lard and onion, then boil for 5 minutes. Cook, covered, over medium heat for 1 hour. Add the pork, remaining water, *epazote* and *chiles*. Cook, covered, over medium heat for another hour. If too much water cooks off, add up to 2 cups (16 fl oz/500 ml) more hot water. Add the salt and cook for 30 minutes. Correct the seasonings.

✱ Serve hot, accompanied by the *salsa de tomate verde cocida* and finely chopped radishes.

SERVES 6

GUANAJUATO

LOMO DE CERDO CON ANÍS

Roast Pork Loin with Anise

Anise is primarily considered a medicinal herb in Mexico, with the star-shaped variety called Anis estrella *made into a tea for collicky babies.* Torta de elote *(page 94) goes well with this unusual pork dish.*

1 pork loin, about 3 lb (1.5 kg)
¼ cup (2 fl oz/60 ml) olive oil
1 teaspoon salt
¼ teaspoon freshly ground pepper
½ teaspoon dried oregano
2 small sprigs thyme
1½ teaspoons aniseed
2 tablespoons all-purpose (plain) flour
1 large onion, sliced
3 cups (24 fl oz/750 ml) white wine
3 cups (24 fl oz/750 ml) chicken stock (page 72)
3 cloves garlic, crushed
½ teaspoon ground nutmeg
2 tablespoons (1 oz/30 g) butter
1 teaspoon cornstarch (cornflour)
1 cup (8 fl oz/250 ml) heavy (double) cream

✳ Remove as much fat from the pork as possible. Rub with the oil, salt, pepper, oregano, thyme and aniseed. Sprinkle the entire surface of the meat with the flour, pressing with your hands to make it stick. Place the sliced onions on top of the pork, cover and refrigerate overnight.
✳ Preheat the oven to 400°F (200°C). Place the wine, stock, garlic and nutmeg in a saucepan. Cover, boil for

Roast Pork Loin with Anise

5 minutes, then remove from the heat.
✳ Place the pork loin in a baking pan and roast, uncovered, for 10 to 15 minutes or until the surface is lightly browned. Add the stock and wine mixture, cover the pan and lower the oven temperature to 325°F (165°C). Roast for 1½–2 hours or until the meat is tender. If the liquid in the pan cooks off, add 1 cup (8 fl oz/250 ml) each of white wine and water.
✳ Transfer the pork to a platter. Strain the pan juices into a heatproof bowl. Rinse out the pan with ¼ cup (2 fl oz/60 ml) water and strain into the bowl.
✳ Melt the butter in a saucepan and blend in the cornstarch. Add the pan juices, stirring constantly to dissolve any lumps. Cook for 5 minutes, then add the cream, still stirring constantly. As soon as the mixture begins to simmer, remove from the heat. Correct the seasonings.
✳ Before serving, slice the pork loin and cover with the sauce.

SERVES 6–8

ZACATECAS

CABRITO EN CHILE ANCHO

Young Goat in Chile Sauce

Cabrito, or tender baby goat, is a popular meal throughout the northern and more arid parts of the central states, as the agile and independent animal is able to survive with little attention. Kid can be ordered from most meat markets, especially in the early spring, and can be found in many Greek, Middle Eastern and Latin American markets. Lamb may be substituted.

1 tender young goat (about 9 lbs/4.5 kg), cut into
    pieces, or 2–3 lb (1–1.5 kg) lamb shoulder or butt end
    of lamb leg
6 tablespoons red wine vinegar
salt and freshly ground pepper
1 lb (500 g) *chiles anchos* (about 32), seeds and
    membranes removed
8 oz (250 g) *chiles guajillos* (about 30), seeds and
    membranes removed
8½ cups (68 fl oz/2.12 l) water
2 tomatoes, roasted (see glossary)
3 bay leaves
1 small sprig thyme
1 small sprig marjoram
5 cloves garlic
5 tablespoons (2½ oz/80 g) lard or oil

✳ Rub the goat with 5 tablespoons of the vinegar and sprinkle lightly with salt and pepper. Cover and refrigerate for at least 2 hours, preferably overnight.
✳ Toast the *chiles* (see glossary) on a comal or iron skillet, then soak in hot water to cover for 30 minutes. Drain and transfer to a blender. Add ½ cup (4 fl oz/125 ml) of the water and the tomatoes, bay leaves, thyme, marjoram and garlic. Purée, strain and set aside.
✳ Heat the lard in a large pan or Dutch oven, add the goat two or three pieces at a time and brown on all sides. Transfer to a platter.
✳ Pour off one-half of the fat, add the *chile* purée and cook for 8 minutes. Add the remaining vinegar, 1 tablespoon salt, and pepper to taste. Stir in 8 cups (64

Steak with Onions (top) and Young Goat in Chile Sauce (bottom)

fl oz/2 l) water, return the meat to the pan and cook, covered, over medium heat for 2 hours, stirring occasionally. Add more water if needed to keep the sauce from drying out. It should be thick.

✳ Serve with *salsa de tomate verde con aguacate* (page 198), *frijoles de la olla* (page 208) and corn tortillas.

SERVES 12

DISTRITO FEDERAL

BISTECES ENCEBOLLADOS

Steak with Onions

Steak with onions is a very popular Mexican dish often found in fondas *(small restaurants). It makes a special meal when served with* chiles anchos rellenos de queso *(page 216). Beer may be substituted for the water.*

¼ cup (2 fl oz/60 ml) oil
salt and freshly ground pepper
2 lb (1 kg) boneless beef round steaks (sirloin), trimmed of fat
3 large onions, sliced
3 cloves garlic, minced
½ cup (4 fl oz/125 ml) water

✳ Heat 3 tablespoons of the oil in a large skillet. Salt and pepper the steaks and sauté them over medium-high heat for 1–2 minutes on each side. Transfer to a platter, cut into strips 1 in (2.5 cm) thick and set aside.

✳ Add the remaining tablespoon of oil to the skillet, add the onions and sauté, stirring constantly, for 5 minutes. Add the garlic and, when the onions and garlic are golden brown, add the strips of steak and any juices that have accumulated on the platter. Add the water, correct the seasonings and cook, covered, over low heat for 5 minutes. If too much liquid cooks off, add more water.

SERVES 6

Birria

Stewed Lamb in Chile Sauce

Birria is really just a rustic soup of lamb or mutton—similar to barbacoa (page 142) and served in deep bowls with a rich red broth, or wrapped in tortillas for tacos. The name means "grotesque" or "a mess," and while it may look that way, it is one of Mexico's most delicious regional dishes. It is a good use for tougher cuts of meat.

4 *chiles guajillos*
3 *chiles anchos*
1 cup (8 fl oz/250 ml) hot water
1 lb (500 g) boneless lean lamb, cut into pieces
1 lb (500 g) lamb ribs or shanks (shins), cut into pieces
12 cups (96 fl oz/3 l) water
6 cloves garlic
½ onion
2 bay leaves
1 teaspoon ground cumin
¼ teaspoon dried marjoram
1 small sprig thyme

1½ teaspoons salt
⅛ teaspoon freshly ground pepper

SAUCE

½ cup (4 fl oz/125 ml) red wine vinegar
2 cloves garlic
1½ teaspoons ground *chile piquín*

GARNISHES

1 cup (8 oz/250 g) onion, chopped
3 limes, cut in half
1 cup (1½ oz/45 g) chopped *cilantro* (coriander)

✱ On a *comal* or iron skillet, toast the *chiles* (see glossary), then remove the seeds and membranes. Soak the *chiles* in the hot water for 20 minutes. Transfer the *chiles* and soaking water to a blender and purée. Strain and set aside.

✱ Place the lamb meat and ribs and the water, garlic and onion in a large pot or Dutch oven. Bring to a boil, skim the surface, cover and cook over medium-low heat for 1½ hours or until the meat is tender. Remove and discard the onion and garlic. Add the puréed *chiles,* bay leaves, cumin, marjoram, thyme, salt and pepper.

Birria

✳ Cook for another 30 minutes so that the flavors blend. Meanwhile, purée the sauce ingredients in a blender.

✳ Serve the lamb in deep bowls with hot corn tortillas and a selection of garnishes. Pass the sauce separately.

SERVES 6

OAXACA

ESTOFADO DE RES

Beef Stew

Green beans are often found in the stews of Oaxaca, like this popular one from the coastal area near Guerrero.

2 lb (1 kg) boneless beef shank (shin)
12 cups (96 fl oz/3 l) cold water
½ onion
4 cloves garlic
1 tablespoon salt
4 *chiles guajillos,* seeds and membranes removed
2 large tomatoes, roasted (see glossary) and peeled
¼ small onion
1 tablespoon oil
2 large potatoes, peeled and cubed
2 small zucchini (courgettes), cubed
8 oz (250 g) green beans, trimmed

✳ Place the beef shank in a large pot or Dutch oven, cover with the water and add ½ onion, 3 garlic cloves and the salt. Bring to a boil, cover and cook over medium heat for about 1½ hours or until the meat is tender. Discard the onion and set aside.

✳ On a *comal* or iron skillet, toast the *chiles* (see glossary), then soak in hot water to cover for 20 minutes. Drain and transfer to a blender. Add the tomatoes, 1 garlic clove and ¼ onion and purée.

✳ Heat the oil in a large skillet, add the tomato purée and boil for 5 minutes. Add 2 cups (16 fl oz/500 ml) of the beef stock, bring to a boil and add the meat, potatoes and zucchini. Cook for 3 minutes, adding more broth if the stew seems too thick. Cook, covered, over medium heat for 10 minutes. Correct the seasonings, add the beans, stir and cook, covered, over low heat for 10 more minutes or until the potatoes are tender.

SERVES 6

OAXACA

COSTILLAS EN SALSA VERDE

Pork Ribs in Green Sauce

Pigs brought by the Spaniards to the New World grew fatter and tastier after feeding on native Mexican food such as corn, peanuts and the fallen ripe fruit of the tropics. This pork dish has a typical green sauce that is accented by cumin from the Mideast.

½ teaspoon ground cumin
6 cloves garlic, minced
1 tablespoon salt
4 lb (2 kg) small pork ribs (spare rib chops), cut into 2–3 rib sections
2 tablespoons (1 oz/30 g) lard or oil (optional)

4 cups (32 fl oz/1 l) water
6 cloves garlic
¼ onion, in chunks
8 *chiles serranos*
2 lb (1 kg) *tomates verdes,* husks removed
8 sprigs *cilantro* (coriander)
salt and freshly ground pepper

✳ Mix the cumin, minced garlic and salt together and rub onto the ribs. (This is best done the day before.)

✳ Place the ribs in a large pot or Dutch oven and add cold water to cover. Bring the water to a boil, then lower the heat to medium. Cover and cook until the liquid has evaporated and the meat can easily be pierced with a fork (about 1 hour). There should be fat rendered from the meat in the pot. If there is not, add the lard or oil and fry the ribs for 10 minutes. Pour off and reserve the rendered fat and set aside.

✳ Place the water and garlic cloves in a large saucepan. Bring to a boil, add the onion and *chiles* and cook for 5 minutes. Add the *tomates verdes* and cook for 4 minutes. Transfer the *tomates verdes, chiles,* garlic and onion to a blender, add 2 cups (16 fl oz/ 500 ml) of the water in which the *chiles* cooked and purée. Add the *cilantro* and blend for 3 quick pulses, so that the *cilantro* is roughly ground. If the sauce is too thick, thin with a little more of the *chile* cooking water.

✳ In a large skillet, heat 2 tablespoons of the rendered fat. Add the *tomate verde* sauce, bring to a boil, lower the heat and cook, covered, for 10 minutes.

✳ Add the sauce to the pot containing the ribs, stir well and cook over low heat for 20 minutes. Season with salt and pepper.

SERVES 6–8

Pork Ribs in Green Sauce (top) and Beef Stew (bottom)

Marinated Filet of Beef

GUERRERO

FILETE ADOBADO

Marinated Filet of Beef

There are two methods of Mexican cooking that use adobo, *a marinade of chiles, spices and vinegar. Usually* en adobo *means cooked and served in the sauce, and* adobado *refers to dishes like this one that are grilled or roasted in a thick coating of the marinade and, after slicing, can be topped with additional sauce. Any leftover* adobo *marinade can be kept in the refrigerator for a long time.*

1 teaspoon salt
¼ teaspoon freshly ground pepper
1 teaspoon Dijon mustard
1 beef filet (rib eye), about 3 lb (1.5 kg)
2 *chiles anchos,* seeds and membranes removed
5 *chiles guajillos,* seeds and membranes removed
1 cup (8 fl oz/250 ml) water
2 cloves garlic
¼ small onion
2 black peppercorns
¼ teaspoon each dried marjoram and oregano
¼ teaspoon ground cumin
1 tomato, roasted (see glossary) and peeled
2½ tablespoons (1¼ oz/40 g) butter
1 teaspoon red wine vinegar

✳ Mix the salt, pepper and mustard together and rub into the filet. Place in a shallow dish and let stand for 30 minutes.
✳ Meanwhile, on a *comal* or iron skillet, toast the *chiles* (see glossary). Soak in hot water to cover for 20 min-

utes, then drain, discarding the soaking water. Transfer to a blender, add the water and purée. Add the garlic, onion, peppercorns, marjoram, oregano and cumin and purée again. Set aside. Purée the tomato and set aside.
✳ Melt the butter in a small saucepan, add the *chile* purée and cook over high heat, stirring constantly, for 5 minutes. Add the puréed tomato and cook for 3 minutes. Add the vinegar, stir and cook over medium heat for 25 minutes or until the sauce thickens. Cover the filet with the sauce and marinate for 30 minutes to an hour.
✳ Preheat an outdoor grill. Place the filet, still coated with the *chile* marinade, on the grill. Turn often so that the meat does not burn. The filet will be done in about 25 minutes—less if you prefer it rare. Alternately, the filet can be placed in a baking dish and roasted in an oven preheated to 400°F (200°C) for 20–30 minutes.

SERVES 6–8

HIDALGO

BARBACOA

Meat Cooked in Leaves

The traditional barbacoa of the high central plains east of Mexico City is lamb, goat or mutton slowly cooked in a deep pit, preheated with a wood fire placed over rocks. The meat is wrapped in maguey leaves and steamed underground from the heat given off by the rocks. This version substitutes aromatic bay, plum and avocado leaves and cooks the barbacoa in a pressure cooker or steamer.

4 lb (2 kg) boneless beef, pork or goat
14 dried avocado leaves
14 bay leaves
10 small dried plum leaves (optional)

MARINADE

3 oz (90 g) *chiles guajillos,* seeds and membranes removed
1½ oz (45 g) *chiles anchos,* seeds and membranes removed
4 cloves garlic
⅛ onion
2 small sprigs thyme
2 small sprigs marjoram
1 tablespoon dried oregano
10 whole cloves
1 tablespoon black peppercorns
3 bay leaves
1 teaspoon red wine vinegar
2 cups (16 fl oz/ 500 ml) water
2 tablespoons coarse salt

✳ To make the marinade, cook the *chiles* in a saucepan of boiling water for 10 minutes. Drain and transfer to a blender. Add the garlic, onion, thyme, marjoram, oregano, cloves, peppercorns, bay leaves, vinegar, water and salt. Purée.
✳ Place the meat in a glass or ceramic dish, add the purée and marinate for at least 3 hours or cover and refrigerate overnight. Turn occasionally.
✳ Place the steamer basket in a pressure cooker and add 5 cups (40 fl oz/1.25 l) water. Place a large sheet of heavy-duty aluminum foil in the basket, shaping it into

DISTRITO FEDERAL

Lengua en Salsa de Tomate y Rajas

Tongue in Tomato Sauce with Chile Strips

Beef and veal tongue are savored in Mexico, as they are in Spain. Rice is a good accompaniment, as are small boiled potatoes or the flavorful papitas de cambray al ajo (page 208).

1 beef tongue (ox tongue), about 2 lb (1 kg)
4 cups (32 fl oz/1 l) cold water
¼ onion
4 cloves garlic, 2 whole, 2 minced
1 teaspoon salt
1 tablespoon oil
1 onion, sliced
1½ lb (750 g) tomatoes, peeled and finely chopped
½ teaspoon dried thyme
¼ teaspoon freshly ground pepper
3 *chiles poblanos,* roasted (see glossary), membranes removed and cut into thin strips

✳ Place the tongue in a pressure cooker and add the water, onion quarter, whole garlic cloves and salt. Cook for 1½ hours or until tender. Alternately, simmer the tongue in a covered saucepan for about 3 hours or until tender. Drain, reserving the stock. Peel off and discard the thick skin that covers the tongue, cut the tongue into thin slices and set aside.

✳ Heat the oil in a skillet, add the sliced onion and minced garlic and sauté for 2 minutes. Add the tomatoes, thyme and pepper and cook over medium-high heat for 5 minutes or until soft. Add 1–2 cups (8–16 fl oz/250–500 ml) of the reserved stock and the *chile* strips, correct the seasonings and cook, covered, over medium heat for 5 minutes. Add the sliced tongue and cook another 5 minutes.

SERVES 6

DISTRITO FEDERAL

Cuete Mechado

Pot Roast Stuffed with Bacon

Mechado style means that slices of vegetables and seasonings, such as the bright orange carrot and flavorful bacon used in this recipe, are inserted into cuts in the meat. This mild-tasting pot roast contrasts well with arroz a la mexicana (page 92) made with chiles serranos. Tortitas de papa (page 210) and ejotes con cebolla y jitomate (page 206) make an excellent complement in color and texture.

3 lb (1.5 kg) boneless beef chuck or shoulder (blade) steak
1 large carrot
4 slices bacon
1 tablespoon oil
½ onion, finely chopped
4 cloves garlic, minced
1 teaspoon freshly ground pepper
¼ cup (2 fl oz/ 60 ml) red wine vinegar
3 cups (24 fl oz/750 ml) water
3 bay leaves

1½ teaspoons dried thyme
1 teaspoon dried marjoram
1 tablespoon salt
2 tablespoons cornstarch (cornflour)
2 tablespoons dry white wine

✳ Preheat the oven to 350°F (180°C). With a sharp knife, make 4 cuts lengthwise in the steak without cutting through the edge. Peel the carrot, cut into 4 lengthwise strips and wrap each strip in a slice of bacon. Place a

Pot Roast Stuffed with Bacon (left) and Tongue in Tomato Sauce with Chile Strips (right)

carrot strip in each slit in the steak.

✳ Heat the oil in a large skillet, add the steak and brown on both sides. Transfer to a baking pan and set aside.

✳ In the same skillet, sauté the onion, garlic and pepper for 2 minutes, stirring constantly. Add the vinegar and water to the skillet, swirl it around and pour over the steak with the onion and garlic. Add the bay leaves, thyme, marjoram and salt. Cover the baking pan with aluminum foil, being careful that the foil does not touch the meat.

✳ Place in the oven and bake for 1½ hours or until the meat is tender.

✳ Transfer the steak to a serving platter. Strain the pan juices, return to the pan and add the cornstarch and wine. Boil for 3 minutes or until thickened. Correct the seasonings.

✳ Slice the steak and cover it with the sauce.

SERVES 6–8

CHIHUAHUA

Puntas de Filete a la Mexicana

Beef Tips Mexican Style

The beef industry began in Mexico in 1530 with a group of colonists headed by Vasco de Quiroga. In the small restaurants of the north, where this dish is most often found, queso fundido con champiñones y rajas de poblano (page 33) and frijoles maneados (page 213) might likely share the table along with floppy flour tortillas.

2 lb (1 kg) beef filet (rib eye) tips, cut into strips
3 cloves garlic, crushed
½ teaspoon freshly ground pepper
¼ teaspoon ground cumin
2 teaspoons salt
2 tablespoons oil
1 cup (8 oz/250 g) finely chopped onion
2 cloves garlic, minced
2½ lb (1.25 kg) ripe tomatoes, peeled and finely
   chopped
6 *chiles serranos,* finely chopped

✳ Mix the beef tips with the crushed garlic cloves, pepper, cumin and 1 teaspoon of the salt. Cover and refrigerate for at least 2 hours, preferably overnight.
✳ Heat the oil in a large skillet or Dutch oven, add the onion and sauté for 4 minutes or until transparent. Add the minced garlic and the beef tips, stirring over high heat until the beef is browned, about 7 minutes. Add the tomatoes, *chiles* and remaining teaspoon of salt. Cook, uncovered, over medium heat for 10 minutes or until the sauce thickens and the meat is tender.
✳*Variation:* Substitute 3 pickled *chiles chipotles* for the *chiles serranos.*

SERVES 6

PUEBLA

Tinga Poblana

Shredded Pork and Beef with Chipotle and Tomates Verdes

Bunches of dried thyme, marjoram and oregano are sold as hierbas de olor (scented herbs) in virtually every Mexican market. These spices add flavor to this smoky- and spicy-

Beef Tips Mexican Style (top) and Tinga Poblana (bottom)

tasting meat stew from Puebla. It is also used as a popular filling for tortas *(page 43) or as a topping for crispy* tostadas, *garnished with shredded lettuce and sliced avocado.*

8 oz (250 g) boneless lean pork, cut into chunks
1 lb (500 g) beef flank steak, cut into chunks
2 bay leaves
2 cloves garlic
salt
1 lb (500 g) *chorizo* or other spicy sausage
1 onion, coarsely chopped
1 clove garlic, minced
1½ lb (750 g) ripe tomatoes, peeled and coarsely chopped
8 oz (250 g) *tomates verdes,* husks removed and finely sliced
½ teaspoon dried oregano
1 small sprig marjoram
1 small sprig thyme
¼ teaspoon freshly ground pepper
¼ cup pickled *chile chipotle* juice
3 pickled *chiles chipotles,* cut into strips

✷ Place the meat in a large pot or Dutch oven and cover with cold water. Bring to a boil over high heat and skim the surface. Lower the heat and add the bay leaves, garlic cloves and 1 teaspoon salt. Cover and cook over low heat for 1 hour or until the meat is tender. Let cool in the stock, then drain, reserving the stock. Shred the meat and set aside.
✷ Remove the casing from the *chorizo* and cut into large chunks. Place in a skillet and fry over medium heat until lightly browned and some of the fat has been rendered. Remove the *chorizo* and set aside. Add the onion and minced garlic to the skillet and sauté for 2 minutes. Add the tomatoes, *tomates verdes,* oregano, marjoram, thyme, pepper and 1 tablespoon salt. Simmer over low heat for 5 minutes, stirring occasionally. Add the *chipotle* juice and stir.
✷ Add the shredded meat to the skillet, stir well and add 1 cup (8 fl oz/250 ml) of the reserved stock. Add the *chorizo,* cover and cook over low heat for 15 minutes. If the sauce is too thick, add more stock.
✷ Serve very hot, garnished with *chile* strips.

SERVES 6

DISTRITO FEDERAL

BUDÍN CON PICADILLO

Ground Meat Casserole

This casserole of meat, tortillas and tomates verdes *is very popular among Americans living in Mexico City and is excellent with* ensalada mixta con aderezo de aguacate *(page 203).*

3 cloves garlic
¼ teaspoon freshly ground pepper
1 whole clove
¼ teaspoon dried thyme
2 teaspoons salt
2 lb (1 kg) lean ground (minced) beef
2 tablespoons oil
1 small onion, finely chopped

Ground Meat Casserole

3 *chiles serranos*
1 lb (500 g) *tomates verdes,* husks removed
½ cup (¾ oz/20 g) chopped *cilantro* (coriander)
2 *chiles poblanos,* seeds and membranes removed
8 squash (zucchini) blossoms (optional)
oil for frying
12 corn tortillas
1 cup (8 fl oz/250 ml) sour cream
1½ cups (6 oz/185 g) grated *queso manchego* (or Monterey Jack or medium-sharp Cheddar cheese)

✷ Grind 2 garlic cloves, the pepper, whole clove, thyme and 1 teaspoon of the salt in a mortar or a *molcajete.* Transfer to a large bowl, add the beef and mix well.
✷ Heat the oil in a large skillet. Add the onion and sauté until transparent. Add the beef and sauté, uncovered, over medium heat for 10 minutes. Drain and set aside.
✷ Place the *chiles serranos* in a saucepan of boiling water and cook for 5 minutes. Add the *tomates verdes* and cook until they change color, about 7 minutes. Drain, transfer to a blender and add 1 garlic clove, the *cilantro* and 1 teaspoon salt. Purée and set aside.
✷ Roast the *chiles poblanos* (see glossary) and let sweat for 10 minutes. Cut into strips and set aside.
✷ Remove the stems and pistils from the flowers, being careful not to tear the blossoms. Open the flowers and spread them flat. Place in a skillet with a tablespoon of water and steam for 3 minutes. Set aside.
✷ Preheat the oven to 375°F (190°C). Heat ½ in (1 cm) oil in a skillet and briefly fry each tortilla on both sides. Arrange 6 tortillas, overlapping, in the bottom of a rectangular baking dish. Cover with a layer of meat, a layer of *chile poblano* strips and a layer of flowers. Cover with half of the cream and a third of the grated cheese. Make another layer of tortillas, meat, *chiles,* cream and cheese. Cover with the *tomate verde* purée, transfer to the oven and bake for 10 minutes. Sprinkle with the remaining one-third of the cheese and bake for 5 minutes or until the cheese melts and browns.

SERVES 6–8

DISTRITO FEDERAL

Ropa Vieja

Shredded Beef with Vegetables

The literal name of this dish—"old clothes"—is very apt and descriptive, as it is a good way to use up leftover cooked beef. The traditional ropa vieja *is used as a filling for tacos, but this variation includes a vinaigrette and is served as a cold salad.*

1 lb (500 g) beef flank steak, cut into 2–3 pieces
2 bay leaves
1 clove garlic
1 tablespoon salt
¼ onion
1 carrot
1 sprig parsley
½ onion, sliced and separated into rings
⅓ cup (3 fl oz/80 ml) olive oil
2 tablespoons red wine vinegar, or to taste
1 tablespoon dried oregano
¼ teaspoon freshly ground pepper
2 tomatoes, cut into chunks
1 head of lettuce, chopped
1 avocado, peeled and sliced
6 radishes, cut in half (optional)

✳ Place the beef, bay leaves, garlic, salt, onion quarter, carrot and parsley in a large heavy saucepan. Add water to cover, bring to a boil, lower the heat, then simmer, covered, until the beef is tender, about 1 hour. Let the meat cool in the stock, then drain and shred.
✳ In a bowl, mix the beef with the onion, oil, vinegar, oregano and pepper. Correct the seasonings and let stand for 30 minutes.
✳ Ten minutes before serving, add the tomatoes and a handful of the lettuce and toss to mix. Arrange a bed of lettuce on a platter and place the meat mixture in the center. Arrange the avocado slices on top and garnish with radish halves if desired.

SERVES 4

SAN LUIS POTOSÍ

Albondigón Relleno de Rajas

Stuffed Meat Loaf

This special meat loaf was presented at a culinary festival of Mexican cooking in 1975. On slicing, the red and green strips of chile *make a colorful presentation.*

1 *bolillo* (hard bread roll), sliced and soaked in milk
1 clove garlic
¼ onion
1 teaspoon dried oregano
1 teaspoon ground cumin
3 whole cloves
1 teaspoon salt
½ teaspoon freshly ground pepper
2½ lb (1.25 kg) beef steak, ground (minced) twice
1 lb (500 g) lean pork, ground (minced) twice
3 eggs
1 tablespoon dry breadcrumbs

3 *chiles poblanos,* roasted (see glossary), membranes removed and cut into strips
1 jar (6½ oz/200 g) roasted red peppers, drained and cut into strips
8 oz (250 g) sliced bacon
salsa de jitomate (recipe follows)

✳ Preheat the oven to 350°F (180°C). Drain the *bollillo,* tear into small pieces and transfer to a large bowl. In a food processor or *molcajete,* grind the garlic, onion, oregano, cumin, cloves, salt and pepper. Transfer to the bowl and add the beef, pork, eggs and breadcrumbs. Use your hands to combine thoroughly.
✳ Transfer to a clean board and pat into a rectangle. Arrange the *chile* and pepper strips down the center. Roll up lengthwise to form a loaf, place in a baking pan, top with bacon strips and bake for 1 hour.
✳ Serve with *salsa de jitomate.*

SERVES 6–8

Salsa de Jitomate

Tomato Sauce

2½ lb (1.25 kg) tomatoes, peeled and cut into chunks
1 clove garlic
¼ onion
¼ teaspoon dried thyme
¼ teaspoon ground cumin
1 whole clove
¼ cup (2 fl oz/60 ml) water
1 tablespoon butter
1 teaspoon salt
¼ teaspoon freshly ground pepper

✳ In a blender, purée the tomatoes, garlic, onion, thyme, cumin, clove and water. Melt the butter in a small skillet, add the purée, salt and pepper and boil for 5 minutes. Lower the heat and cook, uncovered, for 10 minutes.

MAKES 2½ CUPS (20 FL OZ/750 ML)

PUEBLA

Lomo de Cerdo Mechado con Chiles Chipotles y Ciruelas

Pork Roast Stuffed with Chiles Chipotles and Prunes

The cooks from Catalonia in northeastern Spain have always paired meat with fruit, especially pears and prunes, in dishes similar to this Mexican version, which adds the picante *flavor of* chile chipotle.

1 pork loin, about 2½ lb (1.25 kg)
6 oz (185 g) pitted prunes (cut in half if large)
4 pickled *chiles chipotles,* each cut into 4 pieces
1 clove garlic, crushed
salt and freshly ground pepper
2 cups (16 fl oz/500 ml) freshly squeezed orange juice
3 tablespoons all-purpose (plain) flour
2 tablespoons oil
1 large onion, sliced

Shredded Beef with Vegetables (top) and Stuffed Meat Loaf (bottom)

✳ With a knife, make regularly spaced slits on the sides and bottom of the pork loin. Place a prune in one, a *chile* in the next, continuing until you have used all the *chiles* and prunes. Place the pork in a dish and rub with the garlic, salt and pepper. Pour the orange juice over the pork, cover and refrigerate for at least 2 hours, preferably overnight.

✳Preheat the oven to 350°F (180°C). Drain the meat, reserving the juice in which it marinated. Sprinkle lightly with the flour. Heat the oil in a large skillet, add the pork and brown lightly on all sides, about 8 minutes.

✳ Arrange a layer of onion over the bottom of a lightly greased baking pan. Place the pork loin on top.

✳ Add the orange juice marinade to the skillet in which the pork was browned and scrape the bottom of the pan. Strain this juice over the pork and sprinkle with salt. Cover with aluminum foil and bake for 40 minutes. Uncover the meat, turn it over and baste with the pan juices. Roast, uncovered, 30 minutes longer or until a meat thermometer registers 170°F (80°C).

SERVES 6–8   *Photograph pages 104–105*

151

Meat Cooked Uruapan Style

MICHOACÁN

CARNITAS ESTILO URUAPAN

Meat Cooked Uruapan Style

In Uruapan, large shallow copper pots from nearby Santa Clara del Cobre are used to cook these "little meats," which are always served with tortillas and a salsa *so that each person can make their own* tacos.

2 lb (1 kg) boneless pork with some fat, cut into 2-in (5-cm) chunks
8 cups (64 fl oz/2 l) water
¼ onion
2 cloves garlic
1 tablespoon salt
1 tablespoon lard
½ cup (4 fl oz/125 ml) freshly squeezed orange juice
½ cup (4 fl oz/125 ml) milk
salsa de tomate verde con aguacate (page 198) (optional)

✽ Place the pork, water, onion, garlic and salt in a large pot or Dutch oven. Cook, covered, over medium heat for 1–1½ hours or until the pork is very tender. Transfer the meat to a colander to drain.

✽ Melt the lard in a saucepan. As soon as it bubbles, add the orange juice and milk, then the pork. Cook, uncovered, over medium heat until the meat is browned, 15–20 minutes (the orange juice and milk will cook off, leaving the pork to brown). Drain the meat immediately and place in a colander to let the excess grease run off.

✽ Serve with hot corn tortillas and *salsa de tomate verde con aguacate.*

SERVES 6

BISTECES RELLENOS (PAJARITOS)

Stuffed Beef Rolls

Mexican beefsteak is cut thin and then pounded even thinner, which is essential for these "little birds," or stuffed beef rolls.

2 lb (1 kg) beef round steaks (sirloin), cut thin
salt and freshly ground pepper
2 carrots, diced
1 lb (500 g) spinach, stems removed
10 thin slices cured ham, about 6 oz (180 g)
5 ripe tomatoes, roasted (see glossary) and peeled
2 cloves garlic, roasted (see glossary)
¼ teaspoon ground cumin
⅛ teaspoon ground cloves
3 tablespoons oil
¼ cup (2 oz/60 g) chopped onion
1 tablespoon all-purpose (plain) flour
1½ cups (12 fl oz/375 ml) unsalted beef stock
½ cup (4 fl oz/125 ml) red wine
2 bay leaves
1 *chile serrano* or to taste
2 tablespoons chopped *cilantro* (coriander)

✽ Cover each steak with a piece of wax paper or plastic wrap and pound until ¼ in (6 mm) thick. Sprinkle lightly with salt and pepper and set aside.

✽ Place the carrots in a saucepan of boiling salted water and cook until crisp-tender. Drain and set aside.

✽ Rinse the spinach, place in a skillet with just the water that clings to the leaves, cover and cook over medium heat for 4–5 minutes or until wilted. Drain and chop finely. In a small bowl, combine the carrots and spinach and set aside.

✽ Place a slice of ham on top of each steak, fill with the spinach-carrot mixture, roll up and tie with a string.

✽ Purée the tomatoes, garlic, cumin and cloves in a blender.

✽ Heat the oil in a skillet, add the steaks and brown lightly, 2–3 minutes. Transfer to a platter and set aside.

✽ Sauté the onion in the same oil, add the flour and stir for 2 minutes. Add the tomato purée and cook over high heat, stirring constantly, for 5 minutes. Add the stock, wine, bay leaves and *chile serrano* and simmer for 5 minutes. Correct the seasonings. Add the steaks and any juices that have accumulated on the platter. Cook, covered, over low heat for 10 minutes or until tender. Sprinkle with the *cilantro* and serve hot.

SERVES 6

Stuffed Beef Rolls

YUCATÁN

COCHINITA PIBIL

Pork Baked in Leaves

In the Mayan language, pibes *are stone-lined pits, and* pibil *refers to the technique of cooking underground, though nowadays the meat is often steamed in a sealed dish in the oven. The savory meat and red onion* salsa *are rolled into tortillas and served with black beans, downed with* horchata *or beer. Pig's ears and cheeks are an authentic and tasty addition and can be ordered from most butchers.*

8 oz (250 g) pig's ears (optional)
8 oz (250 g) pig's cheeks (optional)
3 lb (1.5 kg) boneless lean pork
3 oz (90 g) *achiote* paste (page 121)
½ cup (4 fl oz/125 ml) lime juice
1 cup (8 fl oz/250 ml) freshly squeezed orange juice
2 teaspoons salt
2 large banana leaves
½ cup (4 oz/125 g) lard, melted

ONION SALSA

2 cups (15 oz/470 g) chopped red onion
1 cup (8 fl oz/250 ml) freshly squeezed orange juice
1 cup (8 fl oz/250 ml) lime juice
1 teaspoon salt
6 *chiles manzanos* or *chiles habaneros*

✳ Cut the meat into 2-in (5-cm) pieces and place in a glass or ceramic dish. Place the *achiote* paste in a small glass bowl and add the juices to dissolve it, using your fingers to help break it up. Add the salt. Pour this liquid over the pork, cover and marinate in the refrigerator for at least 3 hours, preferably overnight.
✳ Preheat the oven to 325°F (165°C). Hold the banana leaves directly over the flame on the stove for a few minutes, until they soften. Line a rectangular baking dish with the leaves, placing one the long way and the other the short way, with their ends overlapping the sides of the dish. Place the pork and marinade on the leaves and baste with the lard. Fold the ends of the leaves over the pork, moistening slightly so they do not burn. Cover the dish with aluminum foil.
✳ Bake for 2 hours. Remove from the oven and uncover the meat. It should be tender, almost falling apart; if it isn't, cover and return to the oven for another 30 minutes.
✳ Four hours before serving, prepare the onion *salsa*. Place the onion in a bowl and add the juices and salt. Toast the whole *chiles* (see glossary) and add them to the onions.
✳ Serve the pork hot and pass the onion *salsa* separately.

SERVES 6–8

QUERÉTARO

TERNERA GUISADA

Seasoned Veal

Veal is not common in Mexico, but in this recipe by Kay Mendieta de Alonso, it is cooked in a very typical Mexican fashion.

5 cloves garlic
2 tablespoons salt
5 lb (2.5 kg) boneless veal roast
¼ cup (2 fl oz/60 ml) olive oil
2 onions, thinly sliced

Pork Baked in Leaves

Seasoned Veal

3 carrots, thinly sliced
3 bay leaves
1 small sprig dried thyme
1 small sprig dried marjoram
1 teaspoon freshly ground pepper
2 cups (16 fl oz/500 ml) dry white wine
2 *chiles pasillas,* seeds and membranes removed
1 tablespoon oil
1 tablespoon chopped onion
2 cloves garlic, chopped
4 tomatoes, about 28 oz (840 g), chopped

✹ In a mortar or *molcajete,* grind the garlic with the salt to make a paste. Rub onto the veal and let stand at room temperature for at least 2 hours or, preferably, cover and refrigerate overnight.

✹ Preheat the oven to 375°F (190°C). Pour the olive oil into a baking pan, add the sliced onions and carrots and stir to coat. Place the veal in the pan and lay the bay leaves, thyme and marjoram on top. Sprinkle with the pepper and pour 1 cup (8 fl oz/250 ml) of the wine around the veal. Cover the pan with aluminum foil and roast for 30 minutes. Uncover, turn the veal over, stir the vegetables and add the remaining wine. Roast, covered, for 30 more minutes.

✹ Meanwhile, toast the *chiles* (see glossary) on a *comal* or iron skillet, then soak in hot water to cover for 20 minutes. Drain and set aside.

✹ Heat the oil in a saucepan, add the chopped onion and garlic and sauté for 2 minutes or until transparent. Add the tomatoes and boil for 10 minutes. Lower the heat and cook, covered, for 20 minutes. Uncover and cook 10 minutes more. Transfer to a blender, add the *chiles,* purée and strain.

✹ Remove the veal from the oven, cover with 2 cups (16 fl oz/500 ml) of the tomato purée and roast, un-covered, for about 30 minutes, basting 3 or 4 times with the sauce from the pan. When the veal can easily be pierced with a fork, remove it from the oven, transfer to a platter and set aside. Strain all the liquid from the pan into a small saucepan, pressing the solids through a strainer with a spoon to obtain as much liquid as possible. Add the remaining tomato purée and simmer, covered, over low heat for 3 minutes. Correct the seasonings.

✹ Just before serving, slice the veal, arrange on a platter and cover with the sauce.

SERVES 8–10

PACIFIC COAST

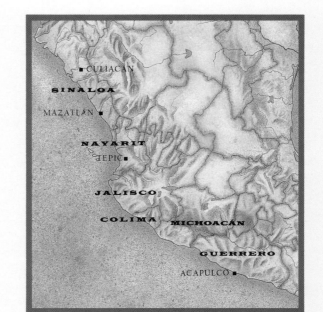

PACIFIC COAST

Picture a scene on the coast of Jalisco. It is a bright hot day in Colimilla, just a twenty-minute boat ride in a small *panga* across the water from the tiny town of Barra de Navidad. A palm-thatched restaurant perched on pilings over the lagoon has tables covered with green cloths and wooden chairs painted an electric yellow. A small heron clutches the uprights on a nearby ramp, poised before spearing its seafood meal. Silent fishermen in dugouts cast their nets. A nearby tern battles with brown pelicans and magnificent frigate birds for the "fish that got away." The quick-turning, dive-bombing tern is the winner!

The meal comes. The first course is *pata de mula* (mule's foot)—sweet black clams served raw in their deep-ridged shells with just a squeeze of lime. Then *camarones a la diabla* (deviled shrimp) are brought with white rice, the flavor of the large shrimp still discernible through a sauce of smoky *chiles chipotles.* A light *ceviche* of freshly caught sierra is brought unasked by the *señora* in apology for the short wait for the final dish, *pescado sarandeado,* the restaurant's specialty. It is a *robalo* (snook) cooked on the grill over white-hot coals, the pungent odors of its thick garlic and *chile ancho* coating serving to stimulate any flagging appetites. Eventually the bones are picked clean and the last tortilla is used to mop the plate and it is time to get back in the small boat and leave.

Previous pages: Sparkling Acapulco Bay, seen from world-famous Las Brisas resort. Left: These small fishing boats in Mazatlán are a quaint footnote to the city's giant fishing industry.

An iguana seller on the way to market in Guerrero, where her reptile friend is destined to become part of a local specialty—iguana stew. With a taste and texture similar to chicken, iguana is popular throughout southern Mexico.

A similar meal can be enjoyed anywhere along the thousand miles of beaches that stretch from Mazatlán to Acapulco. Seafood is a major source of food for the people who live in these six states and for more than one million visitors who come here from colder climes each year in search of fun, sun and sand. The tourists head mainly for the glitzy resort enclaves lining the beaches—Ixtapa, Puerto Vallarta, Manzanillo—but these are not ideal places to seek out regional dishes. The best cooking in the Pacific coast region can be found in the smaller, more remote fishing villages and in the towns that spot the rich, fertile land sandwiched between the coast and the formidable Sierra Madre Occidental.

In Sinaloa, large irrigated plots of tomatoes and other winter vegetables checkerboard the land in competition with fields of rice, wheat and sugar cane. The tortillas here are usually made of *harina* (wheat flour) and are often found wrapped around a filling of *chilorio,* a regional dish of well-cooked and shredded pork in a rich *chile ancho* sauce. *Menudo* (tripe soup) is also a well-loved dish, and in Sinaloa, as in Sonora and other northern states, it is served *blanco,* without the deep red broth characteristic of other regions.

The brackish waters of the coastal lagoons of Sinaloa and Nayarit teem with shrimp, which have made Mazatlán the shrimp capital of the world. All up and down this part of the coast, this succulent crustacean shows up in countless dishes—soups, *ceviche, tamales, tortas*—or may even be pickled or stuffed. This region also boasts sweet scallops and plump, briny oysters, which are eaten raw or *en escaveche* (marinated in vinegar and seasonings).

Tropical fruits are plentiful and may be eaten fresh or prepared in various dishes and drinks. One favorite beverage, *tepache,* is made from sugar and fermented pineapple juice. The cooling, juicy flesh of the mango is particularly prized on this torrid coast, where more than a dozen varieties are grown. There are large, plump ones that have a lemony tang, and some that taste more like a peach. When a refreshing snack is wanted, it is a simple matter to poke a hole through the smooth skin and suck away.

The tiny, tropical state of Colima contains Mexico's only active volcano, El Fuego, and its coastal beaches of powdery black and gray-black sand serve as visual testimony. From Colima's waters come the magnificent sailfish that form the basis of the exceptional *ceviche colimense* and other regional fish dishes such as *tacos* filled with *pez vela con jitomate.*

A low-flying line of pelicans, brown wings trailing in the blue water, often leads to the broad semicircle of sand that separates the town of Barra de Navidad from the bay on one side and the lagoon on the other. It was here that Spanish shipwrights in 1564 constructed a fleet of galleons for the first expedition to the Philippine Islands. When an important official arrived on Christmas Day to check on the progress of the shipbuilding, he named the colony Barra de Navidad (Sandbar of Christmas). Manzanillo and Acapulco, farther to the south, later became major trading ports, leaving Barra de Navidad isolated until 1970, when it was connected to the rest of Mexico by a coastal highway.

The influence of Filipino cooking is apparent in many of the dishes that have originated around the large port city of Manzanillo, thanks to 250 years of trade with Manila. As in the Philippines, pork is the most popular meat, and there is strong resemblance between the pork *adobo* of the islands and the festive *tatemado* of Colima, both of which feature vinegar and garlic as major ingredients and are seasoned with bay leaf and fresh ginger. The difference comes with the Mexican addition of *chile guajillo* and cumin.

Groves of coconut palm trees grow right to the edge of the sea in Colima. On dusty roads the nuts are balanced in precarious piles, awaiting the removal of their husks by women and children who work under sun-sheltering canopies of palm fronds. Rows of palms also protect corn fields and orchards from the same sun. Coconut is the main ingredient in favorite sweets in this region, such as the delicious egg-based *cocadas*. Every beachside *palapa* sells *cocos locos,* a deceptively potent drink in which brandy or rum is added to the

milk in the opened coconut. There is also *crema de coco,* a coconut brandy; a delicious punch of freshly squeezed orange juice, rum and coconut milk; and *tuba,* a mildly fermented drink made from the sap of the coconut palm.

This coastal strip of Mexico is not all fields of crops, coconut and banana plantations and luxuriant tropical vegetation. There are long stretches in Jalisco, Michoacán and other states where the scarcity of water yields only a landscape of dry pine forests and parched chaparral. Turkey vultures circling overhead and a solitary boy tending a herd of goats are about the only movements to be seen. The inhabitants in the few thatched-roof villages eke out an existence by cultivating small plots of vegetables and by fishing.

Guerrero has two cities of significance: Taxco, of silver fame, and Acapulco, which, with the exception of Mexico City, is considered the most cosmopolitan of all the cities in Mexico. Its magnificent natural harbor first served as a supply base for Spanish expeditions along the Pacific Coast, then, starting in 1530, as a port of trade with the Philippines and the Far East.

The Manila galleons, or *Nao de la China,* as they were erroneously called, were among the largest ships of the day. They sailed back and forth across the Pacific, trading Spanish silver bullion and doubloons for silks, spices, ivory, perfumes and fine porcelain. Lasting three to seven months, these were the hardest sea journeys in the world at the time, and on the return voyage the ships usually stopped first in Mendocino, California, and then in Cabo San Lucas and other missions along the coast, where Jesuits and Franciscan monks provided citrus fruit to help cure scurvy among the sailors and passengers.

A mule path had been built across the mountains from Mexico City to Acapulco, and when a ship was due, the population of the little village was tripled to 12,000 by an influx of traders and merchants. Thus, from its early days, Acapulco practiced the art of hospitality and its inhabitants developed the lucrative business of providing food, lodging and amusement. Although all commerce with Spain came to a halt after the Mexican War of Independence (1810–21), Acapulco was left with an ability to assimilate foods from other places and with a love of entertaining visitors. Here, as in other resorts, the bounty of the sea provides the basis for most of the dishes presented in restaurants, but many are international in origin.

Guerrero is not without its traditional dishes, however. Its *ceviche, pozole verde* and iguana stew are considered treats in the outlying regions of the state and the mountainous highlands around Taxco. Two *tamales* are special to the state—one made of *ciruela,* a small type of plum, and another of *jumiles,* little beetles fried with lime. The real aficionado wraps the live beetles in a tortilla, dashes them with *salsa* and swallows them down.

Iguana or lobster, *tepache* or coconut brandy—the food and drinks of the Pacific coastal states provide a good reason to leave the beach resorts and explore the markets and countryside of this bountiful region.

Considered by some to be the gem of Mexican colonial architecture, the church of San Sebastián y Santa Prisca presides over the silver-working town of Taxco.

Pescados y Mariscos

A dancing shrimp lures customers into a seafood restaurant in Veracruz, where specialties such as pescado a la veracruzana are indeed reason to jump for joy.

PESCADOS Y MARISCOS

Six thousand miles of empty beaches, dramatic cliffs and sandy coves are washed by the nutrient-rich waters that surround Mexico. Small wonder that seafood plays such a major role in Mexican cuisine when more than half of its states have shores on the Sea of Cortés, the Pacific Ocean, the Gulf of Mexico or the Caribbean Sea. How long the abundant supply of sea life will continue is an increasingly asked question. Growing industrial and human pollution has resulted in rivers that run dark and dead from the effluent of upriver sugar mills, and sandy beaches that host hordes of bronzing bodies instead of the exquisite but fast-disappearing red clam.

Nevertheless, the bounty of the sea is displayed early every morning in the white- and blue-tiled fish markets of port cities, where blackboards list the day's catches and their going prices. In the many villages lining the coast, buyers surround incoming fishing boats and choose their purchases from piles of fish lying in the bows of the boats.

Seafood should be cooked only to develop its flavor, never to make it tender, and the quickest, simplest methods often produce the best results. About as simple as you can get is *ceviche* (or *cebiche* or *seviche*), a spirit-reviving dish of bite-size pieces of raw fish cooked by the acidic juice of freshly squeezed lime rather than heat. Its flavor and appearance are further brightened by chopped *chile,* tomato or avocado.

Authorities differ as much on the origin of the dish as they do on the spelling of its name, but most agree that it was first seen in Mexico in the port city of Acapulco during the 1500s. The most persistent theory is that *ceviche* originated among the prehistoric people of northern Chile and Peru, was passed up the coast by far-ranging fishermen, and reached Mexico after Cortés built a small fleet of ships in Acapulco and sailed to aid Francisco Pizarro in his conquest of Peru. There is evidence that Peruvian vessels may have reached Mexico at an earlier date, bringing with them the technique of cooking fish without fire. Other experts favor the theory of the Oriental influence brought by trade between Acapulco and Manila.

Quickly sautéed *huachinango* (red snapper) or skewered *robalo* (snook) grilled over white-hot coals may be served directly from the fire with just a squeeze of lime or flavored with garlic or *chile chipotle.* Shellfish is similarly prepared, and a platter of *camarones al mojo de ajo* (garlic shrimp) is about as sensual a dish as has ever been devised.

A simple but unforgettable meal is a plate full of *acamayes* (freshwater crayfish), which are sold by the kilo and eaten by hand in little restaurants such as the one overlooking the Río Pescadore in the high country of Veracruz. Here a swaying narrow rope bridge leads to hillside groves of decadently sweet mangoes, whose juices are mingled with the flavor of *chiles* and *acamayes,* and greedily sucked off the fingers at the end of the meal.

Shrimp and other seafood are often shredded and made into fillings for *tacos, tamales* or *empanadas.* In

Previous pages: Snook with Parsley and Crayfish (left, recipe page 177) and Crab and Cactus Paddle Cocktail (right, recipe page 174)

164

Fishermen in Campeche with their catch of the day—small sharks (dogfish) called cazones. *This local delicacy is used to make* pan de cazón *(shark's bread), a layered tortilla dish popular throughout the Yucatán peninsula.*

A two-handed Gulf coast treat: boiled shrimp ready for peeling, with a squirt of tangy lime.

Sinaloa they are even heaped into *chiles*. And in the Gulf ports of Tampico and Veracruz, unusual azure-colored crabs are stuffed with a mixture of crabmeat, capers, onions, tomatoes and *chiles serranos*. In Puerto Angel, a small fishing village on the Oaxacan coast, pompano is filled with potatoes and onions, seasoned with herbs, wrapped in foil and cooked on a hot griddle until steam causes the foil to puff up, signaling that the fish is ready to eat. In Morelos stuffed carp may be wrapped in corn husks before cooking, and in many places in the southern states, fish is enclosed in large leaves of *hierba santa,* which impart a slightly licorice flavor.

In contrast to the fresh fish, mollusks and shellfish of the east coast, preserved seafood is eaten throughout Mexico, especially at the time of major holidays. The use of dried shrimp, prevalent in the Orient, probably found its way to Mexico by way of the Manila-Acapulco trade route that was established early in colonial history. Lent, with its forty days of penitential fasting, brings pyramids of dried shrimp, or *camarón seco,* to the markets, varying in size, color and degree of dryness. The drier they are, the more penetrating their

After a day on the beaches of Cancún, tourists head to the local seafood
restaurants, where lobster, shrimp and steak dominate the menus.

Jaibas (crabs), bundled and ready for the market. These live blue crabs
from the waters off Tamaulipas and Veracruz are the main ingredient in
chilpachole de jaiba, a spicy crab soup.

salty taste. The most traditional dish combines them
with fleshy green *romeritos* in fritters with a mildly spicy
tomato sauce.

It is paradoxical that *bacalao,* or dried salt cod, a
favorite food in both Spain and Mexico, originally came
from the faraway Grand Banks fishing grounds off the
coast of Newfoundland. Because of its "keeping"
qualities, salt cod was once the major fish eaten in
Europe. For the same reason it was brought by the
Spanish to the New World, where it became a dietary
standby for people living far from the shore. The cod is
split from head to tail, salted and dried until hard as a
board. A long soak is required to soften the flesh and
remove the salt before the fish can be combined with
such New World ingredients as *chiles,* tomatoes and
potatoes in the tasty stew traditionally served at
Christmastime.

Fish or shellfish, fresh or dried, from fresh or salt
water—all have a bland quality that cries out for an
appropriately piquant condiment. That is why the
flavors of Mexico are the perfect complement to
seafood.

Fish lovers on the Pacific coast skewer their catch and grill it right on the beach. The ever-present lime provides the perfect accompaniment.

*Marinated Strips of Fish (left) and Shrimp
Cocktail with Avocado Dressing (right)*

Cóctel de Camarones con Aderezo de Aguacate

Shrimp Cocktail with Avocado Dressing

*Martha Chapa, a well-known painter and food writer,
created this rich and unusual version of a shrimp cocktail.*

1 lb (500 g) small shrimp (prawns)
2 cups (16 fl oz/500 ml) fish stock or bottled clam juice
1 bouquet garni
2 large avocados
½ onion
2 cloves garlic
1 cup (8 fl oz/250 ml) thick cream (*crème fraîche*)
1 *chile serrano,* seeds and membranes removed
2 tablespoons lime juice
½ cup (4 fl oz/125 ml) olive oil

✱ In a covered saucepan, poach the shrimp in the stock
with the bouquet garni. When the shrimp are cooked,
in 2–3 minutes, drain, remove their shells and refrigerate.
✱ While the shrimp cool, prepare the dressing by
puréeing the remaining ingredients in a blender until a
velvety texture is achieved. Arrange alternate layers of
shrimp and dressing in tall glasses. Refrigerate until
ready to serve.
✱*Variation:* When this cocktail is enriched by the addition of poached lobster medallions, a truly extra-
ordinary result is guaranteed.

SERVES 4

Tiritas de Pescado

Marinated Strips of Fish

*This version of ceviche is a specialty in the beachside
restaurants of Zihuatanejo.*

1 lb (500 g) red snapper fillets
¾ cup (6 fl oz/180 ml) lime juice
3 *chiles serranos,* seeded and cut into thin strips
1 cup (8 oz/250 g) thinly sliced red onion
1 tablespoon salt
¼ teaspoon freshly ground pepper
1 tablespoon dried oregano

✱ Cut the fish into strips 2 in (5 cm) long and ¼ in (5
mm) wide. Place in a glass bowl and add the lime juice,
chiles, onion, salt, pepper and oregano. Stir and marinate for 10 minutes. Drain off the excess lime juice and
correct the seasonings.
✱ Serve cold or at room temperature

SERVES 6

TAMAULIPAS

GUATAPE DE CAMARONES

Shrimp Guatape

Hierba santa is prized throughout southeastern Mexico for its unusual flavor. If it is not available, just eliminate it or try adding the lacy tops of fresh fennel, which have a similar taste. This recipe from Socorrito Zorrilla contrasts well with molded white rice.

3 *chiles poblanos* or green bell peppers (capsicums), seeds and membranes removed
4 *tomates verdes,* husks removed
2 cups (3 oz/90 g) fresh parsley
3 small leaves *hierba santa* (optional)
4 cups (32 fl oz/1 l) water
¼ cup (2 fl oz/60 ml) olive oil or lard
1 large onion, finely chopped
1½ tablespoons cornstarch (cornflour), dissolved in a little water
salt and white pepper
2 lb (1 kg) shrimp (prawns), preferably with heads attached
juice of 1 lime

✳ In a blender, purée the *chiles, tomates verdes,* parsley and *hierba santa* with the water. Strain and set aside.
✳ Heat the oil in a large saucepan, add the onion and sauté until transparent. Add the purée, bring to a boil and stir in the cornstarch. Simmer until thickened, then season with salt and pepper.
✳ Peel only the bodies of the shrimp and add them to the mixture. Simmer, covered, until they are cooked through, about 5 minutes. Serve hot, sprinkled with a few drops of lime juice.

SERVES 6

Shrimp Guatape

Avocados Stuffed with Scallops

BAJA CALIFORNIA NORTE

CALLO DE HACHA CON AGUACATE

Avocados Stuffed with Scallops

It is more customary to find avocados stuffed with tiny shrimp than with scallops, but this combination is, if anything, even more tasty. The original recipe uses chocolata scallops, a dark-shelled species found mostly around the Sea of Cortez, but small bay scallops may be substituted.

12 oz (375 g) shucked (opened) scallops
⅓ cup (3 fl oz/80 ml) fresh lime juice
1 tablespoon minced fresh oregano
1 tablespoon minced fresh *cilantro* (coriander)
⅔ cup (5 fl oz/160 ml) olive oil
salt and freshly ground pepper
3 large avocados, ripe but slightly firm
minced *chile serrano* (optional)

✳ Place the scallops in a bowl and add the lime juice, oregano, *cilantro* and oil. Season with salt and pepper and let stand for 15–20 minutes or until opaque.
✳ Cut each avocado in half, remove the pit and spoon out balls of the pulp, reserving the shells. Mix the avocado balls with the scallops and spoon into the avocado shells. If you wish, sprinkle minced *chile serrano* on top.

SERVES 6

TAMAULIPAS

CAMARONES A LA MEXICANA

Mexican-Style Shrimp

When a dish is referred to as a la mexicana, *it is made with tomatoes, onions and* chiles, *combined here with the plentiful shrimp from the coastal waters of Mexico.*

2 tablespoons oil
¾ cup (6 oz/185 g) finely chopped onion
4 cloves garlic, minced
2 lb (1 kg) ripe tomatoes, peeled and chopped
½ teaspoon freshly ground pepper
2 bay leaves
1½ tablespoons dried thyme
1 tablespoon salt
2 tablespoons canned *chile güero* juice
2 tablespoons (1 oz/30 g) butter
2 lb (1 kg) shrimp (prawns), shelled and deveined
3 tablespoons chopped parsley
canned *chiles güeros*

✳ Heat the oil in a large saucepan, add the onion and garlic and sauté for 2 minutes or until transparent. Add the tomatoes and cook over medium heat for 5 minutes, stirring constantly. Add the pepper, bay leaves, thyme, salt and *chile* juice. Cook, covered, over low heat for 5 minutes. Correct the seasonings.
✳ Before serving, melt the butter in a skillet and lightly sauté the shrimp. Add the shrimp to the hot sauce and simmer for 3–4 minutes or until the shrimp are cooked. Sprinkle each serving with chopped parsley and garnish with a *chile güero.*

SERVES 6

GUERRERO

FILETE DE PESCADO EMPAPELADO CON JITOMATE, CILANTRO Y CEBOLLA MORADA

Fish Fillets Baked in Foil with Tomatoes, Cilantro and Red Onions

Braising fish that is wrapped in paper, or now more efficiently in foil, is a little-known but very effective technique for preparing seafood dishes like this great favorite from Acapulco.

6 fillets of sea bass or other firm-fleshed white fish, about 5 oz (155 g) each
salt and freshly ground pepper
1 tablespoon Maggi or Worcestershire sauce
2½ cups (20 fl oz/625 ml) mayonnaise
¼ cup (2 fl oz/60 ml) dry white wine
1 tablespoon minced *cilantro* (coriander)
1 teaspoon dried tarragon
2 tablespoons Pernod
1 tablespoon lime juice
1 tablespoon Worcestershire sauce
1 large red onion, thickly sliced
3 tomatoes, peeled and thickly sliced
12 pitted green olives
6 canned *chiles güeros*

✳ Rinse the fish and pat dry. Season with salt, pepper and Maggi sauce. Cover and refrigerate for at least 1 hour.
✳ In a bowl, combine the mayonnaise, wine, *cilantro,* tarragon, Pernod, lime juice and Worcestershire sauce.
✳ Preheat the oven to 375°F (190°C). Cut 6 sheets of aluminum foil to measure 8 by 10 in (20 by 25 cm). Coat each sheet with a tablespoon of the mayonnaise mixture. Place a fish fillet on the foil and cover lightly with more of the mayonnaise mixture. Top with 2 slices of onion, 2 slices of tomato and 2 olives. Fold the foil to form an envelope and roll the sides so that the juices will not seep out.
✳ Place the foil packets in a baking pan and bake for 10–20 minutes, depending on the thickness of the fillets. Open each foil packet and garnish with a *chile.* Serve immediately.

SERVES 6

TAMAULIPAS

JAIBAS RELLENAS GRATINADAS

Crab and Vegetables au Gratin

Little blue crabs thrive in the shallow waters and estuaries along Mexico's Gulf coast, where they form an integral part of the local cuisine. Traditionally, this crab mixture is served in the shells, but it could be put in individual ramekins or in a larger shallow baking dish. Easily multiplied, it is a good recipe to serve for a crowd.

2 tablespoons (1 oz/30 g) unsalted butter
½ onion, chopped
1 clove garlic, chopped
3 carrots, peeled and grated
3 plum tomatoes, peeled and chopped
¼ cup (2 oz/60 g) tomato paste
1 *chile jalapeño,* diced
1 green bell pepper (capsicum), roasted (see glossary), peeled and diced
1 potato, peeled and diced
salt and freshly ground pepper
1 lb (500 g) crabmeat, picked over to remove shell and cartilage

CHEESE SAUCE

¼ cup (2 oz/60 g) unsalted butter
¼ cup (1 oz/30 g) all-purpose (plain) flour
2 cups (16 fl oz/500 ml) milk
2 tablespoons grated sharp Cheddar cheese
salt and white pepper

TOPPING

½ cup (2 oz/60 g) grated sharp Cheddar cheese
1 tablespoon dry breadcrumbs

✳ Melt the butter in a large skillet. Add the onion and garlic and cook over medium heat until soft. Add the carrots, tomatoes, tomato paste, *chile* and bell pepper. Cook until the tomatoes release their juices and the mixture is well blended. Set aside.
✳ Place the diced potato in a saucepan of boiling water, cover and cook until crisp-tender. Drain and add to the vegetable mixture. Add salt and pepper to taste, then stir in the crabmeat.

✱ To prepare the sauce, melt the butter in a large saucepan. Add the flour and stir until blended. Add the milk and whisk over medium heat until the sauce thickens. Stir in the cheese and add salt and pepper to taste.

✱Preheat the oven to 350°F (180°C). Fill individual shells or a shallow baking dish with the crab mixture and cover with the sauce. For the topping, mix the cheese with the breadcrumbs and sprinkle over the sauce. Bake until the sauce begins to bubble. Turn the oven up to 425°F (220°C) and brown the top for about 2 minutes, being careful not to let it burn.

SERVES 8

Mexican-Style Shrimp (left), Fish Fillets Baked in Foil with Tomatoes, Cilantro and Red Onions (center) and Crab and Vegetables au Gratin (right)

GUERRERO

Huachinango al Perejil

Red Snapper with Parsley Cream

Parsley, preferably the flat-leafed Italian variety, is the flavoring for this sauce, accenting the fresh, light taste of the fish. If whole red snapper is not available, any fish with firm white flesh can be substituted.

1 red snapper, about 3 lb (1.5 kg), cleaned, with head and tail left on
2 tablespoons lime juice
1 clove garlic, finely chopped
salt and freshly ground pepper
2 cups (16 fl oz/500 ml) light (single) cream or half & half (half milk and half cream)
1 cup (1½ oz/45 g) chopped fresh parsley

✱ Preheat the oven to 325°F (165°C). Rinse the fish and pat dry.

Ingredients for Red Snapper with Orange Sauce (top), Fish Veracruz Style (center) and Red Snapper with Parsley Cream (bottom)

✱ Combine the lime juice, garlic and salt and pepper to taste. Rub the entire fish, inside and out, with this mixture and let it marinate for 20 minutes.
✱ Meanwhile, purée the cream and parsley in a blender until smooth. Add salt and pepper to taste.
✱ Place the fish in a greased baking dish. Cover with the parsley cream and bake for about 30 minutes or until the fish is cooked (the time will vary depending on the thickness of the fish).

SERVES 4

SINALOA

Huachinango a la Naranja

Red Snapper with Orange Sauce

The magnificent true red snapper is a Gulf coast fish, but other species abound all along Mexico's Pacific coast and are prepared in myriad ways. This unusual version has an orange sauce that gives the fish a tangy flavor. A slice of olive can be used to replace the eye if the appearance is a bother. Arroz verde con rajas (page 91) makes a pleasant accompaniment.

1 red snapper, about 4 lb (2 kg), cleaned
juice of 1 lime
2 cloves garlic, crushed
2 teaspoons salt
½ teaspoon freshly ground pepper
2 cups (16 fl oz/500 ml) orange juice
⅓ cup (3 oz/90 g) grated onion
1 cup (8 fl oz/250 ml) thick cream (*crème fraîche*)
1 orange, sliced

✱ Rub the fish with the lime juice and crushed garlic. Season with the salt and pepper and let stand for 1 hour.
✱ Preheat the oven to 375°F (190°C). Place the fish in a greased baking dish and cover with the orange juice. Sprinkle with the grated onion.
✱ Bake, uncovered, basting frequently with the pan juices, for 35 minutes or until the fish flakes easily when it is pierced with a fork.
✱ Remove the fish from the oven and cover it with the cream. Garnish with orange slices and serve.

SERVES 6

VERACRUZ

Pescado a la Veracruzana

Fish Veracruz Style

This famous fish dish combines chiles and tomatoes from the New World with the very Spanish addition of capers and olives. It is traditionally served with a scoop of white rice.

1 tablespoon oil
4 cloves garlic, chopped
½ cup (4 oz/125 g) finely chopped onion
2 lb (1 kg) tomatoes, peeled and finely chopped
1 green bell pepper (capsicum), cut into strips
1 teaspoon salt

½ teaspoon freshly ground pepper
2 bay leaves
1 teaspoon dried oregano
½ cup (2½ oz/75 g) chopped green olives
¼ cup (2 oz/60 g) capers
6 fillets of sea bass or other firm-fleshed fish, about
    4 oz (125 g) each
2 tablespoons (1 oz/30 g) butter
6 canned *chiles güeros* or *jalapeños*, for garnish

✳ Heat the oil in a large saucepan, add the garlic and onion and sauté for 3 minutes. Add the tomatoes and bring to a boil. Add the bell pepper and stir for 2 minutes. Add the salt, pepper, bay leaves and oregano. When the mixture returns to a boil, cover and cook over low heat for 8 minutes. Add the olives and capers and cook another 5 minutes. Correct the seasonings and remove from the heat.
✳ Twenty minutes before serving, preheat the oven to 375°F (190°C). Rinse the fillets, pat dry and sprinkle lightly with salt and pepper. Melt the butter in a large skillet, add the fillets and brown lightly on both sides. Transfer to a greased baking dish and cover with the sauce. Cover the dish with aluminum foil and bake for 10–15 minutes. Garnish each fillet with a *chile* before serving.
✳*Note:* You can use a whole fish if you prefer, but you will need to increase the baking time.

SERVES 6

GUERRERO

HUACHINANGO A LA TALLA

Grilled Red Snapper

Fish grilled in this manner is a specialty in the palapas *(palm-roofed beach restaurants) of Barra Vieja, on the outskirts of Acapulco. It is cooked on a wood-fired stove made of clay.*

1 red snapper, about 5 lb (2.5 kg)
5 tablespoons mayonnaise
2 tablespoons lime juice
1 tablespoon salt
¼ teaspoon freshly ground pepper
½ cup (4 oz/125 g) butter, melted

SAUCE

10 *chiles guajillos,* seeds and membranes removed
5 *chiles anchos,* seeds and membranes removed
1 cup (8 fl oz/250 ml) water
4 tomatoes, peeled and seeded
4 cloves garlic
1 tablespoon white vinegar
3 whole cloves
⅓ onion
½ teaspoon each dried oregano, thyme and marjoram
½ teaspoon ground cumin
2 tablespoons (1 oz/30 g) butter
2 tablespoons oil
salt and freshly ground pepper

✳ Have your fish dealer slice the fish open to prepare a "butterfly" cut; remove the gills and intestines from the fish but leave on the scales. Rinse the fish and pat dry.
✳ In a bowl, combine the mayonnaise, lime juice, salt

Grilled Red Snapper

and pepper. Rub the fish with this mixture and marinate at room temperature for 20 minutes.
✳ To prepare the sauce, soak the chiles in hot water to cover for 10 minutes. Drain, transfer to a blender and purée with the water, tomatoes, garlic, vinegar, cloves, onion, oregano, thyme, marjoram and cumin until smooth.
✳ Heat the butter and oil in a small saucepan and add the puréed *chiles*. When the purée comes to a boil, lower the heat and cook for 20 minutes or until the sauce thickens. Add salt and pepper to taste. Let cool to room temperature.
✳ Preheat an outdoor grill and lightly grease the rack. Position the rack about 8 in (20 cm) over a charcoal fire. Place the opened fish, scales side down, on the rack and grill for 15–20 minutes, basting regularly with the sauce. Turn the fish over, baste with the melted butter and grill for 10–15 minutes or until the fish is cooked.

SERVES 4

OAXACA

SALPICÓN DE JAIBA Y NOPALITOS

Crab and Cactus Paddle Cocktail

*A Spanish dictionary will translate salpicón as "medley,"
"splashing" or even "salmagundi," which all comes down to
any number of mixtures of shredded meat and fish served in
different parts of Mexico. This tasty dish from Martha Chapa
is easy to prepare on hot days.*

1 cup (8 fl oz/250 ml) tomato sauce (puréed tomatoes)
8 oz (250 g) tomatoes, peeled and diced
½ teaspoon Worcestershire sauce
½ teaspoon Tabasco sauce
3 paddles of nopal cactus (8 oz/250 g), cooked and
    diced (see glossary)
10 oz (315 g) cooked crabmeat, flaked
3 tablespoons finely chopped *cilantro* (coriander)

*Lobster Salad with Guava Dressing (left) and
Cold Red Snapper (right)*

❋ This tasty dish is easy to prepare on hot days. Just
combine all the ingredients, mix well and chill for
several hours. Serve in tall glasses.

SERVES 4–6   *Photograph pages 162–163*

DISTRITO FEDERAL

ENSALADA DE LANGOSTA CON ADEREZO DE GUAYABA

Lobster Salad with Guava Dressing

*The "new" Mexican style of cooking now in fashion in
Mexico City is exemplified by this salad from the kitchen of
Martha Chapa. The guava, which may be hard to find*

outside Mexico except in the fall, provides a nice balance to the richness of the lobster.

5 small guavas, pitted
½ cup (4 fl oz/125 ml) cider vinegar
1 cup (8 fl oz/250 ml) olive oil
1 tablespoon sugar
½ cup (4 fl oz/125 ml) thick cream (*crème fraîche*)
1½ tablespoons chicken bouillon granules
1 head romaine (cos) lettuce
½ head butter or iceberg lettuce
1 head escarole (curly endive/chicory) lettuce
2 lobster tails, cooked, shelled and cut into medallions
2 guavas, sliced, for garnish

✳ Place the guavas, vinegar, oil and sugar in a blender and purée. When the mixture is smooth, stir in the cream and chicken bouillon granules. Chill.
✳ Just before serving, coat the three kinds of lettuce with a little olive oil and place in a salad bowl. Add the

dressing and toss. Arrange the lobster medallions on top of the lettuce and garnish with the guava slices.
✳*Note:* This recipe can be made with any mixture of lettuce.

SERVES 6

GUERRERO

HUACHINANGO EN FRÍO

Cold Red Snapper

Berro (watercress) is a relative newcomer to the Mexican cooking scene, but it has been enthusiastically welcomed. Instead of the more common avocado that is often used to coat a fish served cold, this dish uses watercress for its distinct, brighter flavor.

1 red snapper or sea bass, about 4 lb (2 kg), cleaned
4 bay leaves
¼ onion, in a chunk
2 cloves garlic
3 stalks celery with leaves
1 carrot, cut into chunks
1 tablespoon coarse salt
8 black peppercorns

MAYONNAISE

1 tablespoon lime juice
½ teaspoon salt
¼ teaspoon freshly ground pepper
1 tablespoon white vinegar
1 clove garlic
1 egg
1 cup (1½ oz/45 g) watercress leaves
1 cup (8 fl oz/250 ml) oil

✳ Rinse the fish and set aside.
✳ Pour at least 6 in (15 cm) of water into a pan large enough to hold the fish. Add the bay leaves, onion, garlic, celery, carrot, salt and peppercorns and bring to a boil over high heat. Add the fish, lower the heat and cook for 25 minutes (if the water does not cover the fish completely, the fish must be turned over using 2 slotted spoons to prevent breaking). Pierce the thickest part of the fish with a fork to see if it is done; if the fish is still somewhat raw, cook for another 15 minutes.
✳ Remove the fish from the pan, transfer to a platter and immediately peel off the skin with a fork, leaving the skin on the head and tail. Cover the fish so it does not dry out and let cool to room temperature.
✳ To prepare the mayonnaise, process the lime juice, salt, pepper, vinegar, garlic and egg in a blender. Add the watercress and process for 30 seconds. With the blender running, add the oil in a thin stream so that it emulsifies and the mayonnaise reaches the desired consistency. Transfer to a bowl, correct the seasonings and chill.
✳ To serve, garnish the platter with watercress and cover the fish with one-third of the chilled mayonnaise. Pass a bowl containing the rest of the mayonnaise.

SERVES 6

Pickled Oysters

Ostiones en Escabeche

Pickled Oysters

An excellent combination of pickled seafood and vegetables to serve as an appetizer or a light main dish preceded by quesadillas. It is best made a day in advance.

20 small cloves garlic
salt
1 cup (2 oz/60 g) cauliflower florets
¾ cup (6 oz/185 g) thinly sliced carrots
¾ cup (6 fl oz/180 ml) olive oil
½ cup (4 oz/125 g) thinly sliced small white onions
2 bay leaves
½ teaspoon each dried marjoram and thyme
½ teaspoon black peppercorns
2 teaspoons dried oregano, crumbled
1½ pints (1½ lb/750 g) shucked (opened) small oysters with their juice
½ cup (4 oz/125 g) thinly sliced sour pickles (preferably cornichons)
¼ cup (2 fl oz/60 ml) cider vinegar
⅔ cup (5 oz/155 g) cooked green peas
⅔ cup (5 oz/155 g) pickled cocktail onions
freshly ground pepper
lime slices, for garnish
pickled *chiles jalapeños*, sliced

* Place the garlic in a small saucepan and add cold water to cover. Add salt and simmer for 4–5 minutes. Drain and set aside.
* Drop the cauliflower and carrots into a large saucepan of boiling salted water and simmer for 1 minute. Drain and set aside.

✳ Heat the oil in a large saucepan and add the sliced onions. Sauté until wilted, about 5 minutes, but do not brown. Add the parboiled garlic, cauliflower and carrots and the bay leaves, marjoram, thyme, peppercorns, oregano and salt to taste.

✳ Add the oysters with their juice. Simmer until the edges of the oysters curl, 5 minutes or less. Remove from the heat and let cool.

✳ Add the pickles, vinegar, peas, cocktail onions and pepper to taste. Chill. To serve, pour the mixture into a serving dish and garnish with lime slices. Serve the *chiles* on the side. This dish is usually eaten with a spoon.

SERVES 6 OR MORE

COLIMA

ROBALO AL PEREJIL CON LANGOSTINOS

Snook with Parsley and Crayfish

Langostinos are freshwater crustaceans, similar to crayfish, that grow especially well in the estuaries of Colima, where they are also called chacales. *On the Gulf coast, where they may reach ten inches in size, they are called* acamayas.

8 cloves garlic, crushed
2 teaspoons salt
2 tablespoons lime juice
6 fillets of snook, sea bass or other firm-fleshed fish, about 5 oz (155 g) each
1 lb (500 g) crayfish or large shrimp (or marron, scampi or Balmain bugs)
⅓ cup (3 fl oz/80 ml) olive oil

Lobster Crêpes with Pine Nut Sauce

1 cup (8 oz/250 g) finely chopped onion
2 tablespoons chopped garlic
1⅓ cups (2 oz/60 g) finely chopped parsley
2–3 *chiles serranos* (optional)
2 cups (16 fl oz/500 ml) white wine
1 cup (8 fl oz/250 ml) fish stock or bottled clam juice
1 teaspoon salt

✳ Combine the crushed garlic, salt and lime juice in a glass dish, add the fillets and the crayfish and marinate, refrigerated, for at least 2 hours, turning occasionally.

✳ Heat the oil in a small *paella* pan or a *cazuela*. Add the onion and chopped garlic and sauté for 4 minutes or until transparent. Add the parsley and *chiles* and stir for 2 minutes. Add the wine, fish stock and salt. When the mixture comes to a boil, lower the heat and add the crayfish. Cover and cook for 5 minutes. Add the fish and cook for 7 minutes or until done. Serve immediately.

✳ If you want a thicker sauce, dust the fillets lightly with flour.

SERVES 6   *Photograph pages 162–163*

SONORA

CREPAS DE LANGOSTA CON SALSA DE PIÑONES

Lobster Crêpes with Pine Nut Sauce

These elegant crêpes of Martha Chapa's are filled with lobster from the Sea of Cortez and pine nuts from the small pines growing on the dry open slopes of the Sierra Madre Occidental. They call for a light but equally elegant dessert such as gelatina de café con licor de café *(page 240).*

2½ cups (10 oz/315 g) pine nuts
2 cups (16 fl oz/500 ml) thick cream *(crème fraîche)*
3 *chiles anchos,* toasted (see glossary), seeds and membranes removed, then soaked
6 tablespoons (3 oz/90 g) butter
2 tablespoons oil
1 onion, finely chopped
3 *chiles poblanos,* roasted (see glossary), peeled, seeds and membranes removed, then diced
8 oz (250 g) cooked lobster meat, flaked
salt and freshly ground pepper
24 crêpes*
1⅓ cups (5 oz/155 g) grated Parmesan cheese

✳ Preheat the oven to 350°F (180°C). To make the sauce, place half of the pine nuts in a blender, add the cream and *chiles anchos* and purée. Set aside.

✳ Heat the butter and oil in a skillet, add the onion and sauté until transparent. Add the *chiles poblanos,* lobster and remaining pine nuts and stir; add salt and pepper to taste, let cool and allow the flavors to blend.

✳ Fill the crêpes with this mixture, roll up and arrange in a greased baking dish. Cover with the reserved sauce and sprinkle the top with Parmesan cheese. Bake for 15 minutes.

* *To make the crêpes, use your own recipe or follow the one in* crepas de mole *(page 96).*

SERVES 8

1 teaspoon ground cumin
¼ cup (2 fl oz/ 60 ml) red wine vinegar
1 cup (1½ oz/45 g) chopped parsley
4 tablespoons chopped *epazote*
2 tablespoons dried oregano
5 or 6 pickled *chiles jalapeños,* chopped
3 tablespoons pickled *chile* juice
1 cup (4 oz/125 g) green peas, cooked (optional)

✱ Place the water, whole garlic cloves, onion quarter, bay leaves, thyme, marjoram and 1 teaspoon of the salt in a large pot or Dutch oven. Bring the water to a boil, add the sailfish, cover and cook over medium heat for 35–45 minutes or until the fish can easily be pierced with a fork. Drain and shred the flesh. Set aside.
✱ Heat the oil in a large saucepan, add the chopped onion and garlic and cook for 3 minutes. Add the tomatoes, peppercorns, clove, cumin, vinegar and ½ teaspoon salt and cook for 5 minutes, stirring constantly. Add the sailfish, parsley, *evazote,* oregano, *chiles* and *chile* juice and correct the seasonings. Boil for 5 minutes. Cover and cook over low heat for 10 minutes. Before serving, stir in the peas if you wish. Serve hot.
✱*Variation:* Use as a filling for *tacos* or serve in *cazuelitas* or on a platter, covered with cream and garnished with strips of *chiles chipotles.*

SERVES 8

Sailfish with Tomato Sauce

COLIMA

PEZ VELA CON JITOMATE

Sailfish with Tomato Sauce

Sailfish is known to most of the world as a prized catch of sports fishermen, but in Mexico it is fished as a food source.

12 cups (96 fl oz/3 l) water
6 cloves garlic, 3 whole, 3 chopped
¼ onion
3 bay leaves
1 small sprig thyme
1 small sprig marjoram
1½ teaspoons salt
3 lb (1.25 kg) boned sailfish, swordfish or marlin, cut into 4 pieces
¼ cup (2 fl oz/60 ml) oil
1½ cups (12 oz/375 g) finely chopped onion
2½ lb (1.25 kg) tomatoes, finely chopped
3 black peppercorns
1 whole clove

OAXACA

TORTITAS DE CAMARÓN SECO

Dried Shrimp Patties

A classic Lenten dish of dried shrimp patties in a dark red mole *sauce. The shrimp are ground, shell and all, in small amounts so that they do not become pulverized. They should still have some texture. Many Oriental and Mexican markets carry these dried shrimp, ground and ready for use.*

6 oz (185 g) dried shrimp, unsalted
1 lb (500 g) paddles of nopal cactus
2 cloves garlic
½ onion, cut in half
1½ teaspoons salt
1 teaspoon baking soda (bicarbonate of soda)
2 oz (60 g) *chiles guajillos,* seeds and membranes removed
1 oz (30 g) *chiles anchos,* seeds and membranes removed
6 whole cloves
½ teaspoon black peppercorns
1 teaspoon each dried thyme and marjoram
1 cup (8 fl oz/250 ml) water
2 tablespoons oil
2 tomatoes
3 eggs, separated
oil for frying

✱ Remove the heads and tails from the shrimp, break the shrimp into small pieces and purée without water in a blender. There should be about 1 cup powdered shrimp. Set aside.
✱ Remove the spines and finely dice the cactus paddles (there should be about 1½ cups). Place in a saucepan with 1 garlic clove, 1 onion quarter, ½ teaspoon salt and the baking soda and add water to cover. Bring to a

boil, then simmer, covered, for 10 minutes or until the cactus is soft enough to pierce with a fork. Drain and set aside.

* Toast the *chiles* (see glossary) on a *comal* or iron skillet. Transfer to a bowl and add hot water to cover. Let soak for 5 minutes and drain.

* Roast the remaining onion quarter and garlic clove (see glossary) with the cloves, peppercorns, thyme and marjoram for about 3 minutes. Transfer to a blender, add the water and purée. Add the drained *chiles* and purée again.

* Heat the oil in a skillet, add the *chile* purée and cook for 5 minutes, stirring constantly. Add 1 teaspoon salt.

* Roast the tomatoes (see glossary) and remove their cores. Peel, then purée the tomatoes in a blender. Add to the *chile* sauce, stir and cook over medium heat for 5 minutes. Correct the seasonings. Add the cactus.

* To prepare the patties, beat the egg whites in a large bowl until they hold stiff peaks. Fold in the yolks, being careful not to stir too much or the whites will lose volume. Sprinkle the dried shrimp over the eggs a tablespoon at a time and fold in.

* Heat 1 cup (8 fl oz/250 ml) of oil in a deep skillet and drop in the egg-shrimp mixture, a tablespoon at a time. As soon as one side of the patty is lightly browned, turn it over. (A fork and slotted spoon work well for turning.) Fry no more than 3 patties at a time so that they don't burn or stick together. After frying, transfer the patties to a colander to drain. There should be about 12 patties.

* Before serving, heat the cactus paddle sauce. Add the patties, so that they float on the sauce.

SERVES 6

Dried Shrimp Patties

Garlic Shrimp

CAMARONES AL MOJO DE AJO

Garlic Shrimp

Garlic is seldom used in prodigious amounts in Mexican cooking, but in this popular shrimp dish it provides a perfect balance of flavors. Rice is a natural accompaniment.

36 medium shrimp (prawns) in their shells
15 cloves garlic, 3 whole, 12 minced
¾ teaspoon salt
¾ teaspoon freshly ground pepper
¾ teaspoon white vinegar
3 tablespoons olive oil
5 tablespoons (2½ oz/80 g) butter
3 tablespoons lime juice

180

✳ From the underside, split the shrimp down the middle without separating them completely. Remove the dark vein if apparent.

✳ In a blender, purée the whole garlic cloves, salt, pepper and vinegar. Marinate the shrimp in this mixture for 30 minutes.

✳ Heat the oil and butter in a skillet. Add the minced garlic and sauté until golden brown, about 3 minutes. Add the shrimp with the shell sides up. Lower the heat, cover and cook for 2–3 minutes or until the shrimp are opaque. Sprinkle with the lime juice and remove from the heat.

SERVES 6

GUERRERO

CAMARONES EN ESCABECHE

Soused Shrimp

Rosario Madero, daughter of the late president Francisco I. Madero, serves these spicy shrimp as an appetizer.

8 cups (48 fl oz/2 l) water
1 onion, cut into chunks
1 tablespoon coarse salt
1 small sprig thyme
1 small sprig marjoram
2 bay leaves
8 cloves garlic
4 lb (2 kg) whole shrimp (prawns) in their shells

SOUSE

3 *chiles poblanos,* roasted (see glossary) and peeled
6–8 *chiles serranos,* sliced
5 oz (155 g) canned roasted red peppers
8 cloves garlic
3 large onions
2 tomatoes, roasted (see glossary), peeled and seeded
4 green (spring) onions, with half the tops
1¼ cups (10 fl oz/310 ml) fresh orange juice
1 cup (8 fl oz/250 ml) lime juice
¾ cup (6 fl oz/180 ml) olive oil
1 cup (8 fl oz/250 ml) red wine vinegar
1 tablespoon each dried tarragon, marjoram and thyme
3 tablespoons chopped parsley
1 tablespoon chopped fresh basil
⅛ teaspoon ground nutmeg
¼ teaspoon each ground cinnamon and cloves
2 tablespoons Worcestershire sauce
1 tablespoon Tabasco sauce
2 tablespoons ketchup (tomato sauce)
3 tablespoons grated *piloncillo* (raw sugar) or brown
    sugar
salt and freshly ground pepper
3 tablespoons *salsa* (recipe follows)

✳ In a large pot or Dutch oven, place the water, onion, salt, thyme, marjoram, bay leaves and garlic. Bring to a boil over high heat and add the shrimp. Return to a boil, cook the shrimp for 1 minute and drain. When the shrimp are cool enough to handle, remove their heads and tails, shell and devein.

✳ To make the souse, purée all the ingredients through the *piloncillo* in a blender. Add salt and pepper to taste and stir in the *salsa.*

✳ Cut the shrimp into ½-in (1-cm) pieces and place in a dish with a cover. Add the souse, cover and refrigerate overnight.

SERVES 6

Salsa for Camarones en Escabeche

This recipe makes more than is needed for the camarones en escabeche, *so use the extra for basting fish or poultry before grilling. Or serve it as a table* salsa *to accompany a succulent cut of steak.*

1 tomato
3 cloves garlic
1½ onions, cut into chunks
13 oz (410 g) *tomates verdes,* husks removed
3 *chiles guajillos,* seeds and membranes removed
1 *chile pasilla,* seeds and membranes removed
2 *chiles de árbol,* seeds and membranes removed
2 whole cloves
1 1-in (2.5-cm) stick cinnamon
⅛ teaspoon ground nutmeg
1 teaspoon each dried thyme and marjoram
2 cups (16 fl oz/500 ml) water
3 tablespoons grated *piloncillo* (raw sugar) or brown
    sugar

✳ Roast the tomato, garlic, onions and *tomates verdes* (see glossary). Peel the tomato and place in a saucepan with the other roasted vegetables.

✳ Toast the *chiles* (see glossary) on a *comal* or iron skillet and add them to the saucepan. Add the cloves, cinnamon, nutmeg, thyme, marjoram and water. Cover and simmer over low heat for 1 hour. Add the sugar, cover and cook over low heat for another hour. Let cool, then purée in a blender.

MAKES ABOUT 4 CUPS (32 FL OZ/1 L)

Soused Shrimp

Fish in Almond Sauce

PESCADO ALMENDRADO

Fish in Almond Sauce

This dish is well known among jet-setters, as it is based on a recipe from the famous Pipo's restaurant in Acapulco.

8 red snapper or sea bass fillets, about 4 oz (125 g) each
juice of 2 limes
1 teaspoon salt
¼ teaspoon freshly ground pepper
2 cups (16 fl oz/500 ml) thick cream (*crème fraîche*)
1 cup (5 oz/155 g) blanched almonds
2 tablespoons grated Parmesan cheese
¼ cup (2 oz/60 g) butter
1 cup (4 oz/125 g) grated *queso Chihuahua* (or Monterey Jack or medium-sharp Cheddar cheese)
8 small slices pickled *chiles jalapeños* (optional)
toasted slivered almonds, for garnish (optional)

❋ Marinate the fillets in the lime juice, salt and pepper for 1 hour in the refrigerator.
❋ Meanwhile, in a blender, purée the cream, almonds and Parmesan cheese. Set aside.
❋ Preheat the oven to 375°F (190°C). Melt the butter in a large skillet, add the fillets and sauté lightly on both sides. Transfer to a greased baking dish and cover with the almond sauce. Sprinkle with the *queso Chihuahua* and bake for about 15 minutes or until the cheese melts.
❋ Garnish with the sliced *chiles* and slivered almonds.

SERVES 8

CEVICHE

Marinated Fish

Almost every Pacific coastal state has its own version of this raw fish cocktail, which naturally cooks itself in lime juice. This recipe is typical of the ceviche *served in Acapulco. All kinds of firm fish can be used, as well as shrimp and scallops.*

2 lb (1 kg) mackerel, sea bass or red snapper fillets, cut into ½-in (1-cm) cubes
2 cups (16 fl oz/500 ml) fresh lime juice
⅓ cup (3 fl oz/80 ml) olive oil
3 cloves garlic
2 lb (1 kg) ripe tomatoes
1 cup (8 oz/250 g) chopped onion
⅓ cup (½ oz/15 g) chopped fresh *cilantro* (coriander)
½ cup (4 fl oz/125 ml) ketchup (tomato sauce)
2 tablespoons Buffalo sauce (mild red pepper sauce) (optional)
1 tablespoon dried oregano
½ teaspoon salt
¼ teaspoon freshly ground pepper
2 tablespoons finely chopped pickled *chiles serranos*
⅔ cup (3 oz/90 g) chopped green olives
whole olives, for garnish (optional)

❋ Place the fish in a glass bowl, cover with the lime juice and marinate at room temperature for 2½ hours.
❋ Heat the oil in a small skillet, add the garlic and sauté for 3 minutes. Discard the garlic and let the oil cool.
❋ Chop the tomatoes, removing the seeds but reserving the juice. Place in a large glass bowl, add the onion, *cilantro,* ketchup, Buffalo sauce, oregano, salt, pepper, *chiles* and olives and combine. Add the oil from the skillet and set aside.
❋ Rinse the fish 3 times in cold water. Cover with water, let stand for 5 minutes and rinse again. Add the fish to the tomato mixture. Add more salt and pepper if needed.
❋ If you like, garnish with whole clives. Serve cold with lime wedges and salt crackers.

SERVES 6–8

Ceviche

Country-Style Carp

ESTADO DE MÉXICO

CARPA CAMPIRANA

Country-Style Carp

Freshwater carp is a magnificent fish with a long and distinguished culinary history. In this unusual version of a marketplace favorite, the fish is encased in corn husks before baking. Catfish or even a firm-textured saltwater fish such as sea bass could be substituted for the distinctive-flavored carp. This recipe is by Mónica Patiño, who owns La Taberna del León restaurant in Valle de Bravo.

8 dried corn husks
2 tablespoons (1 oz/30 g) lard or oil
10 small white onions, quartered
6 *chiles serranos,* finely chopped
6 sprigs *epazote,* chopped
12 *tomates verdes,* husks removed and chopped
1 teaspoon salt, or to taste

¼ cup (2 fl oz/60 ml) olive oil
4 lb (2 kg) whole carp, boned

✳ Soak the corn husks in lukewarm water to cover for 1 hour. Rinse, drain and set aside.
✳ Melt the lard in a skillet. When hot, add the onions and sauté for 2 minutes. Add the *chiles, epazote* and *tomates verdes* and cook for 3 minutes, stirring constantly. Add the salt and set aside to cool. Mix in the olive oil, reserving some to lightly oil the fish.
✳ Preheat the oven to 400°F (200°C). Lay 4 of the corn husks in a rectangular glass baking dish and place the carp on top. Stuff as much of the *tomate verde* mixture as you can into the fish cavity. Sew the opening closed with a trussing needle and string. Lay the remaining corn husks on top. Tie the bottom and top husks together to enclose the whole fish.
✳ Bake for 30 minutes.
✳ To serve, remove the husks from the top. Cut and discard the string. Pass the fish in the baking dish.

SERVES 6

TABASCO

Arroz con Mariscos

Rice with Seafood

Although variations of this paella-like dish are popular on both coasts, it is most typical in Tabasco with its abundance of rice and fish. Different seafoods may be substituted.

2 lb (1 kg) octopus, cleaned
1 cup (8 fl oz/250 ml) water
1 lb (500 g) clams in their shells

2 cloves garlic
1 small chunk onion
2 tomatoes
½ cup (4 fl oz/125 ml) oil
2 cups (11 oz/345 g) long-grain white rice
3 cups (24 fl oz/750 ml) hot water
1 sprig parsley
2 teaspoons salt
12 medium shrimp (prawns) in their shells
1 lb (500 g) fish fillets
3 *chiles poblanos,* roasted (see glossary), membranes
   removed and cut into strips

Rice with Seafood

✳ Cook the octopus in a pressure cooker with ½ cup (4 fl oz/125 ml) of the water for 10 minutes or until tender. (Or place in a saucepan with 6 cups (48 fl oz/1.5 l) water, bring to a boil, cover and simmer for 45–60 minutes.) Drain the octopus, then use a tablespoon to scrape off the suckers and thick skin. Cut into 2-in (5-cm) pieces and set aside.

✳ Steam the clams in the remaining ½ cup (4 fl oz/125 ml) water in a covered saucepan just until they open. Strain, reserving their juices, and set aside.

✳ In a blender, purée the garlic, onion and tomatoes; strain and set aside.

✳ Heat the oil in a small *paella* pan or a large flame-proof casserole. Add the rice and sauté until the grains separate. Drain off the excess oil. Add the puréed tomatoes and cook, stirring constantly, for 2 minutes. Add the hot water, the juice from the clams and the parsley and salt. When the mixture comes to a boil, add the shrimp, fish and clams. Cook, covered, over low heat for 10 minutes. Correct the seasonings. Add the octopus and *chiles*. Cook, covered, for another 10 minutes or until the rice is tender but not mushy. If necessary, add more water.

SERVES 6–8

TAMAULIPAS

COCO CON MARISCOS

Seafood in Coconut Shells

Seafood stews are popular all along the Gulf coast, but this one from Tampico is unusual in that it is served in a hollowed coconut. Local cooks open coconuts with a machete, but a small saw works just as well. The shellfish can vary depending on what is available.

6 coconuts
2 lb (1 kg) octopus, cleaned
2 cups (16 fl oz/500 ml) water
2 cloves garlic
1 lb (500 g) medium shrimp (prawns)
20 clams in their shells
6 tablespoons (3 fl oz/90 ml) olive oil
1¾ cups (14 oz/440 g) chopped onion
1 tablespoon minced garlic
2½ lb (1.25 kg) tomatoes, peeled and chopped (5 cups)
1 teaspoon salt
8 oz (250 g) shucked (opened) scallops
1 cup (1½ oz/45 g) chopped parsley
10 oz (315 g) shucked (opened) small oysters
6 tablespoons (1½ oz/45 g) dry breadcrumbs
2 tablespoons (1 oz/30 g) butter, melted

✳ With a sharp heavy cleaver, cut off the tops of the coconuts. Pour out and save a total of 2 cups (16 fl oz/500 ml) coconut milk (coconut water) and set aside.

✳ Cook the octopus in a pressure cooker with ½ cup (4 fl oz/125 ml) of the water for 10 minutes or until tender. (Or place in a saucepan with 6 cups (48 fl oz/1.5 l) water, bring to a boil, cover and simmer for 45–60 minutes.) Drain, then scrape the octopus with a spoon to remove the suckers and cut into 1-in (2.5-cm) pieces. Set aside.

✳ Meanwhile, place 1 cup (8 fl oz/250 ml) of the water and the cloves of garlic in a saucepan, bring the water to a boil and add the shrimp. Cover and cook until the shrimp turn pink, about 4 minutes. Drain, reserving the cooking stock. Shell the shrimp and devein if needed.

✳ Rinse the clams and steam in the remaining ½ cup (4 fl oz/125 ml) water in a covered saucepan until they open. Drain, reserving all the liquid. Remove the clams from their shells and set aside.

✳ Preheat the oven to 375°F (190°C). Heat the oil in a large saucepan, add the onion and minced garlic and sauté until transparent. Add the tomatoes and salt and cook for 5 minutes. Add the coconut milk and reserved stock from the shrimp and clams. Bring to a boil and add the octopus, shrimp, clams, scallops and parsley. Cook, covered, for 5 minutes and correct the seasonings. Add the oysters and cook for 2 minutes.

✳ To serve, divide the seafood "soup" among the 6 coconut shells. Sprinkle with the breadcrumbs, drizzle with the butter and bake for 7 minutes.

SERVES 6

Seafood in Coconut Shells

Dried Cod Mexican Style

DISTRITO FEDERAL

BACALAO A LA MEXICANA

Dried Cod Mexican Style

This recipe from María Dolores Torres Yzábal is based on the traditional bacalao a la viscaína, Basque-style salt cod from the north of Spain. The original uses dried sweet red peppers and is considered one of the supreme dishes of that region. When preparing this dish, remember that reheated codfish is even better than freshly prepared.

2 lb (1 kg) dried salt cod
1 *chile ancho,* toasted (see glossary)
2 lb (1 kg) tomatoes
½ cup (4 fl oz/125 ml) olive oil
1 large onion, finely chopped
6 cloves garlic, finely chopped
1 bay leaf
pinch of ground cinnamon
pinch of freshly ground pepper
1 jar (7 oz/220 g) roasted red peppers

½ cup (2 oz/60 g) sliced blanched almonds
¼ cup (1 oz/30 g) raisins (optional)
½ cup (2½ oz/75 g) pimiento-stuffed olives
2 tablespoons capers (optional)
2 tablespoons chopped parsley
1 lb (500 g) small potatoes, cooked and peeled
salt (optional)
canned *chiles güeros*

✹ Soak the cod in cold water to cover for 12 hours, changing the water 2 or 3 times. Drain. Place in a saucepan, cover with water and bring just to a boil. Drain, remove the skin and bones, shred the flesh and set aside.
✹ Remove the stem and seeds from the *chile ancho* and soak in hot water for 10 minutes. Drain, then purée in a blender with the tomatoes and strain.
✹ Heat the oil in a large skillet, add the onion and garlic and sauté until transparent. Add the purée and cook over low heat until it thickens. Add the cod, bay leaf, cinnamon, pepper, red peppers, almonds, raisins, olives, capers and parsley. Stir, then cook over medium heat, covered, for 15 minutes. Add the potatoes, cover and cook over high heat for 10 more minutes to heat through. Add salt if required.
✹ Garnish with the *chiles güeros.*

SERVES 8

MICHOACÁN

PESCADO BLANCO DE PÁTZCUARO

White Fish from Pátzcuaro

Pescado blanco is considered the sublime fish delicacy of Mexico. Once plentiful in several lakes, it is now found, in reduced numbers, only in the high Lake Pátzcuaro. Its fame was increased by numerous publicity photos of the local Purépecha (Tarascan) Indians fishing with butterfly nets, now only brought out for special occasions. Another delicate white fish such as sole or flounder may be substituted.

6 white fish from Pátzcuaro, 5 oz (155 g) each, cleaned
juice of 4 limes
⅛ teaspoon salt
½ teaspoon freshly ground pepper
6 eggs, separated
all-purpose (plain) flour, about 1½ cups (6 oz/185 g)
2 cups (16 fl oz/500 ml) oil
2 limes, sliced
chopped tomato (optional)

✹ Rinse the fish and pat dry. Cover both sides with the lime juice, salt and pepper. Let stand for 30 minutes.
✹ In a deep glass bowl, beat the egg whites with a pinch of salt until they form stiff peaks. Add the yolks one at a time and beat lightly. Gradually add 1½ tablespoons flour and stir slowly.
✹ Heat the oil in a large skillet. Dredge both sides of the fish in the flour and shake off the excess. Dip the fish in the beaten eggs and fry one at a time until golden brown. Drain on absorbent paper.
✹ Serve garnished with slices of lime and, if you like, chopped tomatoes.

SERVES 6

COLONIAL TABLELANDS

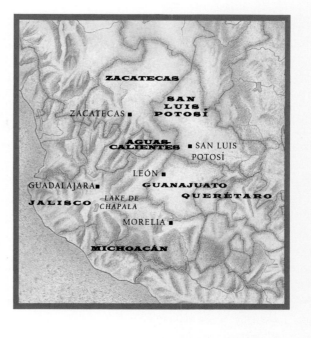

COLONIAL
TABLELANDS

Traveling to Mexico's high, fertile, mineral-rich plateau is like traveling to another time and place. Vestiges of its colonial past stand as reminders of Spain in an earlier era. In Morelia and Querétaro, graceful arches span Romanesque aqueducts, and in Guanajuato, flowerpots adorn wrought-iron balconies that overhang a maze of narrow hillside cobblestone streets. Dark cypresses brood over small tucked-away plazas in the cities, and massive churches and cathedrals dominate the skylines. In the mining city of Zacatecas, rows of mansions built by silver barons line the twisting cobblestone streets, studded here and there with churches of deep rose-colored stone. In the countryside, plodding oxen plow the sun-baked fields, and vineyards line the hills circling Aguascalientes and Querétaro.

Set somewhat apart from the rest of the region and long independent of Mexico City, Guadalajara is often thought of as "more Spanish than even Spain." Elaborately costumed *charros* (horsemen) still skillfully perform on their finely bred mounts in the gallant tradition of their Spanish ancestors, and the bullfight remains a regular Sunday activity.

The cuisine of this region is mostly simple, rustic dishes made from an abundant supply of vegetables and meat. A bowl of *pozole* (pork and hominy soup) is a favorite meal, and each state has its own version. In Jalisco and Aguascalientes, *birria,* a dish similar to the central region's *barbacoa,* is also popular. For *birria,* whole or large pieces of lamb or kid are thickly coated

Previous pages: The mazelike configuration of Guanajuato, an old silver-mining town. Left: The narrow cobblestone streets and elegant colonial architecture of Querétaro, a city of fascinating legends and patriotic memories.

with a rich purée of *chiles,* spices and other seasonings, sealed with a little liquid in a large container and slowly steamed for hours. *Birria* is served in its own spicy broth in hefty-size bowls and may be topped with chopped onions and dried oregano or *cilantro*—or shredded and served as a *taco.* Either way, it is delicious.

Pico de gallo ("rooster's beak"), a colorful combination of orange and *jícama* slices served with a scorchingly hot sprinkle of ground *chile piquín,* is a *botana* (snack) that goes well with Jalisco's most famous beverage, tequila. Outside Guadalajara, in the small towns of Tequila and Tepatitlán, this potent liquor is made from the fermented juice of *Agave tequilana,* a local species of maguey plant.

Before the coming of the Spanish, there were few settlements in the northern parts of this region. Only roaming bands of Chichimecs ("people descended from a dog") would pass through in search of wild animals, their diet supplemented by the plentiful prickly-pear cactus and various insects and their larvae. The lakes of Jalisco and Michoacán abounded in fish, and in the twelfth century the Purépecha, or Tarascan Indians, as they were called by the Spanish, settled around the beautiful Lago de Pátzcuaro, amid forest-draped hills and extinct volcanoes. They were one of the few tribes never conquered by the Aztecs, but when they offered their services to Cortés, his men, acting without orders, ruthlessly plundered their land. Worse still, a decade or so later one of the most brutal of the conquistadors, Nuño de Guzmán, sold many of the Indians into slavery, took the more beautiful of the women for his own use, and tortured and then killed their leaders. He then headed for Jalisco and Colima, plundering as he went, driven by a tale of a land ruled by women of great beauty and strength—the legendary Amazons. Disappointed in his search but ever ambitious, Guzmán founded the city of Guadalajara, which he named after his Arabic-rooted birthplace in Spain, Wad-al-had-jarah.

In an attempt to redress the horrors inflicted upon the Tarascans, Don Vasco de Quiroga was sent to Michoacán. This unusual man helped the Indians become more self-sufficient by developing their crafts—woodworking, copperware, weaving, pottery and lacquerware—all of which are found today in the markets and stores of the region. The Purépecha continue to live in the valleys scattered around the lake, much as they have for centuries. In boats hollowed out of tree trunks, early morning fishermen paddle silently through the reeds to toss their nets in deep water to catch the memorable *pescado blanco* (whitefish). Once plentiful in Jalisco's Lake Chapala, this delicate fish can now be caught only in Lake Pátzcuaro. Lakeside restaurants feature *pescado blanco rebozado,* in which the fish is lightly dipped in an egg batter and sautéed. Heaping mounds of *charales fritos,* crunchy fried little fish the size of sardines, are devoured like popcorn—head, tail and all.

Michoacán also has its share of unusual *tamales:* puffy, triangular ones called *corundas,* wrapped in fresh corn leaves instead of dried husks; delicious unfilled fresh-corn *uchepos,* served with thick cream and *salsa;* and innumerable sweet *tamales,* often colored in shades of pink or green and consumed with cups of frothy chocolate. Morning in Pátzcuaro finds housewives standing outside an open door of the cathedral's convent, waiting for the nuns to bring them their special

mixture of *chocolate de metate,* prepared from cacao, cinnamon and vanilla.

The tallest cathedral in Mexico soars over Michoacán's capital city of Morelia. Nearby, in a peaceful tree-lined plaza, dusk brings out vendors who prepare the very special *pollo de plaza,* a piquant chicken dish served with *enchiladas,* carrots and potatoes.

The people of Michoacán love sweets, and an entire market in Morelia is devoted to candies. One of the sweetest desserts ever devised, *chongos* (milk curds swimming in cinnamon-flavored syrup), was first made in Zamora in the northern part of the state.

The state of Guanajuato, like Michoacán, has had a tumultuous history. In the mid-1500s, when a group of friars was sent north to pacify the combative Chichimec Indians, they learned that silver was to be found nearby. Soon mines were established in Zacatecas, San Luis Potosí and Guanajuato. During the colonial period, a single mine in the state of Guanajuato produced one-fourth of the silver in the world. Named Cuanax-huato (Hilly Place of the Frogs) by earlier Tarascan settlers, the city of Guanajuato grew topsy-turvy up the side of a steep hill. The streets went every which way, skirting a deep ravine that cut through the center of the town. Many of Guanajuato's

A typical early morning vignette in Tequila. The town is best known for a more potent drink, however. Tequila is made from the locally grown small blue maguey plant.

On summer Sundays in Guadalajara, the crowds flock to the charreada, *Mexico's version of a rodeo, where the dashing* charros *thrill with lasso skills and other feats of superb horsemanship.*

residents became fabulously wealthy during this period, but the Indians were forced to work in the mines under inhuman conditions. They would remember such abuses well, and in 1810, under Father Hidalgo, joined with wealthy Creoles resentful of Spain's refusal to appoint them to leadership positions. In this city began the ten years of war and strife that eventually led to independence from Spain.

Although the town of Guanajuato was ravaged, the mines damaged and flooded, much of its past glory remains. It has the most architecturally splendid market in Mexico, constructed in 1910 from plans by Alexandre Eiffel. The Mercado Hidalgo resembles nothing so much as an old-fashioned train station, with Eiffel's distinguishing trademark of iron cross beams and glass. Under its vaulted roof, two floors of stalls sell every imaginable item of food, clothing, trinkets and household goods.

The miners' special *enchiladas* of fried chicken, potatoes and carrots are still served from smoking braziers outside the markets. The roads outside the city are lined with small stands selling fresh-picked strawberries and jewellike crystallized ones, for this is one of the world's largest strawberry-producing areas. The nearby town of Celaya is famous for *cajeta,* the soft, caramellike candies traditionally made of goat's milk and packed in little wooden boxes. Another very special dish from Guanajuato and the neighboring state of San Luis Potosí is *fiambre,* a purposefully jumbled mixture of sliced cold marinated meats—pork, chicken, beef tongue and pigs' feet—and colorful pieces of pickled vegetables.

In the nearby little state of Aguascalientes, fighting bulls are bred on the lush land, where large numbers of sheep and cattle graze. It is little surprise that the main courses set out on family tables are meat dishes—special versions of *birria, pozole* and *menudo.* A rejuvenating soup made from tripe, *menudo* is popular throughout the region, both as a filling breakfast or a late supper. An unusual version from the shoe-making city of León differs from those of other areas by including orange juice, red wine and almonds.

Peach and avocado orchards, fields of corn and globular heads of garlic and onions share the fertile valleys of Aguascalientes with clusters of small vineyards that produce some of the best wines in the country.

Verduras, Ensaladas, Frijoles y Salsas

Mexico's marketplaces provide a palette for the colorful spectrum of fresh produce.

Verduras, Ensaladas, Frijoles y Salsas

Tottering mounds of maize, baskets of beans—red, black, white, multicolored, speckled and striped—cacao, peppers, onions, a thousand kinds of green stuff, fruits, sweet potatoes and squashes greeted Hernán Cortés and the chronicler Bernal Díaz del Castillo when they first reached the great marketplace of Tlatelolco at the center of the Aztec empire. "As we had never seen anything like it, we stood amazed by the infinity of people and goods," wrote Díaz. It was said that 20,000 to 25,000 buyers and sellers came every day and that every fifth day there were twice that many.

The same vegetables are prized today. While they only occasionally show up as a salad or as a cooked side dish, they appear in just about every course put on the table except for dessert—and even that may be a dish of mashed and flavored sweet potato.

With a history going back thousands of years, squash has always played an important role in the Mexican diet. The *pepitas* (dried seeds) are eaten plain as snacks, or ground for flavoring and thickening the many varieties of *pipianes.* Squash flowers have long been considered a delicacy, and in Oaxaca the delicate young squash vines are made into a popular soup. Another member of this family is the pear-shaped *chayote,* which alone does not have a distinctive flavor

or texture. In fact, it can only be called bland, but with a little garlic or tomato or *chile,* turns out to be a very interesting vegetable.

Around the world, whenever Mexican food is mentioned, *guacamole* immediately comes to mind. Made from the nutritious avocado, it is served freshly made with most *antojitos.* Much less known than the avocado, *nopales* (cactus paddles) are beginning to appear more and more in the produce departments of supermarkets. The crisp new growth of the prickly-pear cactus, minus its prickles, is cooked and used in salads, *tacos* and scrambled eggs. The fruit, or cactus pear, is tremendously popular in Mexico and in much of the rest of the world.

Cilantro (coriander) is used to season virtually every type of dish. Also called Chinese parsley because of its use in many Oriental cuisines, it has a unique pungent flavor that complements spicy dishes. In the southern states of Mexico, the pungency of *epazote* is craved—a pot of black beans without this herb is simply incomplete. It is also in the south that the musky *hierba santa* is used to season *tamales,* chicken and, particularly in Veracruz, fish. This giant plant has velvety leaves that impart a sarsaparilla flavor to food.

The luscious, sensual spiciness of *chiles* is the seasoning most identified with Mexican cooking. All the *chiles* now grown throughout Mexico, the southwestern United States and Central America are derived from only five domesticated species that originated in South America. The same *chile* may be known by different names in Mexico, depending on whether it is fresh or dried or depending on the region in which it is grown. Eating any *chile,* whether it is described as mild or *picante,* is a little like an imaginary game of *chile* roulette, with wide variations in the degree of hotness due to such factors as soil and climate.

Tomatoes and *chiles,* onions and garlic—these four vegetables are the basis for the *salsas* that accompany virtually every meal in Mexico—every plate of eggs, every bowl of soup or piece of meat. The roughly chopped *salsa mexicana cruda* sits on the counters of neighborhood *taquerías,* and there is no end to the other fresh and cooked *salsas* that can be used to liven up a meal.

Salsas are also made from the wonderful but confusing *tomate verde* (green tomato), which is not a true tomato, though it is a member of the same nightshade family. Enclosed in a papery husk, this small lime-green fruit has a tart taste that blends perfectly with other ingredients when it is dehusked and cooked. It is available canned in specialty food stores, and many supermarkets and greengrocers now carry the fresh *tomate verde* under the name *tomatillo.*

Although *frijoles* (beans) may be considered the poor man's meat, they are eaten by all classes of people and in all parts of Mexico and the world. While a few—the fava, chick pea and soybean—originated in the Old World, most of the protein-rich legumes that we eat today have long been a part of the Mexican diet.

The Mexican people still painstakingly plant and cultivate their crops—most using the time-honored methods of the past. They have paid heed to the words of the ancient Maya leader Huehuetlalli, who admonished:

> Take care of the things of the earth;
> do something, cut wood, work the soil,
> plant the cactus, plant the maguey.
> You will have to drink, to eat, to dress.
> Thus you will stand on your feet, be real,
> thus you will stride,
> thus they will speak of you, praise you,
> thus you will be known.

A profusion of chiles *often leads to confusion: there are more than one hundred varieties in Mexico, and these dried* chiles *in Oaxaca may be called by a completely different name elsewhere in Mexico.*

GUERRERO

SALSA COSTEÑA

Chile Costeño Sauce

This table salsa is made with the searing-hot chile costeño, which is difficult to find outside the Pacific coast region of Mexico. The equally hot but shorter and wider dried chile de árbol can be substituted. Serve this sauce with fish, meat or chicken.

6 chiles costeños
8 tomates verdes, about ½ lb (250 g), husks removed
1 clove garlic
½ cup (4 oz/125 g) chopped onion
⅓ cup (½ oz/15 g) chopped *cilantro* (coriander)
½ teaspoon salt

✳ Toast the chiles on a *comal* or iron skillet (see glossary). They should turn dark but not be allowed to burn.
✳ In a saucepan, cook the *tomates verdes* in boiling salted water for 5 minutes. Drain.
✳ In a blender, purée the *chiles* with the *tomates verdes* and garlic. Do not strain. Transfer to a sauce dish, add the onion, *cilantro* and salt and stir. Correct the seasonings.

MAKES 1 CUP (8 FL OZ/250 ML)

MICHOACÁN

SALSA DE TOMATE VERDE CON AGUACATE

Tomate Verde Sauce with Avocado

Avocado has been added to this green table salsa, which makes it a richer condiment. The rest of the salsa can be made in advance, refrigerated and combined with avocado before serving.

5 chiles serranos
10 oz (315 g) *tomates verdes,* husks removed
1 clove garlic
1 tablespoon vinegar from pickled *chiles*
1 pickled *chile serrano,* seeds removed
1 teaspoon salt
½ cup (¾ oz/20 g) coarsely chopped *cilantro* (coriander)
1 avocado, peeled, pitted and cubed
⅓ cup (3 oz/90 g) finely chopped onion

✳ Place the fresh *chiles* in a large saucepan of boiling water. After 5 minutes, add the *tomates verdes.* After about 3 minutes, remove the *chiles* and *tomates verdes* and drain.
✳ Purée the *chiles, tomates verdes,* garlic, vinegar and pickled *chile* in a blender. Add the salt and *cilantro* and blend for 2 short cycles.
✳ In a bowl, combine the purée, avocado and onion. Correct the seasonings.

MAKES ABOUT 1½ CUPS (12 FL OZ/375 ML)

SALSA DE MOLCAJETE

Molcajete Sauce

While most table salsas are either fresh or cooked, in this version the flavor of the chiles and tomatoes is intensified by roasting. Some salsas can be made in a blender, but the texture of this one is much better when made in the traditional molcajete, as it is important that it be chunky, not smooth. This salsa complements any of the masa antojitos in Chapter 2.

5 chiles serranos
2 ripe tomatoes
1 clove garlic
1 teaspoon salt

✳ On a *comal* or iron skillet, roast the *chiles* and tomatoes (see glossary) for 8 minutes or until they are soft. Peel off and discard the burned skin from the tomatoes. In a mortar or *molcajete,* grind the *chiles* and garlic. When they are roughly chopped, add the tomatoes and continue grinding. Add the salt. Serve in the *molcajete* or a small bowl.

MAKES 1½ CUPS (12 FL OZ/375 ML)

VERACRUZ

SALSA DE CACAHUATE

Peanut Sauce

Ground peanuts and chiles are the base for this unusual table salsa, which is used on grilled meats and eggs and to add flavor to plain rice.

5 chiles anchos
3 chiles pasillas
3 chiles costeños
2 cups (16 fl oz/500 ml) hot water
2½ cups (12 oz/375 g) unsalted peanuts, skins removed
4 cloves garlic
¼ onion, cut in half
1 tablespoon oil
1 tablespoon salt
½ cup (4 fl oz/125 ml) chicken stock (page 72) (optional)

✳ Toast the *chiles* on a *comal* or iron skillet (see glossary), remove the seeds and membranes and soak in the hot water for 20 minutes. Transfer the *chiles* and water to a blender, add the peanuts, garlic and one piece of the onion and purée.
✳ Heat the oil in a skillet, add the remaining piece of onion and sauté for 2 minutes. Remove and discard. Add the *chile* purée to the skillet and boil for 5 minutes. Stir in the salt and boil for 10 more minutes. If the sauce is too thick, thin with the stock.

MAKES 2 CUPS (16 FL OZ/500 ML)

Top to bottom: Chile Costeño Sauce, Molcajete Sauce, Tomate Verde Sauce with Avocado, Peanut Sauce

Top to bottom: Mexican Sauce, Guajillo Chile Sauce,
Deviled Sauce, Cooked Tomate Verde Sauce

Salsa Endiablada

Deviled Sauce

Versions of this bottled salsa *are found throughout Mexico,
sprinkled on beans, broiled meats or any dish needing a little
more fire. It is very* picante *and lasts forever. This version is
from Socorrito Zorrilla.*

20 *chiles pasillas,* seeds and membranes removed
1 large onion
2 heads garlic
2 cups (16 fl oz/500 ml) cider vinegar
1 tablespoon each dried marjoram, oregano and
   crumbled bay leaf
5 black peppercorns
3 whole cloves
1 cup (8 fl oz/250 ml) olive oil
salt

✳ Toast the chiles (see glossary) on a *comal* or iron skillet
with the onion and garlic. Place in a saucepan with the
vinegar, herbs, peppercorns and cloves and boil for 20
minutes.
✳ Transfer the mixture to a blender and purée until
perfectly smooth. Strain, return to the blender, add the
olive oil and purée again. Season with salt.

✳ Store in closed bottles. The longer the sauce ages, the
more flavor it will have.

MAKES 3½ CUPS (28 FL OZ/875 ML)

Salsa Mexicana

Mexican Sauce

*If the sweet field-ripened tomato is used to make this classic
condiment, which is served in every Mexican restaurant, it is
the perfect complement to* antojitos. *Notice that the
ingredients for this* salsa *should be finely chopped and not
put in a blender.*

3 ripe tomatoes, chopped
½ cup (4 oz/125 g) chopped onion
4–6 *chiles serranos,* chopped
½ cup (¾ oz/20 g) chopped *cilantro* (coriander)
2 teaspoons salt
2 teaspoons lime juice

✳ Combine the tomatoes, onion, *chiles, cilantro,* salt and
lime juice in a sauce dish. Stir well and correct the
seasonings. This *salsa* is best if prepared 1 hour in
advance so the flavors will blend.

MAKES ABOUT 1½ CUPS (12 FL OZ/375 ML)

GUERRERO

Salsa Chile Guajillo

Guajillo Chile Sauce

This simple salsa *does wonderful things for grilled meats or* tacos. *If any is left over, it will last in the refrigerator for several days.*

12 *chiles guajillos,* seeds and membranes removed
1 large tomato, about 8 oz (250 g), roasted (see glossary) and peeled
1 clove garlic
2 teaspoons salt
¼ cup (2 fl oz/60 ml) water

✻ On a *comal* or iron skillet, toast the *chiles* well, about 2 minutes (see glossary). Rinse but do not soak.
✻ In a blender, purée the *chiles* with the tomato, garlic, salt and water.
✻ *Variation:* Instead of the tomato, use 5 *tomates verdes,* husked and boiled for 5 minutes. Blend with the *chiles,* garlic, salt and water, then stir in 1 cup (1½ oz/45 g) finely chopped *cilantro* (coriander) and ½ cup (4 oz/125 g) chopped onion.

MAKES 1 CUP (8 FL OZ/250 ML)

Refried Beans

Salsa de Tomate Verde Cocida

Cooked Tomate Verde Sauce

An earthy, everyday salsa *found sitting in bowls on the tables of small restaurants throughout Mexico.*

3 cups (24 fl oz/750 ml) water
2½ teaspoons salt
2 cloves garlic
4 *chiles serranos*
1 lb (500 g) *tomates verdes,* husks removed
½ cup (¾ oz/20 g) loosely packed *cilantro* (coriander)
¼ cup (2 oz/60 g) chopped onion

✻ In a saucepan, bring the water and 1 teaspoon of the salt to a boil. Add the garlic, *chiles* and *tomates verdes* and simmer, uncovered, for 8–10 minutes. Drain, reserving ½ cup (4 fl oz/125 ml) of the liquid.
✻ Transfer the garlic, *chiles, tomates verdes* and liquid to a blender. Add the *cilantro* and remaining salt and purée briefly. Transfer to a bowl.
✻ Stir in the onion and let the sauce cool before serving. It can be refrigerated for up to 3 days.

MAKES 2 CUPS (16 FL OZ/500 ML)

Frijoles Refritos

Refried Beans

Here is one dish where using a flavorful homemade lard definitely makes a difference. Canned beans, in a pinch, can be substituted for the frijoles de la olla, *using approximately 1 cup water (in place of the bean liquid) to 3 cups beans. Don't think that refritos means to fry twice; it simply means "well fried"—until all the liquid is gone.*

½ cup (4 oz/125 g) lard or oil
½ onion, cut into chunks
4 cups (32 fl oz/1 l) *frijoles de la olla* (page 208) with their liquid
crumbled *queso fresco* (or feta cheese) (optional)
fried tortilla strips* (optional)

✻ Melt the lard in a large skillet, add the onion and sauté, stirring frequently, for 5 minutes or until golden and soft. Remove and discard onion. Add half of the beans with their liquid and mash in the skillet with a potato masher. Gradually add the remaining beans and liquid and continue mashing to make a coarse purée. Stir and cook over medium-high heat until the purée begins to dry out.
✻ Transfer to a warm platter and, if desired, sprinkle with cheese and garnish with tortilla strips.
✻ *Variation:* If you like the taste of onion, you can use finely chopped onion, in which case do not discard.

*Cut 4 day-old corn tortillas in half, then cut into ½-in (1.5-cm) strips. Heat ½ in (1 cm) oil in a small skillet and, when hot, add the tortilla strips a few at a time and fry, turning at least once, for about 3 minutes or until golden brown. Remove from the oil with a slotted spatula and drain on absorbent paper. (If using fresh tortillas, dry first in a preheated 250°F/120°C oven for an hour.)

SERVES 6

Hacienda-Style Artichokes

GUANAJUATO

ALCACHOFAS DE LA HACIENDA

Hacienda-Style Artichokes

Artichokes were fashionable in nineteenth-century Mexican cuisine—stuffed with almonds, ham or mushrooms, or fried in an egg batter. This particular recipe was served at the table of Count de Valenciana, who owned the biggest silver mine in Mexico.

6 large artichokes
2 tablespoons salt
2 bay leaves
1 teaspoon baking soda (bicarbonate of soda) (optional)

DRESSING

4 hard-boiled (hard-cooked) eggs, finely chopped
1 cup (8 oz/250 g) finely chopped onion
¾ cup (6 fl oz/180 ml) mayonnaise
1½ tablespoons Dijon mustard
2 teaspoons red wine vinegar
2 teaspoons olive oil
⅓ cup (½ oz/15 g) minced parsley
½ teaspoon salt
¼ teaspoon white pepper

✻ Cut the stems of the artichokes flush with the bottoms and cut off the tips of the leaves.
✻ Place about 3 quarts (3 l) of water in a large pot with the salt, bay leaves and baking soda. Bring to a boil and add the artichokes. Cover and cook for 15–20 minutes or until an artichoke leaf can easily be removed from the base. Drain. With a spoon or small knife, pull out the fuzzy choke in the center of each artichoke and discard. Place the artichokes upside down on a platter and chill.
✻ To make the dressing, combine the eggs, onion, mayonnaise, mustard, vinegar, oil, parsley, salt and pepper. If the mixture is too thick, thin with water to the desired consistency. Chill.
✻ Immediately before serving, spoon the dressing into the center of each artichoke.

SERVES 6

ENSALADA CESAR

Caesar Salad

Caesar salad has had a following ever since the late 1920s, when it was created by two Italian brothers, Alex and Caesar Cardini, in their Tijuana restaurant. It is now featured in many restaurants worldwide, although few versions bear a close resemblance to the original.

2 large heads of romaine (cos) lettuce
5 cloves garlic
1 can (2 oz/56 g) anchovy fillets
3 egg yolks
¼ teaspoon freshly ground pepper
½ teaspoon Maggi (or Worcestershire) sauce
½ teaspoon Worcestershire sauce
¼ cup (2 fl oz/ 60 ml) lime juice
1 cup (8 fl oz/250 ml) plus 2 tablespoons olive oil
⅓ cup (1½ oz/45 g) grated Parmesan cheese
12 slices of *bolillo* (hard bread roll) or *baguette*

✻ Remove the outer leaves from the lettuce; use only the tender centers. Rinse the lettuce, drain and set aside.
✻ Mash the garlic in a mortar or *molcajete*. Place the anchovies in a large bowl and finely shred with a fork. Add the garlic and mix together. Whisk in the egg yolks, then the pepper and the Maggi and Worcestershire sauces. Stir well and add the lime juice. The mixture should be pale yellow in color.
✻ Add the cup of olive oil in a thin stream while whisking constantly. Add 2 tablespoons of the Parmesan cheese.
✻ Heat the remaining oil in a skillet, add the bread slices and fry briefly. Drain and set aside.
✻ To serve, gently toss the lettuce in the dressing and arrange on each plate with 2 slices of fried bread on top. Sprinkle with the remaining cheese and serve immediately.

SERVES 6

Caesar Salad

SINALOA

Ensalada Mixta Con Aderezo de Aguacate

Mixed Salad with Avocado Dressing

Avocado adds a Mexican touch to this green salad popular in the coastal resorts. Romaine lettuce would be used in Mexico, but any greens can be substituted.

1 large head of romaine (cos) lettuce, torn into bite-size pieces
1½ avocados, cut into thick slices
2 large firm, ripe tomatoes, cut into wedges
3 green (spring) onions, sliced (optional)

DRESSING

2 tablespoons mayonnaise
6 cloves garlic
¼ cup (2 oz/60 g) chopped onion
1 tablespoon lime juice
½ teaspoon dried thyme
½ teaspoon salt
¼ teaspoon freshly ground pepper
1 bay leaf
½ avocado, peeled and pitted
½ cup (4 fl oz/125 ml) water
1 cup (8 fl oz/250 ml) corn oil

✻ To make the dressing, purée the mayonnaise, garlic, onion, lime juice, thyme, salt, pepper, bay leaf, avocado and water in a blender. With the motor running, add the oil in a thin stream until the mixture forms an emulsion, about 2 minutes. Chill.
✻ Arrange the lettuce on a platter and top with the avocados and tomatoes. Cover with the dressing, garnish with the green onions and serve immediately.

SERVES 6

DISTRITO FEDERAL

Ensalada de Chile Ancho con Queso Fresco

Ancho Chile Salad with Cheese

This salad of marinated chiles anchos *makes an easy accompaniment to many Mexican meals, especially simple, mild-flavored fish dishes such as* huachinango a la naranja *(page 172). This recipe comes from Sara Luisa García Sabaté de Naranjo.*

5 oz (155 g) *chiles anchos*
3 tablespoons red wine vinegar
2 tablespoons oil
¼ teaspoon salt
⅛ teaspoon freshly ground pepper
4 oz (125 g) *queso fresco* (or feta cheese), crumbled
1 head of Boston or bibb (butterhead) lettuce

✻ Remove the seeds from the *chiles.* Cut the *chiles* into slices 1 in (2 cm) wide. Rinse and drain.
✻ Combine the *chiles,* vinegar, oil, salt and pepper in a deep bowl. Stir, then let stand for 24 hours.
✻ Stir the mixture and correct the seasonings. Arrange leaves of the lettuce on salad plates, spoon the *chile* mixture on top and sprinkle with the crumbled cheese. Garnish, if you like, with thin strips of *jícama* (yam bean).

SERVES 6

Mixed Salad with Avocado Dressing (left)
and Ancho Chile Salad with Cheese (right)

Rosaura Salad

Ensalada Rosaura

Rosaura Salad

María Dolores Torres Yzábal won an award for this surprising salad at a Christmas food festival held at the Museum of Popular Cultures in Mexico City. Among its unusual ingredients is acitrón, *a candied cactus fruit native to the Baja Californias used mainly in* picadillos *(meat fillings) and Christmas breads.*

1 lb (500 g) red cabbage, thinly sliced
2 small raw beets, peeled and shredded
8 oz (250 g) spinach, thinly sliced
1 jícama (yam bean), about 10 oz/315 g, peeled and cut into sticks
½ onion, thinly sliced
3½ oz (100 g) *acitrón* (candied cactus), diced (if unavailable, use candied pineapple)
1 cup (3 oz/90 g) croutons
½ cup (2 oz/60 g) amaranth seeds or toasted sesame seeds

VINAIGRETTE

1½ teaspoons soy sauce
½ cup (4 fl oz/125 ml) corn oil
2 tablespoons cider vinegar
1 teaspoon (or to taste) chicken bouillon granules
1 teaspoon dried tarragon
½ teaspoon dried oregano
½ teaspoon *fines herbes*

AVOCADO DRESSING

1 cup (8 fl oz/250 ml) milk
1 clove garlic
1 tablespoon lime juice
1 cup (8 fl oz/250 ml) cream (any kind)
2 avocados
salt
1 tablespoon finely chopped chives

✱ Fifteen minutes before serving, combine the cabbage, beets, spinach, *jícama,* onion and *acitrón* in a salad bowl.
✱ To prepare the vinaigrette, mix all the ingredients together. (The vinaigrette can be made 6 hours in advance.)
✱ To prepare the avocado dressing, purée the milk and garlic in a blender. Add the lime juice, cream, avocados and salt to taste and blend until smooth. Pour into a small bowl and stir in the chives. (This dressing can be made half an hour in advance.)
✱ Add the vinaigrette to the salad and mix well. Sprinkle the croutons on top.
✱ Place the avocado dressing on one side of the salad bowl and a bowl of the amaranth or sesame seeds on the other. Each person takes a serving of the salad, adding the avocado dressing and a few of the seeds to taste.

SERVES 12

DISTRITO FEDERAL

ENSALADA DE NOPALITOS Y JÍCAMA

Cactus and Jícama Salad

This is a refreshing composed salad that makes a colorful display of nopal cactus, jícama, tomato and avocado.

1 tablespoon oil
2 paddles of nopal cactus (12 oz/375 g), cut into strips
 ½ in (1 cm) wide
3 cups (1½ lb/750 g) peeled and grated *jícama* (yam
 bean)
¼ cup (2 fl oz/ 60 ml) fresh lime juice
1 teaspoon salt
6 tablespoons olive oil
3 tablespoons red wine vinegar
½ teaspoon salt
¼ teaspoon freshly ground pepper
ground *chile piquín* (optional)
2 cups (3 oz/90 g) watercress, stems removed and
 rinsed
2 avocados, peeled, pitted and cut into strips
3 tomatoes, cut into wedges

✱ Heat the oil in a skillet, add the cactus and sauté for 3 minutes. Cover and cook over low heat for 8 minutes or until crisp-tender. Set aside.
✱ In a bowl, combine the *jícama,* lime juice and salt. Set aside.
✱ Combine the oil, vinegar, salt and pepper. Stir well and correct the seasonings.
✱ To serve, place the *jícama* in the center of a platter, sprinkle lightly with *chile piquín* and arrange the watercress, avocados and tomatoes around it. Place a circle of cactus strips around the edge of the platter. Pour the vinaigrette dressing over the salad and serve.

SERVES 6

Cactus and Jícama Salad

Spinach Salad with Jamaica Flower Dressing

GUERRERO

ENSALADA DE ESPINACA CON JAMAICA

Spinach Salad with Jamaica Flower Dressing

Dried jamaica *and watercress are an unusual addition to this spinach salad by Kay Mendieta de Alonso. The deep-red* jamaica *flowers can be purchased in most Hispanic markets.*

10 oz (315 g) fresh spinach
1 small bunch watercress (optional)
6 slices bacon
1 clove garlic
⅓ cup (2 oz/60 g) dried *jamaica* flowers
½ cup (4 fl oz/125 ml) plus 1 tablespoon corn oil
2 tablespoons red wine vinegar or to taste
¼ teaspoon salt
¼ teaspoon freshly ground pepper
6 green (spring) onions, thinly sliced

✱ Rinse the spinach, drain, cut into strips and set aside. Rinse the watercress, remove the stems and set aside.
✱ In a large skillet, fry the bacon until it is brown and crisp. Remove and crumble into bits. Set aside.
✱ Grind the garlic with the *jamaica* flowers in a mortar or *molcajete.* Add a tablespoon of the oil and grind to form a paste. Rinse the mortar with the rest of the oil and transfer to a bowl. Add the vinegar, salt and pepper, stir well and let stand for 2 hours.
✱Strain the dressing and correct the seasonings. (*Note:* The dressing can be served without straining if you prefer.)
✱ To serve, arrange the spinach on a plate, place the watercress on top, then the green onion. Cover with the dressing and sprinkle with the bacon bits.

SERVES 4

HIDALGO

Nopalitos

Cactus Paddles

The paddles or joints of the nopal cactus are cultivated as a green vegetable throughout Mexico. They do exude an okra-like slimy substance when cooked, which needs to be washed off in cold running water. Serve the cactus paddles with tortillas for making tacos or as a side dish.

3½ cups (11 oz/345 g) finely chopped paddles of nopal cactus
1 teaspoon baking soda (bicarbonate of soda)
3 cloves garlic
½ onion
6 *chiles serranos*
1 lb (500 g) tomatoes
1 tablespoon oil
½ cup (¾ oz/20 g) finely chopped *cilantro* (coriander)
½ teaspoon salt

✳ Place the chopped cactus paddles in a saucepan and add water to cover. Add the baking soda, garlic and onion, cover and cook over medium heat for 10–15 minutes. Drain and remove the garlic and onion.
✳ Cook the *chiles* in boiling water for 5 minutes. Add the tomatoes, cook for 3 more minutes and drain. Peel the tomatoes and purée with the *chiles* in a blender.
✳ Heat the oil in a skillet, add the purée and sauté for 5 minutes. Add the cactus and boil for 5 minutes. Stir in the *cilantro* and salt.

SERVES 4

Cactus Paddles

MORELOS

Ensalada de Chayotes

Chayote Salad

This simple salad makes use of the versatile chayote, the fresher the better. In some rural areas, the campesinos (peasants) fry the leaves of the chayote plant as a tasty filling for quesadillas.

2 lb (1 kg) *chayotes* (vegetable pears/chokos)
salt
6 tablespoons oil
3 tablespoons red wine vinegar
½ teaspoon salt
¼ teaspoon freshly ground pepper
1 teaspoon dried oregano
½ red onion, thinly sliced and separated into rings

✳ Place the *chayotes,* unpeeled, in a large saucepan. Cover with water, add a pinch of salt and cook, covered, for 30–40 minutes or until they can easily be pierced with a fork. Drain and let cool for 5 minutes. Peel the *chayotes,* cut in half, then cut each half into 3 or 4 strips. Chill.
✳ Combine the oil, vinegar, salt, pepper and oregano. Stir well and correct the seasonings.
✳ Before serving, mix the *chayotes* with the dressing, top with the onion and sprinkle with more oregano if desired. Let stand for 5 minutes before serving.

SERVES 6

GUANAJUATO

Ejotes con Cebolla y Jitomate

Green Beans with Onion and Tomato

In the large haciendas of Guanajuato, cooked fresh vegetables were often prepared as side dishes, served lightly chilled or at room temperature.

2 lb (1 kg) green beans, cut into 1½-in (4-cm) lengths
2 cloves garlic
3 tablespoons red wine vinegar or to taste
1 small sprig thyme or 1 teaspoon dried thyme
½ teaspoon salt
¼ teaspoon freshly ground pepper
½ cup (4 fl oz/125 ml) olive oil
1 large tomato, chopped
¼ cup (2 oz/60 g) chopped onion
1 tablespoon dried oregano

✳ In a large saucepan, boil the beans in salted water for 8–10 minutes or until crisp-tender. Drain, then soak in ice water for 10 minutes. Drain, pat dry and set aside.
✳ Purée the garlic, vinegar, thyme, salt and pepper in a blender. With the motor running, add the oil in a thin stream.
✳ About 20 minutes before serving, combine the beans, tomato and onion. Add the vinaigrette and sprinkle with the oregano.

SERVES 6

DISTRITO FEDERAL

ESCABECHE VICTORIOSO

Marinated Vegetables

This substantial pickled vegetable salad has been in the family of chef Victor Nava for four generations. The recipe uses shrimp but is often made with pig's feet—cooked with garlic, onions and herbs.

1 onion, quartered
2 bay leaves
2 sprigs thyme
2 sprigs marjoram
2 slices lime
1 teaspoon salt
20 shrimp (prawns)
1 cup (8 fl oz/250 ml) corn oil (or ½ corn, ½ olive oil)
4 onions, sliced
1 tablespoon prepared mustard
1 teaspoon chicken bouillon granules
1 tablespoon sugar
1½ teaspoons ground allspice
1½ teaspoons freshly ground pepper
2 sprigs parsley
½ cup (4 fl oz/125 ml) red wine vinegar
½ cup (4 fl oz/125 ml) water
20 small new potatoes, cooked but not peeled
12 small young carrots, cooked

12 small round squash or zucchini (courgettes), cooked
10 florets of cauliflower, cooked
½ cup (2 oz/60 g) fresh or frozen green peas, cooked
1 small can (7 oz/220 g) mushrooms
2 red bell peppers (capsicums), roasted (see glossary), peeled and cut into strips
dried oregano

✳ In a large saucepan, place the quartered onion, 1 bay leaf, 1 thyme sprig, 1 marjoram sprig, the lime slices and salt in 2 qt (2 l) water. Bring to a boil and add the shrimp. When the water returns to a boil and the shrimp turn pink, drain. Peel the shrimp and set aside.

✳ In a large pot or Dutch oven, heat the oil over medium heat. Add the sliced onions and sauté until transparent, stirring constantly. Transfer the onions to a plate and set aside. In the same oil, sauté the mustard, bouillon granules and sugar for 2 minutes. Add the allspice, pepper, parsley, vinegar, water and remaining bay leaf, thyme sprig and marjoram sprig. Return the onion to the pan and boil for 5 minutes.

✳ Remove from the heat and add the shrimp, potatoes, carrots, squash, cauliflower, peas, mushrooms and bell peppers. Sprinkle with oregano, correct the seasonings and let the combined vegetables cool.

✳*Variation:* Substitute cooked pig's feet for the shrimp.

SERVES 10

Marinated Vegetables (left), Chayote Salad (center) and Green Beans with Onion and Tomato (right)

New Potatoes with Garlic

ESTADO DE MÉXICO

ACELGAS CON PAPA Y CHORIZO

Chard with Potatoes and Chorizo

Swiss chard, a very popular green in Mexico, is the star of this hearty side dish, which is also used almost like an herb to add flavor to soups and broths.

1½ lb (750 g) chard (silverbeet), stems removed
1 tablespoon oil
10 oz (315 g) *chorizo* or other spicy sausage, casings removed, cut into chunks
½ cup (4 oz/125 g) finely chopped onion
2 potatoes, peeled and cubed
1¼ lb (625 g) tomatoes, puréed and strained
½ teaspoon salt

✱ Rinse the chard, place in a saucepan with just the water that clings to the leaves and cook, covered, for 5 minutes over low heat. Chop the chard coarsely and set aside.
✱ Heat the oil in a large skillet, add the *chorizo* and sauté over medium heat until the fat is rendered, 3–4 minutes. Remove the *chorizo,* add the onion and sauté in the skillet drippings for 2 minutes. Add the potatoes and sauté for 4 minutes, being careful not to let the onion burn.
✱ Add the chard, tomatoes and salt. Boil vigorously for 2 minutes. Add the *chorizo,* cover and cook over medium heat for 10–15 minutes or until the potatoes are tender.

SERVES 4–6

GUERRERO

PAPITAS DE CAMBRAY AL AJO

New Potatoes with Garlic

In the markets throughout Mexico, it is a common sight to see pyramids of very tiny potatoes arranged on mats on the ground. This dish can accompany grilled meats; it also makes a popular party appetizer.

2 lb (1 kg) very small new potatoes, unpeeled
½ cup (4 oz/125 ml) butter
1 tablespoon oil
8 cloves garlic, minced (about 2 tablespoons)
1 tablespoon salt
1 teaspoon freshly ground pepper
1½ tablespoons lemon juice (optional)
½ teaspoon Tabasco sauce

✱ Cook the potatoes in boiling salted water until tender, 20–25 minutes. Drain and set aside.
✱ In a large saucepan, heat the butter and oil. Add the potatoes and sauté for 8–10 minutes. Add the garlic, salt, pepper, lemon juice and Tabasco sauce, lower the heat and cook for 3–4 minutes or until the garlic turns a golden color; be careful not to burn the garlic.

SERVES 6

TABASCO

FRIJOLES DE LA OLLA

Pot Beans

Since, as it is said in Mexico, "not even mice will eat raw beans," the simmering olla *(clay pot) of beans is a constant in most kitchens. In modern Mexican homes, however, beans are often cooked in a pressure cooker, but they always seem to taste better made the traditional way.*

2 cups (12 oz/375 g) dried black, pinto or pink beans
10 cups (80 fl oz/2.5 l) water
⅓ onion
3 tablespoons (1½ oz/50 g) lard or bacon drippings
1 sprig *epazote*
2 teaspoons salt
3 *chiles serranos*

✱ Rinse the beans, cover with room-temperature water and let soak for at least 3 hours. Discard any beans that float, then drain.
✱ Place the beans in a large pot or Dutch oven and add the water, onion and lard. Cook, covered, over medium heat for 1½–2 hours or until tender. Make sure that there is always enough water to cover the beans; add more *hot* water if needed (be sure it is hot). When the beans are tender, uncover, add the *epazote,* salt and *chiles* and cook, uncovered, for 20 minutes. Correct the seasonings.

SERVES 6

*Chard with Potatoes and Chorizo (left)
and Pot Beans (right, with chorizo)*

Chopped Zucchini with Corn (left), Potato Patties (center) and Mushrooms with Epazote (right)

MORELOS

TORTITAS DE PAPA

Potato Patties

Vegetable fritters are a popular way of preparing vegetables in Mexico, particularly during Lent. They also accompany simple chicken and fish dishes such as huachinango a la talla *(page 173). These potato patties can be served with a fresh* salsa mexicana *(page 200) or a cooked* salsa.

2 lb (1 kg) baking potatoes, unpeeled
2 cups (8 oz/250 g) grated *queso manchego* (or Monterey Jack or medium-sharp Cheddar cheese)
3 eggs
¼ teaspoon freshly ground pepper
1 cup (8 fl oz/250 ml) corn oil
salt

✳ Cook the potatoes in boiling salted water for about 20 minutes or until they can easily be pierced with a fork. Drain, peel and mash the potatoes well. Knead the potatoes with your hands, working in the grated cheese. Form into 3-in (7.5-cm) patties.
✳ In a bowl, beat the eggs lightly and stir in the pepper. Dip both sides of the patties into the beaten eggs.
✳ Heat the oil in a large skillet until very hot. Add the patties 2 at a time and fry on both sides until they are lightly browned. Sprinkle lightly with salt and drain. Serve hot or at room temperature, accompanied by *salsa de jitomate* (page 150).

SERVES 6

ESTADO DE MÉXICO

HONGOS AL EPAZOTE

Mushrooms with Epazote

This basic recipe for cooking the many different wild mushrooms found in the markets of the central highlands during the rainy season can be used as a wonderful filling for quesadillas or

omelets. *If wild mushrooms are not available, the more easily obtained cultivated mushroom is a perfectly good substitute.*

2 tablespoons oil
¼ cup (2 oz/60 g) chopped onion
2 cloves garlic, chopped
10 oz (315 g) large wild mushrooms
2 *chiles serranos,* chopped
3 tablespoons chopped *epazote*
1 teaspoon salt
½ teaspoon freshly ground pepper

✳ Heat the oil in a large skillet, add the onion and garlic and sauté until transparent. Add the mushrooms, *chiles, epazote,* salt and pepper. Lower the heat, cover and cook for 5 minutes to blend the juices. Serve with warm corn tortillas, as a snack or a side dish.

SERVES 4–6

OAXACA

CALABACITAS PICADAS CON ELOTE

Chopped Zucchini with Corn

This is a very typical and simple way of cooking three of Mexico's contributions to the culinary world: squash, corn and tomato.

2 tablespoons oil
1 clove garlic, chopped
¼ onion, chopped
1½ lb (750 g) zucchini (courgettes), chopped (about 6 cups)
kernels from 2 ears (cobs) of corn (about 1 cup)
2 tomatoes, peeled and finely chopped
2 small sprigs *cilantro* (coriander)
1 teaspoon salt
½ teaspoon freshly ground pepper

✳ Heat the oil in a skillet, add the garlic and onion and sauté over medium-high heat for 2 minutes. Add the zucchini and corn and sauté for 2 minutes, stirring constantly. Add the tomatoes and cook over high heat until the mixture begins to bubble. Add the *cilantro,* salt and pepper, lower the heat and cover. Cook for 5 minutes or until the zucchini is tender.
✳*Variation:* Add strips of roasted *chile poblano* and sprinkle with *queso fresco* (or feta cheese) before serving.

SERVES 6

OAXACA

COLIFLOR Y CALABACITAS CAPEADAS

Cauliflower and Zucchini Fried in Batter

Cauliflower was probably introduced to Mexican cuisine by the French; it appeared on a menu in Emperor Maximilian's court in 1865. This recipe is prepared year-round but is especially popular during Lent.

6 small zucchini (courgettes)
1 small head of cauliflower, broken into 6 pieces
1 tablespoon milk
2 lb (1 kg) ripe tomatoes
¼ small onion
3 cloves garlic
½ cup (4 fl oz/125 ml) water
1 tablespoon oil
1 bay leaf
salt and freshly ground pepper
2 cups (8 oz/250 g) grated *queso manchego* (or Monterey Jack or medium-sharp Cheddar cheese)
5 eggs, separated
½ cup (4 oz/125 g) all-purpose (plain) flour
oil for frying

✱ In separate saucepans, cook the zucchini and cauliflower in boiling water, adding the milk to the cauliflower pan. When they are crisp-tender, drain and set aside.

✱ In a blender, purée the tomatoes, onion, garlic and water. Strain. Heat 1 tablespoon oil in a saucepan, add the tomato purée and boil vigorously over high heat for 5 minutes.

Add the bay leaf and salt and pepper to taste, cover and cook over medium heat for 8 minutes. Set aside.

✱ Cut the stem end off each zucchini and, with a long, thin knife, remove some of the center to form a "tunnel." Fill the tunnels with grated cheese and set aside. Push grated cheese into the cauliflower florets and set aside.

✱ Beat the egg whites until they form stiff peaks, then stir in the yolks one at a time. Spread the flour on a plate. Lightly dredge the vegetables in the flour, then dip into the beaten eggs, so that each piece is completely coated.

✱ Heat ½ in (1 cm) oil in a skillet. When hot, add the vegetables one or two at a time and fry, turning, so that each vegetable browns evenly. Transfer to a colander to drain.

✱ Before serving, heat the tomato sauce, place the fried vegetables in it, cover and cook over medium heat for 5 minutes.

SERVES 6

Cauliflower and Zucchini Fried in Batter

Pickled Chiles and Vegetables

CHILES Y VERDURAS EN ESCABECHE

Pickled Chiles and Vegetables

Attractive glass jars of pickled vegetables are displayed throughout central Mexico, and their enticing contents are used to accompany almost any main dish. They will last for several months in the refrigerator.

½ cup (4 fl oz/125 ml) oil
5 cloves garlic
4 carrots, sliced
8 oz (250 g) *chiles jalapeños,* cut in half, seeds and
    membranes removed
30 small white onions
3 small zucchini (courgettes), about 8 oz (250 g), sliced
8 oz (250 g) small mushrooms
1 sprig thyme
1 sprig marjoram
5 bay leaves
2 teaspoons salt
¼ teaspoon freshly ground pepper
2 teaspoon dried oregano
2 cups (16 fl oz/500 ml) white vinegar
¾ cup (6 fl oz/180 ml) water

✱ In a large skillet, heat the oil, add the garlic and carrots and sauté for 2 minutes. Add the *chiles,* onions, zucchini and mushrooms and sauté 3 more minutes. Add the thyme, marjoram, bay leaves, salt, pepper and oregano and stir well. Add the vinegar and water, bring to a boil, lower the heat and simmer, covered, for 7 minutes. Remove from the heat and let stand, covered, for 15 minutes.

✱ Transfer to a heatproof bowl and let cool. Marinate for at least 12 hours before serving.

SERVES 6

GUERRERO

Chiles Rellenos de Atún

Tuna-Stuffed Chiles

Although cheese, meat or beans are the traditional fillings for chiles poblanos, this unusual version uses a tuna-potato salad. It is served as a cold dish and, when combined with a soup such as sopa de ajo (page 84), makes a pleasant light lunch or supper.

6 *chiles poblanos*
salt
2 teaspoons white vinegar
1 tablespoon oil
1 bay leaf
¼ teaspoon dried oregano
1 clove garlic
1 red onion, thinly sliced
½ teaspoon freshly ground pepper
⅓ cup (3 fl oz/80 ml) water
1 tablespoon red wine vinegar

FILLING

2 potatoes, cooked, peeled and cubed (about 2 cups)
1 can (6½ oz/200 g) tuna fish, drained and flaked
2 tablespoons finely chopped onion
½ cup (4 fl oz/125 ml) mayonnaise
1 tablespoon lime juice
1 tablespoon red wine vinegar
salt and freshly ground pepper

✳ Roast and peel the *chiles* (see glossary). Make a lengthwise slit in each one, being careful not to break it, and remove the seeds and membranes. Soak the *chiles* in water to cover with 1 tablespoon salt and the white vinegar for 20 minutes. Rinse, drain and set aside.
✳ Heat the oil in a skillet, add the *chiles* and sauté lightly. Add the bay leaf, oregano, garlic, onion, ½ teaspoon salt, pepper, water and red wine vinegar. Cook, uncovered, over medium-high heat for 8 minutes. Remove from the heat and let cool. Reserve the cooking liquid.
✳ To make the filling, combine the potatoes, tuna, onion, mayonnaise, lime juice and vinegar in a bowl. Add salt and pepper to taste.
✳ Fill the *chiles* with the tuna mixture, arrange on a platter and cover with the cooking liquid from the skillet. Chill for at least 2 hours.

SERVES 6

CHIHUAHUA

Frijoles Maneados

Creamed Bean Dish

Popular in the dairy-rich north, this bean dish is an old family recipe from María Dolores Torres Yzábal. It is important that it be served very hot.

1 lb (500 g) dried pinto or pink beans
8 cups (64 fl oz/2 l) water
½ onion
1 cup (8 fl oz/250 ml) plus 3 tablespoons oil

⅔ cup (5 fl oz/160 ml) milk
2 teaspoons salt or to taste
2 *chiles anchos*, seeds and membranes removed
1 cup (4 oz/125 g) diced *queso manchego* or *queso Chihuahua* (or medium-sharp Cheddar cheese)

✳ Rinse the beans, cover with room-temperature water and let soak for at least 3 hours. Discard any beans that float, then drain.
✳ Place the beans in a large pot or Dutch oven with the water, onion and 3 tablespoons oil. Bring to a boil and simmer, covered, over medium heat until tender, about 20 minutes.
✳ Preheat the oven to 350°F (180°C). Using a slotted spoon, scoop a portion of the beans (along with a little of the cooking liquid) into a blender or food processor. Purée with about 3 tablespoons of the milk. Continue puréeing portions of the beans with the milk until all the beans are puréed and all the milk is used. As the beans are puréed, pour them into a casserole.
✳ Heat the remaining cup of oil, and when it is very hot, almost smoking, stir it into the beans. Not all of the oil will combine with the beans, but this does not matter. Stir in the salt.
✳ If the *chiles* are not soft, heat them briefly on a *comal* or iron skillet without allowing them to cook. Tear or break the chiles into strips and add them to the beans. Cover the casserole, place in the oven and bake for 1½–2 hours.
✳ Remove the casserole from the oven and add the cheese, pushing the pieces into the beans rather than stirring them in. The idea is to have bits of melted cheese, not to blend the cheese with the beans. Return the casserole to the oven for about 5 minutes or until the cheese melts. Serve very hot.

SERVES 8 *Photograph page 214*

Tuna-Stuffed Chiles

Creamed Bean Dish (top, recipe page 213) and Chile Strips with Cream (bottom)

DISTRITO FEDERAL

RAJAS CON CREMA

Chile Strips with Cream

These are an integral accompaniment to many grilled meat dishes and are also a good filling for tacos.

¼ cup (2 oz/60 g) butter or oil
1 onion, sliced
6 *chiles poblanos,* roasted (see glossary), peeled and cut
   into strips
½ teaspoon salt
⅓ cup (3 fl oz/80 ml) thick cream *(crème fraîche)*

✳ Melt the butter in a large skillet, add the onion and sauté until transparent. Add the *chiles* and cook over low heat for 10 minutes, stirring occasionally. Add the salt and cream. When the cream begins to bubble, remove from the heat and stir. Serve with tortillas.

SERVES 6

PUEBLA

CHILES EN NOGADA

Chiles in Walnut Sauce

This dish, resplendent with the red, white and green colors of the Mexican flag, was created by the imaginative Augustine nuns of Puebla for a visit by Mexico's very own emperor, Don Augustín de Iturbide, who, after the War of Independence, lasted a mere eleven months in office. It is featured as a main dish during August and September, when the new crop of walnuts is available. Although this dish appears complicated, the sauce and filling are best prepared the day before, and the chiles can be stuffed several hours in advance.

12 *chiles poblanos*
2 tablespoons salt
1 tablespoon white vinegar
5 eggs, separated
½ cup (2 oz/60 g) all-purpose (plain) flour
oil for frying
seeds of 1 pomegranate
sprigs of parsley, for garnish

NUT SAUCE

30 walnuts in their shells or 1 cup (3 oz/90 g) walnut halves
1½ cups (12 fl oz/375 ml) milk
1 cup (8 fl oz/250 ml) thick cream *(crème fraîche)*
6 oz (185 g) *queso fresco* (or feta cheese)
2–3 tablespoons sugar
pinch salt

FILLING

1 lb (500 g) pork loin
4 cups (32 fl oz/1 l) water
¼ onion, in a chunk
5 cloves garlic, 3 whole, 2 chopped
1 sprig parsley
1 tablespoon salt
⅓ cup (3 fl oz/80 ml) oil
¾ cup (6 oz/185 g) finely chopped onion
2 cups (1 lb/500 g) peeled and finely chopped tomatoes
4 tablespoons minced parsley
1 apple, peeled and chopped (about 1 cup)
1 large pear, peeled and chopped (about ¾ cup)
1 peach, peeled and chopped (about ½ cup)
1 plantain or large firm banana, peeled and chopped
   (about ¾ cup)
⅓ cup (2 oz/60 g) raisins
⅓ cup (2 oz/60 g) chopped blanched almonds

✳ To prepare the nut sauce, shell the walnuts, place in a heatproof bowl, cover with boiling water and let soak for 5 minutes. Drain, then peel the thin tan skin from the nuts. Place the walnuts in a small bowl, cover with 1 cup (8 fl oz/250 ml) of the milk and let soak for 12 hours.
✳ Drain the walnuts, discarding the milk. (If packaged nuts are used, reserve ½ cup/4 fl oz/125 ml of the soaking milk for use in puréeing the nuts.) Transfer the walnuts to a blender and purée with the cream, the remaining ½ cup (4 fl oz/125 ml) milk and the *queso fresco,* sugar and salt. Refrigerate.
✳ To prepare the filling, place the pork, water, onion quarter, 3 garlic cloves, parsley and half of the salt in a large saucepan. As soon as the water comes to a boil, cover and cook over medium heat for 40–60 minutes or until the pork is tender. Drain, reserving ½ cup (4 fl oz/125 ml) of the cooking stock. Let the pork cool briefly, then chop finely and set aside.
✳ Heat the oil in a large skillet or saucepan. Add the chopped onion and garlic and sauté for 4 minutes or until transparent. Add the tomatoes and minced parsley and cook for 5 minutes, stirring constantly. Mix in the remaining salt and the apple, pear, peach, plantain, raisins and almonds and cook over medium heat for 4 minutes. Add the pork and the reserved stock. Correct the seasonings and cook, uncovered, over low heat for 7–10 minutes or until the fruit is

cooked and the mixture has thickened. Set aside.

✴ Roast and peel the *chiles* (see glossary). Make a lengthwise slit in each one, being careful not to break it, and remove the seeds and membranes. Soak the *chiles* in water to cover with the salt and vinegar for 20–60 minutes, depending on how "hot" they are.

✴ Rinse the *chiles,* drain well and pat dry with paper towels. Use a spoon to place some of the meat mixture inside each *chile,* being careful not to overstuff or the filling will spill out when the *chile* is cooked. Set aside.

✴ Beat the egg whites until they form stiff peaks, then stir in the yolks one at a time. Spread the flour on a plate, turn each *chile* in it to coat lightly, then dip into the beaten eggs, so that the *chile* is completely coated.

✴ Heat ½ in (1 cm) oil in a skillet. When hot, add the *chiles* one or two at a time and fry on each side until lightly browned. Drain on absorbent paper. The *chiles* can be served cold or at room temperature. Arrange them on a platter, cover with the nut sauce and sprinkle with the pomegranate seeds. Garnish with sprigs of parsley.

✴*Variations:* There are as many minor variations of this recipe as there are people who prepare it. Some cooks add chopped citron, cinnamon and black pepper to the chopped meat mixture and a little sweet sherry or white wine to the nut sauce. Some use coarsely ground pork instead of cooked and chopped pork loin. The major difference is whether the *chiles* are covered with batter or not. Traditional recipes call for coating the *chiles,* but you may leave them uncoated, according to your taste and the amount of time you have to prepare them.

SERVES 12

Chiles in Walnut Sauce

PUEBLA

CHILES RELLENOS DE QUESO

Chiles Stuffed with Cheese

It is said that Emperor Maximilian liked a similar version of these cheese-stuffed chiles, *only prepared with* jocoque, *a rich, very thick soured cream.*

6 *chiles poblanos*
salt
2 teaspoons white vinegar
3 large ripe tomatoes
¼ small onion
1 clove garlic
1 tablespoon oil
2 bay leaves
½ teaspoon freshly ground pepper
3 cups (12 oz/375 g) grated *queso Chihuahua* (or
    Monterey Jack or medium-sharp Cheddar cheese)
3 eggs, separated
½ cup (2 oz/60 g) all-purpose (plain) flour
oil for frying

✳ Roast and peel the *chiles* (see glossary). Make a lengthwise slit in each one, being careful not to break it, and remove the seeds and membranes. Soak the *chiles* in water to cover with 1 tablespoon salt and the vinegar for 20 minutes. Rinse, drain and set aside.
✳ In a blender, purée the tomatoes, onion and garlic, then strain. Heat 1 tablespoon oil in a skillet, add the tomato purée and bring to a boil. Lower the heat, add 1 teaspoon salt, the bay leaves and pepper and cook, covered, for 10 minutes. If the sauce is too thick, thin with up to ¾ cup (6 fl oz/180 ml) of water. Set aside.
✳ Fill each *chile* with ½ cup (2 oz/60 g) of the grated cheese and set aside.
✳ Beat the egg whites until they form stiff peaks, then stir in the yolks one at a time. Spread the flour on a plate, turn each *chile* in it to coat lightly, then dip into the beaten eggs, so that the *chile* is completely coated.
✳ Heat ½ in (1 cm) oil in a skillet. When hot, add the *chiles* one or two at a time and fry on each side until lightly browned. Drain on absorbent paper.
✳ Before serving, heat the tomato sauce and arrange the *chiles* carefully so that each is almost covered with sauce. Cover and simmer for 5 minutes.

SERVES 6

DISTRITO FEDERAL

CHILES RELLENOS DE PICADILLO

Chiles Stuffed with Seasoned Meat

The ubiquitous chile relleno *is found throughout Mexico— with or without batter, with or without sauce. This is one of the most traditional versions. While care should be taken not to tear the* chile, *the batter is an effective sealer; for large openings, toothpicks can be inserted to close the gap. Chiles can be stuffed in advance and refrigerated. Bring to room temperature before frying.*

6 *chiles poblanos*
1 tablespoon salt
2 teaspoons white vinegar
½ cup chopped plantain or large firm banana
½ recipe for *picadillo* (page 132)
3 eggs, separated
½ cup (2 oz/60 g) all-purpose (plain) flour
oil for frying
3 large ripe tomatoes, peeled
¼ small onion
2 cloves garlic
salt and freshly ground pepper

✳ Roast and peel the *chiles* (see glossary). Make a lengthwise slit in each one, being careful not to break it, and remove the seeds and membranes. Soak the *chiles* in water to cover with the salt and vinegar for 20 minutes. Rinse, drain and set aside.
✳ Meanwhile, in a large saucepan, stir the plantain into the *picadillo,* cover and cook over low heat for 5 minutes. Fill each *chile* with 2 heaping tablespoons of *picadillo* and set aside.
✳ Beat the egg whites until they form stiff peaks, then stir in the yolks one at a time. Spread the flour on a plate, turn each *chile* in it to coat lightly, then dip into the beaten eggs, so that the *chile* is completely coated.
✳ Heat ½ in (1 cm) oil in a skillet. When hot, add the *chiles* one or two at a time and fry on each side until lightly browned. Drain on absorbent paper.
✳ In a blender, purée the tomatoes, onion and garlic, then strain. Heat 1 tablespoon oil in a large skillet, add the tomato purée and sauté briefly. Lower the heat and cook, covered, for 15 minutes. If the sauce is too thick, thin with water to the desired consistency. Add salt and pepper to taste.
✳ Place the *chiles* in the tomato sauce, cover and heat for 5 minutes. Serve covered with the sauce.

SERVES 6

PUEBLA

CHILES ANCHOS RELLENOS DE QUESO

Ancho Chiles Stuffed with Cheese

It is not just fresh green chiles *that are stuffed in Mexican cooking but also the dried. The* chile ancho *used here is the dried form of the* chile poblano. *For ease in stuffing, select* chiles *that are fat and not too twisted or brittle. This recipe is from Margot Rosenzweig de Palazuelos.*

6 *chiles anchos*
1 tablespoon oil
10 oz (315 g) *tomates verdes,* husks removed and
    quartered
½ large onion, cut into chunks
2 large tomatoes, each cut into eighths
1 teaspoon salt
1 cup (8 fl oz/250 ml) thick cream *(crème fraîche)*
1½ cups (6 oz/185 g) grated *queso manchego* (or
    Monterey Jack or medium-sharp Cheddar cheese)
½ cup (2 oz/60 g) all-purpose (plain) flour
3 eggs, separated
oil for frying

✳ Make a lengthwise slit in each *chile* and remove the seeds and membranes. Toast the *chiles* (see glossary),

Ancho Chiles Stuffed with Cheese (top), Chiles Stuffed with Seasoned Meat (center)
and Chiles Stuffed with Cheese (bottom)

then soak in warm water to cover for 5 minutes. Drain and set aside.

✳ Heat the oil in a large skillet. Add the *tomates verdes* and cook, stirring, for 3 minutes. Add the onion, cook for 3 minutes, then add the tomatoes and cook another 3 minutes. Stir in the salt and cream, cover and cook over medium heat until the sauce begins to bubble. Remove from the heat and set aside.

✳ Stuff the *chiles* with the cheese. Spread the flour on a plate.

✳ Beat the egg whites until they form stiff peaks, then stir in the yolks one at a time. Turn the *chiles* in the flour, shaking off the excess. Dip each *chile* in the beaten eggs, so that it is well coated.

✳ Heat ½ in (1 cm) oil in a skillet. When hot, add the *chiles* one or two at a time and fry on each side until lightly browned. Drain in a colander.

✳ Before serving, heat the sauce. Add the *chiles* to it, cover and cook over low heat for 3 minutes, just until the *chiles* are hot. Serve immediately.

SERVES 6

THE FRONTIER

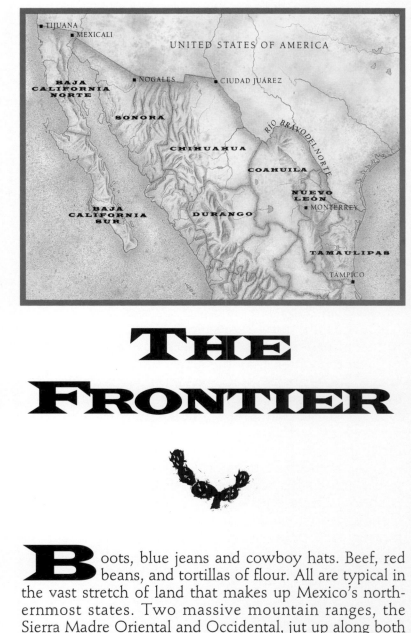

THE FRONTIER

Boots, blue jeans and cowboy hats. Beef, red beans, and tortillas of flour. All are typical in the vast stretch of land that makes up Mexico's north-ernmost states. Two massive mountain ranges, the Sierra Madre Oriental and Occidental, jut up along both coasts of Mexico, imprisoning between them a land of monotonous, empty deserts slashed by deep gorges, where sand devils spiral back and forth with nothing but dead brush for dance partners. It is a land rich in minerals, though, and when provided with water it is fertile and productive.

When soldiers and priests from Spain searched north-ward for gold and souls, they found an inhospitable land with tribes of Indians whose eating habits reflected their primitive, nomadic way of life. Even as late as the 1700s, a Jesuit priest described the natives as "all bar-barians and savages. In their foods, they don't use any condiments. They eat fresh meat, almost raw or dried or even burnt. They eat things that for us would not be edible such as roots, worms, lobsters, spiders, snakes, cats and even dried skins. A dog is as appreciated as a goat is to us."

As always, the Spanish brought their own food sources with them, and on these great plains of the north the herds of cattle increased rapidly, often running wild by the hundreds. The Spanish horses of Moorish breeding were the best in the world, and the cattle were fast and lean. Both the Indians and their conquerors literally swung into the saddle, and the great cattle industry of Mexico and Texas was born. Today the herds are more likely to be comprised of Angus, Holsteins or Herefords, but cattle ranching is just as

Previous pages: Punta Balandra, near La Paz, one of the dramatic rock formations that dot the wild Baja coast. Left: Ranchers take a break to enjoy a cup of coffee and perhaps a bowl of soup at Sonora's marketplace.

important to the economy and diet of Mexico as it was four hundred years ago.

Remembering the methods used by their families in Spain to preserve meat during long and hot periods of time, the settlers cut most of the beef into thin strips and dried it. Even though refrigeration has eliminated the need for drying, variations of dried beef, such as *carne seca, cecina* and *machaca,* still provide the basis for many regional dishes, and are used as a filling for *antojitos,* or shredded and scrambled with eggs.

While cattle are important, there is more to northern Mexico than ranching. Irrigation has brought large areas into cultivation, and modern agricultural and industrial cities (Monterrey is Mexico's third largest city) present a side of Mexico most tourists never see.

Dairy products abound in Mexico's four largest states—Sonora, Chihuahua, Coahuila and Durango. *Jocoque,* rich clabbered cream, is slathered on *antojitos* in Chihuahua and may be atypically flavored with *achiote* from Yucatán. No Mexican cheese has a greater international reputation than the giant wheels of Chihuahua cheese made in the state's Mennonite farming communities. Because of its melting qualities, Chihuahua is a favorite for stuffing *quesadillas* and fat green *chiles poblanos,* as is the more easily found *queso asadero,* or broiling cheese.

In the hottest arid parts of Coahuila and Nuevo León, it was hard to raise even cattle, but the nimble little goat is able to thrive on the meager vegetation it can find. Consequently, *cabrito,* or baby goat, is an especially favored food. Monterrey, the capital of Nuevo León, is known as the goat capital of Mexico. Here, *cabrito al pastor* (spit-roasted suckling kid) is served with flour

The north is ranch country, and beef is the most popular meat. Open-air steak restaurants serve grilled steaks with frijoles charros *(cowboy beans), downed with the local beer. Sharing the tabletop is a basket of* tortillas de harina, *the wheat-flour tortillas of the region.*

tortillas and *frijoles borrachos* (drunken beans), which are spiked with the local beer.

Mescal, distilled from the ever-present maguey, complements the simple foods of the rugged north, as do the many varieties of local beer. The famed margarita cocktail was created in 1942 by a barman in Chihuahua, but the idea of mixed drinks is far more popular with tourists than with the average Mexican, who prefers drinking tequila straight.

Early in the 1900s in the little border town of Tijuana, Caesar Cardini created the salad that still bears his name on restaurant menus around the world. An unusual dressing of garlic, anchovy, Worcestershire sauce and Parmesan cheese is poured over crisp romaine lettuce and tossed with crunchy croutons and a coddled egg to make a salad with a well-deserved reputation.

In the state of Chihuahua, high in the canyons of the Sierra Madre Occidental, is found the heartland of the Tarahumara Indians. The Tarahumaras, along with the Lacandón of Chiapas, are considered the two tribes of Indians most resistant to modern culture, preferring to live in isolated caves and crude huts.

Known as the "running people," the Tarahumaras still hold traditional running races lasting up to three straight days over rough terrain at high altitudes. First identified in the late 1800s, the tribe was thought to be on its way to extinction, a speculation that proved false. Today, more than 50,000 Tarahumaras live as they always have, with no apparent desire to be "assimilated."

Most tourists arrive in this remote land of the Tarahumara on one of the world's great railroad journeys—a twelve-hour, 300-mile-long trip that traverses the awesome Barranca del Cobre. This is North America's deepest series of canyons, more than 900 miles long, with a mile-long vertical drop to the river below. Arizona's Grand Canyon is insignificant by comparison.

Tamaulipas, in the northeasternmost corner of Mexico, is a state of real contrasts. Its very name means "high mountain," and its western boundary is the high mountain range of the Sierra Madre Oriental, yet there are long stretches of desolate beaches and lagoons along its Gulf coast. It has the same barren plains to the north as do the other border states, and pockets of dense tropical forests throughout the southern part of the state. The food of Tamaulipas is just as varied as the topography. There are the traditional beef and cheese dishes of the other border states, and seafood dishes similar to those of Veracruz to the south, but there is also a difference: everything just seems to be prepared on a bigger scale. The best-known dish associated with Tamaulipas is *carne asada a la tampiqueña,* a very large, very thin strip of grilled beef served with *enchiladas* and beans. Even the *tamale* made here is gigantic. Some say this is the influence of the Huaxtec Indians, who settled around Tampico before 1000 B.C. They were originally Maya, but separated from the rest of the tribe and migrated north, where their culture was marked by an emphasis on pleasure, gaiety and excess.

Baja California Norte, the top of the isolated finger of Mexico that protrudes between the Pacific Ocean and the Sea of Cortés, is one of the prime grape-growing regions of Mexico. The largest winery in Mexico, the Bodega de Santo Tomás, founded in 1888, is located in the mild and fertile valleys near Ensenada.

Farther south, on both sides of the mountainous spine of the Baja peninsula, the desolate landscape is broken by huge outcroppings of boulders and the twisted,

Choosing to remain apart from modern Mexican society, the Tarahumara Indians live isolated in the far reaches of the Sierra Madre Occidental in Chihuahua.

fantastic shapes of the *cirio,* or "boojum," trees. One of the few spots of green in this Dr. Seuss world surrounds the Río Mulegé, Baja's only river, barely one mile long. An oasis of date palms has been created here at the foot of the imposing Sierra de la Giganta, and, not surprisingly, dates are frequently used in local cooking.

Some of the most beautiful beaches in Mexico are snuggled into small coves between cactus-covered hills on the eastern side of Baja California Sur. Tall, craggy mountains provide a background for Cabo San Lucas and San José del Cabo, both considered world-class resorts.

The adjacent Sea of Cortés, also known as the Gulf of California, teems with more than 250 species of fish—including yellow-tail, grouper and pompano—as well as an abundance of shellfish. They are usually prepared in a simple manner, as in *ostiones en escabeche* (pickled oysters) or *sopa de almejas* (clam soup). The fish, lobster and shrimp are quickly grilled or served with garlic or a spicy tomato sauce. The large sea turtles that frequent these and other Mexican waters have recently been declared an endangered species by the Mexican government, so *caguama estofado* and other turtle dishes should no longer show up on restaurant menus.

Northern Mexico had no early culinary traditions to draw on. The few Indian tribes were nomadic; for them, eating was a matter of survival, not pleasure. The cuisine was developed by the *vaqueros* (cowboys), adventurers and others searching for opportunity and a new life—in both legal and illegal pursuits. The foods they ate reflected their outdoor and mobile way of life: meat cooked over a campfire of aromatic mesquite wood beside a pot of nourishing beans. Both were flavored with pungent garlic, onions and *chiles.* Fresh or aged cheeses were added, all served up in huge flour tortillas.

In time, new ingredients and new techniques were added, brought by cooks from other parts of Mexico and the world. The dishes became more varied and refined, but even today the foods of the frontier are the simple foods that symbolize the life of the *vaquero.*

PANES Y
POSTRES

Sugar skulls appear in the markets during late October, just in time for the Day of the Dead celebration.

PANES Y POSTRES

Little family-run *panaderías* (bakeries) in rural villages are baking the same breads that for generations have satisfied the souls and stomachs of the Mexican people. Made from wheat brought from the Old World and grown in the highlands around Mexico City, the hearty loaves with superb crust were soon considered "as good and cheap as in Spain."

During the short French occupation of Mexico (1864–67), breads, sweets and pastries assumed a major place in the meals of the ruling class. In Mexico City alone, there were 50 bakeries and 128 pastry and chocolate shops, plus 13 establishments devoted exclusively to making cakes.

It was during this time that the crusty little rolls called *bolillos* came into their own. Today, many restaurants serve covered baskets of this tasty bread with their meals. *Bolillos* are also lightly toasted to accompany *huevos rancheros* at the breakfast table. The *telera,* a flatter version of the *bolillo,* is used to make the remarkable *torta,* a many-layered sandwich found in small backstreet restaurants.

The Spanish brought with them their love for *pan dulce.* All sizes and shapes of wonderfully sweet yeast breads are an integral part of the early morning breakfast ritual. Fried fluted fritters called *churros* are another direct descendant from Spain. A simple dough of flour, water and egg yolks is squeezed into strips and quickly fried in pots of bubbling lime-seasoned oil. Dipped in sugar and eaten hot, *churros* make a perfect mobile breakfast or snack.

The savory smell of baking bread fills the rural villages throughout Mexico. The outdoor adobe ovens found behind family homes are heated with the hardwood of the region.

Previous pages: Oaxacan Egg Bread (left rear, recipe page 237), Day of the Dead Bread (center, recipe page 232) and Round Bread for the Day of Kings (right, recipe page 234)

226

Sweet breads go hand-in-hand with special holidays. In Oaxaca, Christmas Eve is the time for eating *buñuelos,* sweet finger-sticking fritters served in clay dishes. When finished, everyone is expected to joyfully hurl their dish onto the stone-paved street, smashing it into small fragments. In a continuation of the celebration, the eve of Epiphany is celebrated with the serving of *rosca de reyes* (ring of the kings), a traditional bread from Spain commemorating the search of the three kings for the baby Jesus. Hidden inside a crown of semisweet yeast bread decorated with gemlike crystallized fruits is a little doll representing the Christ child. A similar yeast bread is made for All Saints Day and the Day of the Dead during the first days of November.

The pre-Conquest Indians, with only honey available to them, did not have the passion for sweets that Mexicans now have. After a meal, an Aztec noble would be well satisfied by a piece of fruit from a nearby garden or the countryside—melon, papaya, guava, *guanábana* or the luscious pineapple. The Dominican friar Thomas Gage, who chronicled the early eating habits of the Mexicans, reminisced in 1625: "But I cannot forget that which they call piña, or pineapple; not the pineapple of the high pine trees, but a pineapple that groweth upon a lower shrub with prickly leaves, and is bigger than our biggest musk melons in England; when it is ripe, it is yellow without and within. But the better way of eating it is preserved, which is absolutely the best preserve in all that country."

Preserved or candied fruits and nuts are still favorite sweets in Mexico: jewellike *cubitos de ate* (fruit jellies); crystallized figs, pineapples, mangoes and tamarinds; and vivid-green candied limes stuffed with shreds of coconut. Market stands sell great chunks of candied cactus, sweet potatoes and pumpkin, and jars of sugar-coated almonds. Special nut brittles made of peanuts, walnuts, pecans, or sesame or pumpkin seeds are arranged in intricate designs to tempt passersby.

The heavy use of egg yolks is as characteristic of Mexican desserts as those in Spain. The story goes that the nuns of Jerez were challenged by the surplus of egg yolks left over when the whites were used to clarify the sherry wine made in the region. From their kitchens came forth *flans,* candies and custards, which were then re-created in the convents of Mexico.

Magnificent displays of culinary delicacies were prepared by the nuns on the feast days. A description by one guest, Artemio Valle-Arizpc, in the early 1600s, portrayed vast tables of decorated milk puddings alongside puddings of sweet potato and coconut, or

Sticks of canela *(cinnamon) add spice to many desserts, including* arroz con leche *and* huevos reales. *Mexican cooking favors the soft variety of cinnamon bark from Ceylon.*

Helados *(ice creams) and* nieves *(ices) are a familiar treat everywhere, whether flavored with exotic fruits or the vanilla and chocolate that are native to Mexico.*

pineapple, guava and honey. He told of "huge platters filled with sugar pastes, delicate almond fruits, royal eggs [egg sponge], pastes made of molasses, cheese, anise and ginger; other trays were covered with milk and honey candies with coconut, as well as almonds fused to resemble pears and apples, coated with liquid caramel and wrapped in colored paper. The silvery bowls were filled to the brim with honey and sugar buns with almonds, sugar and spices, squash preserves, chilacoyes [gourd sweets], transparent candied citrons decorated with sparkling gold and silver confetti, quince candies, marzipan, and almond toffees, toasted or stuffed pears, and sugar-coated peaches, dipped in rum, sparkling like jewels." All of these sweets can still be found today—but not served at the same time!

There are new delights too. On the streets of every city and village, transparent plastic cups filled with red, green, orange and yellow gelatins are sold as quick,

refreshing treats. Some are even embellished with a layer of *rompope,* a thick eggnog laced with brandy or rum. The same gelatin can be transformed into a spectacular finish to a meal by putting it into a crystal bowl and adding ground nuts or liqueurs.

Helados (ice creams) or *nieves* (ices) come into their own under the portals in the little town of Pátzcuaro in Michoacán. Here, a steady stream of ice cream lovers wait their turn for a cone of their favorite fruit-flavored frost, maybe one of creamy yellow guava or ripe pink mango, or the one everyone comes back to—a vanilla cream called *nieve* paste, or snow cream. Luckily, one can find Michoacán-style ice cream stands throughout the country, although the frozen treat never seems to taste the same.

There is no doubt that the contribution of sweets—whether in the form of breads, candies, or desserts—has been gratefully received into the cuisine of Mexico.

Three-Milk Cake

GUERRERO

PASTEL TRES LECHES

Three-Milk Cake

A very moist and rich-tasting cake, this is a favorite among Mexican housewives, who love to serve it with coffee in the afternoon for friends.

2½ cups (10 oz/315 g) all-purpose (plain) flour
1 teaspoon baking powder
7 eggs, separated
1 cup (8 oz/250 g) sugar
¾ cup (6 fl oz/180 ml) milk
1 teaspoon vanilla extract (essence)
1 can (12 fl oz/354 ml) evaporated milk
1 can (14 oz/396 g) sweetened condensed milk
1 cup (8 fl oz/250 ml) heavy (double) cream
¼ cup (2 fl oz/60 ml) brandy (optional)

FROSTING

6 egg whites
pinch of salt
¼ teaspoon cream of tartar
¾ cup (6 fl oz/180 ml) water
1½ cups (12 oz/375 g) sugar
peel of 1 lime, grated

✳ Preheat the oven to 375°F (190°C). Grease and flour a 9-in (23-cm) springform pan (cake tin). Sift the flour and baking powder together.

✳ In a large bowl, beat the egg whites with an electric mixer until frothy. Add the sugar and beat to form stiff peaks, then add the egg yolks one at a time. Turn down the mixer to a slower speed and add one-third of the flour and one-third of the milk. Repeat until all the flour and milk are incorporated, then add the vanilla. Pour the batter into the prepared pan and bake for 35–45 minutes or until a toothpick inserted into the center comes out clean. Let cool for 5 minutes and remove from the pan. Cut the cake into 3 layers.

✳ In a bowl, combine the evaporated milk, condensed milk and cream. If you wish, stir in the brandy. Pour one-third of the milk mixture over the bottom layer of cake, set the middle layer on top, pour one-third of the milk mixture over it, cover with the top layer of cake and pour the remaining milk mixture over it.

✳ To prepare the frosting, beat the egg whites, salt and cream of tartar in a large bowl until the whites hold soft peaks. Set aside.

✳ Mix the water, sugar and lime peel in a small heavy saucepan. Bring to a boil over medium-high heat and cook until a candy thermometer registers 238°F (120°C) or soft ball. Remove from the heat and add to the beaten egg whites in a thin stream. Beat for 6 minutes or until the mixture is stiff.

✳ Cover the top and sides of the cake with the frosting and refrigerate until just before serving.

SERVES 10

Mamey Cake

OAXACA

ANTE DE MAMEY O DURAZNO

Mamey or Peach Cake

All antes have a base of cake bread soaked in a syrup, but the paste fillings vary. This version from Socorrito Zorrilla uses the large exotic mamey, with its deep apricot color. It is occasionally sold in some markets outside Mexico.

1 *marquesote* (page 231)
⅔ cup (3½ oz/100 g) toasted almonds, for garnish
⅔ cup (3½ oz/100 g) toasted pine nuts, for garnish

MAMEY OR PEACH PASTE

1¼ cups (10 oz/310 g) sugar
1 cup (8 fl oz/250 ml) water
2 large mameys, peeled and seeded, or 2 lb (1 kg) peach
  pulp, puréed
7 tablespoons (3½ oz/100 g) butter

SYRUP

2 cups (1 lb/500 g) sugar
½ cup (4 fl oz/125 ml) water
1 stick cinnamon
2 cups (16 fl oz/500 ml) dry sherry

✳ Remove the crust from the *marquesote*. Slice about ½ in (1 cm) thick and set aside. (If the *marquesote* was baked in a layer cake pan, slice it in half horizontally.)
✳ To make the mamey paste, place the sugar and water in a saucepan and bring to a boil. When the syrup reaches the soft-ball stage (238°F/120°C on a candy thermometer), add the puréed fruit and the butter, lower the heat and beat the mixture until smooth. Set aside.
✳ To make the syrup, mix the sugar, water and cinnamon stick in a heavy saucepan and boil, stirring, until the mixture forms a light syrup. Remove from the heat and stir in the sherry.
✳ Arrange half of the sliced cake bread in a layer on a plate and pour some syrup over it. Spread half of the mamey paste on top and repeat these layers, spreading the mamey paste on top and on all sides. Garnish with the toasted almonds and pine nuts.

SERVES 8

OAXACA

ANTE DE ALMENDRA

Almond Cake

The basic ante, *first made in Puebla, is a dessert of cake bread soaked in syrup and mixed with a paste of wine and fruit preserves. Socorrito Zorrilla serves this almond version at her restaurant, El Vitral, in Oaxaca.*

1 *marquesote* (recipe follows)
⅔ cup (3½ oz/100 g) raisins, for garnish
⅔ cup (3½ oz/100 g) toasted almonds, for garnish
cinnamon stick, for garnish

ALMOND PASTE

1½ cups (8 oz/250 g) blanched almonds
4 cups (32 fl oz/1 l) milk
1½ cups (12 oz/375 g) sugar

SYRUP

2 cups (1 lb/500 g) sugar
½ cup (4 fl oz/125 ml) water
1 large stick cinnamon
2 cups (16 fl oz/500 ml) dry sherry

✳ Remove the crust from the *marquesote*. Slice about ½ in (1 cm) thick and set aside. (If the *marquesote* was baked in a layer cake pan, slice it in half horizontally.)
✳ To prepare the almond paste, grind the almonds very fine in a nut grinder or mortar. Place in a saucepan with the milk and sugar and boil until thick.
✳ To make the syrup, mix the sugar, water and cinnamon stick in a heavy saucepan and boil, stirring, until the mixture forms a light syrup. Remove from the heat and stir in the sherry.
✳ On a glass plate, arrange half of the sliced cake bread in a layer. Pour some syrup over it and top with half of the almond paste. Repeat these layers, spreading the almond paste on top and on all sides. Garnish with the raisins, toasted almonds and shavings of the cinnamon stick.

SERVES 8

MARQUESOTE

Cake Bread

This is one of the classic Mexican cakes, served with just a sprinkle of powdered sugar or as a more elaborate dessert with a wine or fruit syrup (as in ante de almendra*). This traditional version was associated with all-male* pulquerías, *where it was sold to carousing husbands to take home to placate their jealous wives.*

8 eggs, separated
½ cup (4 oz/125 g) sugar
1 tablespoon baking powder

1½ cups (6 oz/185 g) cornstarch (cornflour)
½ cup (4 oz/125 g) butter, melted
sesame seeds (optional)

✱ Preheat the oven to 375°F (190°C). Grease and flour 2 loaf pans or 9-in (23-cm) square baking pans.
✱ In a large bowl, beat the egg whites until they form stiff peaks. Fold in the yolks one at a time, still beating. Combine the sugar, baking powder and starch. Mix thoroughly. Fold this mixture gently into the eggs and add the melted and cooled butter. Pour into the pans, sprinkle with sesame seeds if you like and bake for about 25 minutes.

MAKES 2 CAKES

Almond Cake

MICHOACÁN

PAN DE MUERTO

Day of the Dead Bread

During the weeks around the Days of the Dead (All Saints and All Souls), celebrated on November 1 and 2, this traditional round loaf is baked and decorated with pieces of dough formed into tears or bones. It is one of the many foods placed in the colorful offering for the dead, along with chocolate and vivid yellow marigolds.

1 teaspoon dry yeast
¼ cup (2 fl oz/60 ml) lukewarm water
4 cups (1 lb/500 g) all-purpose (plain) flour
6 eggs
1 teaspoon salt
½ cup (4 oz/125 g) sugar
2 teaspoons aniseed
1 teaspoon ground nutmeg
½ cup (4 oz/125 g) butter, melted
orange-flower water (optional)
egg wash (1 egg white plus ½ egg yolk)
sugar for sprinkling

✳ Combine the yeast with the water and ⅓ cup (1½ oz/45 g) of the flour and let stand until the mixture doubles in volume.
✳ Place the remaining flour in a large bowl, make a well in the center and place the eggs, salt, sugar, aniseed, nutmeg, butter and orange-flower water in the well. Beat together, then add the yeast mixture, combining it with the dough. Knead on a floured board for 15 minutes or until the dough no longer sticks to the surface.
✳ Place the dough in a greased bowl, cover with a cloth and let rise in a warm, draft-free area for 3 hours or until doubled in volume.
✳ Preheat the oven to 450°F (230°C). Pinch off about one-third of the dough and form into a 2-in (5-cm) ball and a long rope. Mold pieces of the rope to resemble little bones. Set aside.
✳ Shape the remaining dough into a round loaf and brush with the egg wash. Place the ball of dough in the center of the loaf and arrange the "bones" in a circular pattern around the ball. Brush with the remaining egg wash.
✳ Bake for 10 minutes in the hot oven, lower the temperature to 350°F (180°C) and continue baking for 30 minutes.
✳ Sprinkle with sugar and serve at room temperature.

SERVES 8   *Photograph pages 224–225*

FLAN

Caramel Custard

This universally known Spanish dessert is also a favorite in Mexico, tracing its origin here to the days of the Conquest, when milk and eggs were introduced by the Spaniards. Egg custards are popular in many cuisines, but the signature of the flan is its caramelized sugar topping. This basic recipe can be contemporized by adding 2 tablespoons of instant coffee and 2 teaspoons of coffee liqueur.

1¼ cups (10 oz/310 g) sugar
4 cups (32 fl oz/1 l) milk
1 teaspoon vanilla extract (essence)
pinch of salt
4 eggs
3 egg yolks
½ teaspoon cornstarch (cornflour)
1 tablespoon cold water

✳ Preheat the oven to 350°F (180°C). Place ¾ cup (6 oz/185 g) of the sugar in a heavy saucepan over medium heat. Swirl the pan constantly until the sugar melts and caramelizes, turning a golden brown. Pour into a 1½-qt (1.5-l) ring mold, Charlotte mold or round baking dish and tilt the mold so that the caramel covers the bottom and sides. Set aside.
✳ In a separate saucepan, combine the milk, remaining ½ cup (4 oz/125 g) sugar, vanilla and salt and bring to a boil. Lower the heat and simmer, uncovered, for 10 minutes or until the milk is reduced by half. Cover to keep warm and set aside.
✳ Lightly beat the eggs and egg yolks in a large bowl. Stir the cornstarch and water together and add to the eggs. Slowly pour in the warm milk, stirring constantly. Mix well, strain and pour into the caramel-coated mold.
✳ Cover the mold with foil, set in a larger pan and pour 1 in (2.5 cm) boiling water into the pan. Place in the oven and bake for 35–40 minutes or until a knife inserted near the center comes out clean.
✳ Let the *flan* cool for 30 minutes to room temperature and then refrigerate, preferably overnight. To serve, invert the mold on a platter. Serve cold.
✳*Note:* If the caramel has hardened on the bottom of the mold, quickly place it in a pan of hot water to soften.

SERVES 6

YUCATÁN

TORTA IMPERIAL

Imperial Torte

This light cake is representative of the European influence in Mérida during the period of colonization.

2 cups (10 oz/315 g) blanched almonds
1 tablespoon all-purpose (plain) flour
6 eggs, separated
1 teaspoon cream of tartar
1¾ cups (14 oz/435 g) sugar
½ teaspoon vanilla extract (essence)
2 cups (16 fl oz/500 ml) water
1 3-in (7.5-cm) stick cinnamon
1 tablespoon grated orange peel
1 teaspoon orange liqueur
¼ cup (1 oz/30 g) toasted chopped almonds

✳ Preheat the oven to 325°F (165°C). Grease and flour a 9-in (23-cm) springform pan (cake tin).
✳ In a nut grinder or food processor, grind the almonds. Mix with the flour and set aside.
✳ In a large bowl, beat the egg whites until frothy. Add the cream of tartar and continue beating, adding 1 cup (8 oz/250 g) of the sugar, 1 tablespoon at a time, until the whites hold stiff peaks. Add the yolks one at a time, then the vanilla. Fold in the almond-flour mixture

Caramel Custard (left) and Imperial Torte (right)

with a spatula. Transfer the batter to the prepared pan and bake for 25–35 minutes. Let cool for 5 minutes, unmold and set aside.

✻Heat the water with the remaining ¾ cup (6 oz/185 g) sugar and the cinnamon stick and orange peel. Cook over medium heat until the mixture thickens slightly.

Stir in the orange liqueur and pour over the torte. Sprinkle with the toasted almonds and serve.

✻*Variation:* The torte can be covered with a custard or pastry cream instead of the syrup.

SERVES 6

233

YUCATÁN

PATAS

Coffee Bread

This rich coffee bread recipe from France has been in the family of Virginia Vázquez for many generations.

3 packages (¼ oz/7 g each) dry yeast
¼ cup (2 fl oz/60 ml) lukewarm water
1½ lb (750 g) all-purpose (plain) flour
4 eggs
⅔ cup (5 oz/155 g) sugar
5 eggs, separated
1½ cups (12 oz/375 g) butter, at room temperature
sugar for sprinkling

✳ Dissolve the yeast in the lukewarm water.
✳ Place 2 cups (8 oz/250 g) of the flour in a bowl and make a well in the center. Place 1 egg and 1 tablespoon sugar in the well and add the dissolved yeast. Use the tips of your fingers to combine the ingredients thoroughly. Knead the mixture on a floured board for 10–15 minutes; when you can hear little bubbles popping, the dough is ready.
✳ Place the egg whites in a bowl by the work surface and moisten your hands in them whenever the dough feels dry.
✳ Form the dough into a ball and make a cross on the top surface with a knife. Place in a lightly greased bowl, cover and let stand in a warm place for 1 hour or until it begins to rise.
✳ Place the remaining 4 cups (1 lb/500 g) flour in a large bowl, make a well and add the remaining 3 eggs, the egg yolks and the sugar. With the tips of your fingers, mix half the ingredients in the well with the flour. Add the dough that has been rising and knead all the ingredients together to form a smooth dough. (Moisten your hands with the eggs whites whenever necessary and lightly grease the dough with butter whenever it begins to stick.)
✳ Knead for about 30 minutes or until the dough produces small bubbles. Roll it into a cylinder or *baguette* 18 by 2½ in (46 by 6.5 cm); cut the cylinder into 12 slices.
✳ Grease the dough slices with butter. Take one slice and, with the tips of your fingers well greased, stretch it, working outward from the center to the edges, until it measures about 11 in (28 cm) square; it should be transparent. Grease the dough liberally with butter and cut into 3 strips. Wind one of these strips around a greased ¾-in (2-cm) cylinder, such as a cannoli form, a bulb baster or a piece of broom handle. Wind the second strip around the first strip and, finally, the third around the first two (the strips wind continuously, like a roll of tape). Slip this roll onto a greased baking sheet. Repeat the procedure until all the slices have been used up. Be careful to leave 2 in (5 cm) of space between the rolls so they do not stick together.
✳ Place the baking sheets in a warm place, cover the dough and let rise for 3 hours.
✳ Preheat the oven to 350°F (180°C). Sprinkle a tablespoon of sugar on the top of each roll. Bake for 25–30 minutes or until the rolls brown lightly. Remove from the pan and let cool slightly. Serve warm.

MAKES 12 ROLLS

ROSCA DE REYES

Round Bread for the Day of the Kings

This crown-shaped sweet bread is served on January 6, the Day of the Kings, or Twelfth Night. A small doll representing the Christ child is randomly inserted when the bread is almost finished baking, and whoever gets the slice with the doll must then hold a party on February 2, the Feast of Candelaria.

2 packages (¼ oz/7 g each) dry yeast
½ cup (4 fl oz/125 ml) lukewarm water
4 cups (1 lb/500 g) all-purpose (plain) flour
3 eggs
3 egg yolks
⅓ cup (3 oz/90 g) sugar
½ teaspoon salt
1 teaspoon grated lime or orange peel
2 tablespoons orange-flower water or milk
¾ cup (6 oz/180 g) butter, softened

FOR DECORATING THE BREAD

6 tablespoons (3 oz/90 g) margarine
½ cup (3 oz/90 g) powdered (icing) sugar
2 egg yolks
¾ cup (3 oz/90 g) all-purpose (plain) flour
3 oz (90 g) citron, cut into strips
3 candied figs, cut into strips
1 candied orange, cut into strips
1 egg, lightly beaten
sugar for sprinkling

✳ Sprinkle the yeast over the lukewarm water, add 2 tablespoons of the flour and let stand for 20 minutes in a warm place.

✳ Place the remaining flour in a large bowl, make a well in the center and place the eggs, egg yolks, sugar, salt, lime peel, orange-flower water, butter and dissolved yeast in the well. Mix the ingredients together with your fingertips, then knead on a floured board until the dough is smooth. When small bubbles start to form, in about 15 minutes, shape into a ball and place in a lightly greased bowl. Cover and let rise in a warm place until doubled in volume.

✳ Meanwhile, to prepare the decoration, cream the margarine in a small bowl, then beat in the sugar, egg yolks and flour. Set aside.

✳ Knead the bread dough one more time and shape into a large ring loaf. Transfer to a greased baking sheet and let rise in a warm place for 45 minutes.

✳ Preheat the oven to 475°F (250°C). Decorate the ring with strips of the powdered sugar mixture and strips of the candied fruit, pressing them into the dough. Glaze the ring with egg, sprinkle the strips with sugar and bake for 10 minutes. Lower the temperature to 400°F (200°C), remove the ring from the oven and press 1 or 2 little plastic dolls into the underside. Return to the oven and bake for another 10 minutes.

SERVES 12   *Photograph pages 224–225*

Coffee Bread

Sugar-Coated Fried Bread

TORREJAS

Sugar-Coated Fried Bread

In the state of Puebla it is customary to feed children this Mexican version of French toast when they get their first tooth.

3 cups (24 fl oz/750 ml) milk
1 3-in (7.5-cm) stick cinnamon

½ cup (4 oz/125 g) sugar or grated *piloncillo* (raw sugar)
14 ½-in (1-cm) slices *bolillo* (hard bread roll) or *baguette*
oil for frying
4 eggs, lightly beaten

SYRUP

2 cups (16 fl oz/500 ml) water
2 cups (1 lb/500 g) grated *piloncillo* (raw sugar) or brown sugar
1 2-in (5-cm) stick cinnamon
1 tablespoon very fine julienne strips of lime peel

✻ Place the milk, cinnamon and sugar in a heavy saucepan and boil for 5 minutes. Let cool.

✻ Place the bread slices in a large baking dish. Cover with 2 cups (16 fl oz/500 ml) of the boiled milk and let stand for 1 hour.

✻ Meanwhile, prepare the syrup. Mix the water, *piloncillo,* cinnamon and lime peel in a saucepan and boil until the *piloncillo* dissolves and the mixture thickens slightly. Set aside and keep warm.

✻ Heat ½ in (1 cm) oil in a skillet. Dip the soaked bread in the beaten eggs and place in the hot oil. Fry for 2–3 minutes on each side or until golden brown. Transfer to a platter.

✻ Serve the fritters covered with the *piloncillo* syrup or sprinkled with white sugar.

SERVES 6

OAXACA

PAN DE YEMA OAXAQUEÑO

Oaxacan Egg Bread

Socorrito Zorrilla's regional variation for egg bread. In Oaxaca it is baked in wood-burning clay ovens. Slices of these large crusty loaves of airy-textured sweet bread are perfect for dunking in hot chocolate or for toasting.

Sweet Potato Dessert

1½ oz (45 g) dry yeast
1 cup (8 fl oz/250 ml) lukewarm water
8 cups (2 lb/1 kg) all-purpose (plain) flour
¾ cup (6 oz/185 g) sugar
1 cup (8 oz/250 g) butter, melted
1 tablespoon salt
5 eggs
10 egg yolks
1 tablespoon aniseed
egg wash (1 egg white plus ½ egg yolk)
sesame seeds (optional)

✻ Dissolve the yeast in the lukewarm water. Add 1 cup (4 oz/125 g) of the flour and 1 tablespoon sugar and let stand for 1 hour.

✻ Place the remaining flour in a large bowl. Make a well in the center and place the remaining sugar, butter, salt, eggs, egg yolks, aniseed and yeast mixture in the well. Mix thoroughly, then knead on a floured board until the dough becomes elastic and bubbles form.

✻ Place the dough in a greased bowl, cover with a cloth and let rise in a warm, draft-free place until doubled in volume.

✻ Punch down the dough, form into 2 round loaves and place on a greased baking pan. Let the dough rise in a warm place until doubled in volume again.

✻ Preheat the oven to 375°F (190°C). Make several slashes across the top of the loaves, brush with the egg wash and, if desired, sprinkle with sesame seeds. Bake for 35–40 minutes.

MAKES 2 LOAVES   *Photograph pages 224–225*

PUEBLA

DULCE POBLANO DE CAMOTES

Sweet Potato Dessert

A true camote is hard to find, but the common sweet potato (not a yam) works well in this light, old-fashioned dessert recipe by María Dolores Torres Yzábal.

3 sweet potatoes (6 oz/180 g each), peeled and cut into
   chunks
½ cup (4 oz/125 g) plus ½ teaspoon sugar
⅓ cup (3 oz/90 g) butter
½ teaspoon ground cinnamon
½ cup (4 fl oz/125 ml) thick cream *(crème fraîche)*
1 teaspoon grated orange peel
⅓ cup (2 oz/60 g) raisins

✻ Cook the sweet potatoes in a saucepan of boiling water for 25 minutes. Drain and mash the hot sweet potatoes with the ½ cup sugar and the butter, cinnamon, cream and half of the orange peel.

✻ Preheat the oven to 325°F (165°C). Grease a baking dish and sprinkle with ½ teaspoon sugar and the remaining orange peel. Spread the sweet potato mixture in the dish and bake for 10 minutes. Garnish with the raisins and let cool.

SERVES 6

COLIMA

COCADA

Coconut Candy

A hard cocada *is sold all along the Pacific coast in cellophane-wrapped bars. This creamier dessert version can be served in small bowls. It keeps well in the refrigerator but should always be served at room temperature.*

1 small coconut
1 cup (8 fl oz/250 ml) coconut milk (coconut water)
1 cup (8 fl oz/250 ml) milk
1 cup (8 oz/250 ml) sugar
3 egg yolks
¼ cup (2 fl oz/60 ml) dry sherry
¼ cup (1 oz/30 g) almonds, blanched and halved

✳ Heat the coconut in a 400°F (200°C) oven for 8–10 minutes so that it will be easier to break. Make a hole in one end to extract the milk, then break the coconut into pieces. Remove both the outer husk and the thin brown skin attached to the white coconut meat, then grate the meat.
✳ Place the coconut meat, coconut milk, milk and sugar in a saucepan and boil until the coconut becomes transparent. Remove from the heat and let cool slightly. Beat the egg yolks with the sherry and stir into the pan. Cook, stirring, over low heat until the mixture thickens. Let cool slightly and transfer to an 8-in (20-cm) square baking pan.
✳ Garnish the candy with almonds. When cool, place in an oven preheated to 500°F (260°C) to brown the top. Cut into squares and serve at room temperature.
✳*Note:* For a large coconut, increase the amount of sugar in proportion to the quantity of coconut milk.

SERVES 6–8

Coconut Candy

Orange "Dusts"

PUEBLA

POLVORONES DE NARANJA

Orange "Dusts"

Each part of Mexico has its own version of these flaky cookies, which take their name from the word polvo *(dust), referring to their light consistency. Maria Dolores Torres Yzábal uses orange for flavoring, but ground nuts and cinnamon are also common. A mix of half butter and half vegetable shortening can be substituted for the lard.*

1 cup (8 oz/250 g) lard
½ cup (4 oz/125 g) sugar
2 large egg yolks
¼ cup (2 fl oz/60 ml) orange juice
peel of 2 oranges, grated
4 cups (1 lb/500 g) all-purpose (plain) flour
powdered (icing) sugar

✳ Preheat the oven to 400°F (200°C). In a large bowl, beat the lard until it is fluffy. Add the sugar a little at a time. When it is thoroughly mixed in, add the egg yolks, orange juice and orange peel. Stir in the flour with a spatula.
✳ On a floured surface, roll out the dough to a thickness of ¾ in (2 cm). Cut out 2½-in (6-cm) circles and place them on a greased baking sheet. Reroll the scraps and continue until all of the dough has been used.
✳ Bake for 25 minutes or until the cookies begin to brown lightly around the edges. Transfer to a rack to cool, then arrange on a platter and sprinkle with the sugar through a fine sieve.

MAKES 36 COOKIES

Buñuelos

BUÑUELOS

Buñuelos

These Mexican fritters are flatter than the traditional puffs of Spain, but they are still light as air. While buñuelos *are served all year long, they play a special role at Christmastime, when they are eaten with hot chocolate.*

½ cup (4 fl oz/125 ml) water
3 orange leaves or ¼ teaspoon orange liqueur
   (optional)
2 cups (8 oz/250 g) all-purpose (plain) flour
1 egg
1 tablespoon sugar
1 tablespoon cold margarine or shortening (vegetable
   lard)
oil for frying
sugar syrup (recipe follows)

❋ In a small saucepan, boil the water and orange leaves for 3 minutes. Discard the leaves and set the water aside. (Or bring the water to a boil, add the orange liqueur and set aside.)
❋ Place the flour in a large bowl, make a well in the center and add the egg, sugar and margarine. With your fingertips, mix all the ingredients together until the texture resembles coarse meal. Add the reserved water by tablespoons as needed, mixing and kneading with your hands until the dough is pliable, about 3 minutes.
❋ Lightly grease a glass bowl, add the dough, cover and let rest for 20 minutes.
❋ Divide the dough into 12 balls, each about 1½ in (4 cm) in diameter.

❋ Flour a working surface and a rolling pin. Roll out each ball to a circle about 7 in (18 cm) in diameter. With your fingers, stretch the dough as much as possible without breaking it, until almost transparent.
❋ Meanwhile, heat ½ in (1 cm) oil in a large skillet. When it is very hot, add 1 *buñuelo*. After 15–20 seconds, turn it over and bathe with the hot oil until it is light golden and has puffed up, about 30 seconds. Transfer to a plate covered with paper towels to drain the excess oil. Repeat with the remaining dough.
❋ Pour some syrup over the *buñuelos* and serve warm or at room temperature.
❋*Note:* These are also delicious sprinkled with sugar while still hot.

MAKES 12 BUÑUELOS

SUGAR SYRUP

3½ cups (28 fl oz/875 ml) water
½ teaspoon aniseed
2 cones (11 oz/345 g) *piloncillo* (raw sugar)
1½ 4-in (10-cm) sticks cinnamon
peel of ¼ orange
4 guavas, cut in half (optional)

❋ Heat the water in a heavy saucepan, add the aniseed, *piloncillo,* cinnamon sticks, orange peel and guavas and boil over medium heat for 10 minutes. Stir, lower the heat and boil for 5 more minutes.

MAKES ABOUT 3½ CUPS (28 FL OZ/875 ML)

GELATINA DE ROMPOPE CON FRESAS

Eggnog Gelatin with Strawberries

This beautiful dessert is made with rompope, *a thick Mexican eggnog. It can be purchased in Hispanic markets or, better yet, made at home.*

2 packages (5 teaspoons) unflavored gelatin
¼ cup (2 fl oz/60 ml) water
1 cup (8 fl oz/250 ml) heavy (double) cream
2 cups (16 fl oz/500 ml) *rompope* (page 54)
¼ teaspoon vanilla extract (essence)
4 egg whites
1 lb (500 g) strawberries, stems removed
2 tablespoons sugar
1 tablespoon anisette

✳ In a small bowl, sprinkle the gelatin over the water and let stand for 5 minutes or until absorbed.
✳ Meanwhile, heat the cream slightly in a small saucepan. Remove from the heat and stir in the gelatin. Mix well to dissolve, then strain into a bowl. Add the eggnog and vanilla, mix well and set aside.
✳ In a large bowl, beat the egg whites until they form stiff peaks. Fold in the eggnog mixture, then pour into a lightly greased 1½-qt (1.5-l) ring mold. Refrigerate for at least 4 hours, preferably overnight.
✳ Meanwhile, place the strawberries in a glass bowl, add the sugar and anisette and let stand for 2 hours. Purée in a blender, strain and set aside.
✳ Just before serving, unmold the gelatin and cover with the strawberry sauce.

SERVES 4–6

GELATINA DE ALMENDRA

Almond Gelatin

This very old recipe from María Dolores Torres Yzábal makes a refreshing dessert accompanied by cookies. Orchards of apples, peaches and Italian prunes cloak the lower slopes of the Sierra Madre Oriental, and many of the desserts of this region feature these fruits. While prunes and almonds make a perfect taste combination, other fruits such as strawberries or poached pears can be substituted.

1 package (2½ teaspoons) unflavored gelatin
2¼ cups (18 fl oz/560 ml) cold milk
⅔ cup (5 oz/155 g) sugar
4 egg yolks
½ cup (3 oz/90 g) blanched almonds
⅛ teaspoon almond extract (essence) (optional)

✳ In a small bowl, sprinkle the gelatin over ¼ cup (2 fl oz/60 ml) of the milk and let stand for 5 minutes or until absorbed.
✳ Meanwhile, place the remaining milk and the sugar, egg yolks and almonds in a blender and purée until the almonds are completely ground. Transfer to a saucepan and cook over low heat until the mixture thickens slightly. Remove from the heat and stir in the almond

Eggnog Gelatin with Strawberries (top) and Almond Gelatin (bottom)

extract. Add the gelatin and stir until it dissolves.
✳ Pour the mixture into a lightly greased 4-cup (1½-pt/1-l) mold. Let cool slightly and refrigerate for at least 3 hours, preferably overnight.
✳ Invert the molded gelatin onto a platter and serve with cooked or canned fruit. A good choice is pitted prunes that have been cooked in water with a little sugar (to make a light syrup), with amaretto added to taste before serving.

SERVES 6

GELATINA DE CAFÉ CON LICOR DE CAFÉ

Coffee Gelatin

Gelatins are extremely popular in Mexico—served in a rainbow of colors or made with milk and fruits. This dessert pays homage to the coffee liqueurs of Mexico, now esteemed in many countries. It is an ideal elegant ending to a rich main course.

1 package (2½ teaspoons) unflavored gelatin
1½ cups (12 fl oz/375 ml) cold water
¼ cup (2 oz/60 g) sugar
3 teaspoons instant coffee granules
1 cup (8 fl oz/250 ml) Kahlua or other coffee liqueur

✳ In a small bowl, sprinkle the gelatin over ½ cup (4 fl oz/125 ml) of the water and let stand for 5 minutes or until absorbed.
✳ Meanwhile, place the remaining water and the sugar and instant coffee in a saucepan over medium heat. Cook, stirring, until the sugar dissolves. When the mixture begins to boil, remove from the heat. Add the gelatin and stir until it dissolves. Add the coffee liqueur and stir to combine.
✳ Pour the mixture into lightly greased individual molds or into a lightly greased 4-cup (1½-pt/1-l) mold. Let

cool slightly and refrigerate for 3 hours or until the gelatin is firm. Unmold the gelatin and garnish each serving with a dollop of whipped cream, a maraschino cherry and a mint leaf. Or garnish with chocolate shavings or a coffee bean.

SERVES 6

FLAN BLANCO

White Flan

While this is not a flan *in the traditional sense—it is missing two of the custard's main ingredients, egg yolks and milk— it has* flan's *caramel coating, with the added surprise of a light meringue-type filling. This recipe is by Rosario Madero, who shares it with her family at their Chihuahua hacienda.*

12 egg whites
⅛ teaspoon salt
½ teaspoon cream of tartar
¾–1 cup (6–8 oz/185–250 g) sugar
1½ teaspoons vanilla extract (essence)
½ teaspoon almond extract (essence)

CARAMEL

1½ cups (12 oz/375 g) sugar
⅛ teaspoon salt
½ teaspoon vanilla extract (essence)
¼ teaspoon almond extract (essence)

TOPPING

1 cup (8 fl oz/250 ml) heavy (double) cream
pinch of salt

1 tablespoon powdered (icing) sugar
½ teaspoon vanilla extract (essence)
¼ teaspoon almond extract (essence)
1 cup (5 oz/155 g) toasted blanched almond halves,
   for garnish

✱ Preheat the oven to 350°F (180°C). Place the ingredients for the caramel in a heavy saucepan over medium heat. Swirl the pan constantly until the sugar melts and caramelizes, turning a light golden brown. Pour into a 2-qt (2-l) ring mold or Bundt pan and tilt so that the caramel covers the bottom and sides. Set aside.

✱ Place the egg whites in a large bowl, add the salt and cream of tartar and beat until the whites form stiff peaks. Fold in the sugar, then add the extracts. Pour this mixture into the caramel-coated mold (the caramel should be hard by this time). Set the mold in a larger pan and pour 1 in (2.5 cm) boiling water into the pan. Place in the oven and bake for 45–60 minutes. Do not remove the mold from the oven immediately; instead, turn off the oven and leave the mold in the oven with the door open for 10 minutes before taking it out. Then be careful to put the mold in a spot where there are no drafts or extreme temperature changes. When the mold cools to room temperature (about 20 minutes), unmold the *flan* onto a platter and cover with the caramel sauce. To remove any caramel that sticks to the mold, place 1 cup (8 fl oz/250 ml) water in the mold and hold it over a hot burner on the stove, stirring until the caramel is loosened; let cool a little and pour the diluted caramel over the *flan*.

✱ To prepare the topping, beat the cream with a pinch of salt. When it begins to thicken, mix in the sugar and the extracts. Beat until stiff. Spoon dollops of cream onto the *flan* and garnish with the toasted almond halves.

SERVES 8

White Flan (left) and Coffee Gelatin (right)

Caramel Crêpes

GUANAJUATO

Crepas de Cajeta

Caramel Crêpes

The original rich-tasting goat's milk cajeta was sold in little wooden cajas (boxes) in the shops of Celaya, Guanajuato, where it was made in huge copper pots. Today it is more commonly sold in glass jars in different flavors and can be used as a dessert topping, as in this recipe for crêpes.

CRÊPES

1½ cups (12 fl oz/375 ml) milk
½ cup (2 oz/60 g) all-purpose (plain) flour
1 egg
1 tablespoon oil
butter

SAUCE

2 tablespoons (1 oz/30 g) butter
1 cup (8 fl oz/250 ml) *cajeta* (recipe follows)
½ cup (4 fl oz/125 ml) orange juice
1 tablespoon white tequila
¾ cup (3 oz/90 g) chopped walnuts

✳ To prepare the crêpes, beat the milk, flour, egg and oil together in a mixing bowl. Let rest for 5 minutes. Lightly butter a nonstick crêpe pan and set over medium heat. Pour 1½ tablespoons of the mixture into the pan and tilt it to cover the bottom. As soon as the edges of the crêpe begin to dry cut, turn it over. When the second side is lightly browned, transfer the crêpe to a plate. Repeat until all the mixture has been used, being sure to butter the pan before making each crêpe. There should be about 12 crêpes. Set aside.

✳ To prepare the sauce, melt the butter in a small saucepan and add the *cajeta* and orange juice. Stir over medium heat for 3–5 minutes or until heated and thoroughly combined. Add the tequila, heat, ignite and let burn off.

✳ Before serving, briefly heat the sauce. Fold each crêpe in half, then fold again to make a triangle. Dip each of the crêpes in the sauce. Place 2 crêpes on each plate and divide the remaining sauce among the 6 plates. Sprinkle with the chopped walnuts. Serve hot.

SERVES 6

Cajeta

Caramel Sauce

¼ cup (2 fl oz/60 ml) water
1 teaspoon baking soda (bicarbonate of soda)
4 cups (32 fl oz/1 l) milk (preferably goat's milk)
1 cup (8 oz/250 g) sugar
1 teaspoon vanilla extract (essence) (optional)

✳ In a cup, stir the water and baking soda together. Set aside.

✳ Stir the milk and sugar together in a saucepan and bring to a boil. Lower the heat to medium and, stirring constantly, pour in the baking soda water in a thin stream; be careful not to let any baking soda sitting in the bottom of the cup be poured in. Continue cooking and stirring for 50–60 minutes or until the mixture coats the back of a spoon, turns a rich caramel color and is clear.

✳ Pour the mixture into a bowl, stir in the vanilla and let cool. The *cajeta* can be made 1 or 2 months in advance, covered and refrigerated.

MAKES ABOUT 3½ CUPS (28 FL OZ/875 ML)

GUERRERO

Merengue Con Natilla y Mango

Meringue with Mangoes and Soft Custard

Kay Mendieta de Alonso serves this delicate contemporary version of meringue cake as a spectacular ending to a special dinner party.

2½ cups (1¼ lb/625 g) sugar
1 cup egg whites (about 7 eggs)
1 teaspoon white vinegar
4 mangoes, peeled, pitted and sliced, for garnish

CUSTARD SAUCE

2 cups (16 fl oz/500 ml) milk
½ cup (4 oz/125 g) sugar
1 teaspoon very fine julienne strips of lime peel
4 egg yolks
2 tablespoons cornstarch (cornflour)
1½ teaspoons brandy

✳ Preheat the oven to 500°F (260°C). Place 1 cup (8 oz/250 g) of the sugar in a heavy saucepan over medium heat. Swirl the pan constantly until the sugar melts and caramelizes, turning a golden brown. Pour into a 1½-qt (1.5-l) ring mold and tilt the mold so that the caramel covers the bottom and sides. Set aside.

✳ Grind the remaining sugar in a blender.

✳ Beat the egg whites in a large bowl and, as soon as they begin to froth, add the vinegar. Add the ground sugar, beating until it is completely incorporated and the whites become stiff. Using a spatula, transfer this meringue to the caramel-coated mold.

✳ Set the mold in a larger pan and pour 1 in (2.5 cm) boiling water into the pan. Place in the oven and bake for 10 minutes or until the meringue puffs up and turns golden brown. Lower the oven temperature to 250°F (120°C) and bake for 40 minutes. Turn off the oven and open the oven door slowly so that the meringue cools gradually and does not collapse. Leave in the oven with the door open for 40 minutes. Let cool to room temperature and then refrigerate for at least 3 hours, preferably overnight.

✳ To prepare the custard, warm the milk, sugar and lime peel in a saucepan. Combine the egg yolks and cornstarch in a small bowl, then pour ½ cup (4 fl oz/125 ml) of the warm milk into the yolks, stirring constantly. Transfer this mixture to the saucepan of milk and cook over low heat, stirring constantly, until the custard thickens, about 8 minutes. Do not let the custard boil. Remove from the heat, stir in the brandy and let cool.

✳ To serve, invert the meringue onto a platter. Scrape out any caramel that remains in the mold and cover the meringue with it. Arrange the mango slices in the center and around the outside of the meringue. Pass the custard in a separate bowl.

SERVES 8–10

Meringue with Mangoes and Soft Custard

Rice Pudding

DISTRITO FEDERAL

MOUSSE DE TEQUILA

Tequila Mousse

Although mousse was not introduced to Mexican cuisine until the arrival of Empress Carlotta and the numerous French immigrants of the nineteenth century, it is now a popular dessert. María Dolores Torres Yzábal has "Mexicanized" it with the unmistakable flavor of tequila.

¾ package (2 teaspoons) unflavored gelatin
1 cup (8 oz/250 g) sugar
pinch of salt
4 eggs, separated
3 tablespoons lime juice
2 tablespoons water
½ cup (4 fl oz/125 ml) white tequila
¼ cup (2 fl oz/60 ml) triple sec
finely grated peel of 1 lime

✳ In a glass or enamel saucepan, mix the gelatin, ½ cup (4 oz/125 g) of the sugar and the salt.
✳ Beat the egg yolks in a large bowl until they are thick and creamy. Add the lime juice and water and continue beating. Pour the mixture over the gelatin and place the saucepan over medium heat for 5 minutes, stirring the mixture constantly until the gelatin dissolves.
✳ Remove from the heat and stir in the tequila, triple sec and the grated rind. Let cool, then refrigerate.
✳ In a large bowl, beat the egg whites, gradually incorporating the remaining sugar, until they form stiff peaks.
✳ When the egg yolk mixture begins to set, fold in the beaten egg whites. Place in a serving bowl or in dessert dishes and chill for at least 2 hours. Garnish with extra grated lime peel.

SERVES 8

Tequila Mousse (top) and Pears with Piloncillo and Tequila (bottom)

ARROZ CON LECHE

Rice Pudding

Rice pudding, the most loved of all Mexican desserts, is found in virtually every marketplace and restaurant in Mexico. A tablespoon of brandy can be added for a special occasion. It is delicious served at any temperature—chilled, warm or room temperature.

1 cup (5 oz/155 g) long-grain white rice
3 cups (24 fl oz/750 ml) water
1 3-in (7.5-cm) stick cinnamon
1 tablespoon very fine julienne strips of lime or orange peel (optional)
pinch of salt
4 cups (32 fl oz/1 l) milk
1½ cups (12 oz/375 g) sugar or to taste
⅓ cup (2 oz/60 g) raisins
1 teaspoon vanilla extract (essence)
ground cinnamon, for garnish (optional)

✳ Place the rice in a large saucepan with the water, cinnamon, lime peel and salt. Bring to a boil, lower the heat and cook, covered, until most of the water has been absorbed. Stir in the milk and sugar and cook, stirring constantly, over low heat until the mixture thickens. Add the raisins and vanilla and cook for 2 minutes. Remove from the heat and let cool for 20 minutes. Transfer to a platter or individual bowls and refrigerate. Sprinkle lightly with cinnamon before serving.
✳ *Variation:* For a richer, more custard-like flavor, beat an egg into the milk before adding it to the pan.

SERVES 6

CHIHUAHUA

PERAS CON PILONCILLO Y TEQUILA

Pears with Piloncillo and Tequila

Martha Chapa, who places great emphasis on the artistic appeal of foods, prepares this dish with whole pears dramatically presented upright, drizzled with syrup and finely grated zest of lime. This recipe can also be made with apples.

2½ cups (20 fl oz/625 ml) water
1 tablespoon very fine julienne strips of lime peel
1 stick cinnamon

1 cone (5–6 oz/150–180 g) *piloncillo* (raw sugar), in chunks
¼ cup (2 fl oz/60 ml) white tequila
6 firm pears, peeled and, if desired, cut in half and cored

✳ Place the water, lime peel, cinnamon and *piloncillo* in a saucepan and boil until the sugar dissolves. Add the tequila and pears, cover and simmer gently, turning occasionally, for 20 minutes or until the pears soften (be careful not to let them overcook and become mushy). Let cool and serve.

SERVES 6

CHIHUAHUA

Capirotada

Syrup-Coated Bread Pudding

Every region of Mexico has its own version of this traditional Lenten dessert. This northern recipe is unusual in that it includes layers of cheese. It is sturdy and nourishing enough to be served as a late supper.

20–25 slices *bolillo* (hard bread roll) or *baguette*, 1–2 days old
⅔ cup (5 oz/155 g) butter
10 corn tortillas, toasted (optional)
2 cups (8 oz/250 g) grated *queso añejo* or *queso Chihuahua* (or Monterey Jack or medium-sharp Cheddar cheese)
1¼ cups (6 oz/185 g) raisins
1½ cups (6 oz/185 g) chopped walnuts or peanuts

SYRUP

1 cone (5–6 oz/150–180 g) *piloncillo* (raw sugar)
3 cups (24 fl oz/750 ml) water
1 stick cinnamon
3 whole cloves
1 cup (8 fl oz/250 ml) milk

✳ To make the syrup, mix the sugar, water, cinnamon stick and cloves in a saucepan and boil, stirring, until the mixture forms a light syrup. Remove from the heat and stir in the milk.
✳ Toast the bread until lightly browned. Spread the butter on the bread.
✳ Preheat the oven to 400°F (200°C). Cover the sides and bottom of a *cazuela* or casserole with the tortillas. Dip each piece of bread into the syrup and arrange a layer of bread in the bottom of the *cazuela*. Sprinkle with part of the cheese, raisins and nuts. Continue making layers of bread, cheese, raisins and nuts until all the ingredients have been used.
✳ Strain the syrup that is left over and pour over the pudding. Cover the *cazuela* with foil and bake the pudding for 20 minutes, uncovering periodically and smoothing the surface of the pudding with a wooden spoon. Lower the oven temperature to 300°F (150°C) and bake for another 30 minutes. Serve lukewarm.
✳*Variation:* Cover the pudding with meringue and bake in a 500°F (260°C) oven for 5 minutes or until the surface is golden brown.

SERVES 6

Syrup-Coated Bread Pudding

PUEBLA

HUEVOS REALES

Royal Eggs

Like mole poblano, *this very sweet dish is attributed to the creative Dominican nuns of the Santa Rosa convent. Egg whites were used to paint the walls of the convent, and it is said that* huevos reales *were dreamed up as a way to use the remaining yolks. It can be prepared a day in advance.*

10 egg yolks
2 teaspoons baking powder
1 teaspoon butter
⅓ cup (2 oz/60 g) raisins, for garnish
cinnamon shavings, for garnish

SYRUP

2 cups (16 oz/500 g) sugar
1 cup (8 fl oz/250 ml) water
7 1-in (2.5-cm) sticks cinnamon
2 tablespoons dry sherry

✳ Preheat the oven to 275°F (135°C). In a large bowl, beat the egg yolks until they are thick and creamy. Stir in the baking powder.
✳ Grease a 13- by 9-in (33- by 23-cm) baking dish with the butter and pour in the egg mixture. Cover the dish with aluminum foil and bake for about 45 minutes or until a toothpick inserted in the center comes out clean (be careful not to overbake). Remove from the oven and let cool for 10 minutes.
✳ To make the syrup, mix the sugar, water and cinnamon in a small heavy saucepan and boil, stirring, for 5 minutes until the mixture forms a light syrup. Remove from the heat and stir in the sherry.
✳ Cut the eggs in the baking dish into 1-in (2.5-cm) squares. Cover with the syrup and garnish with raisins and cinnamon shavings. Serve chilled or at room temperature.

SERVES 8

PUEBLA

TURRÓN DE CIRUELA PASA

Prune Nougat

Turrón *is a Spanish confection of Arab origin, usually made with honey and almonds. This softer Mexican version is often made at the same time as the yolk-rich* huevos reales *(see previous recipe) to make use of the leftover egg whites.*

4 oz (125 g) pitted prunes
1½ cups (12 fl oz/375 ml) water
2 cups (1 lb/500 g) sugar
1 stick cinnamon
10 egg whites
½ teaspoon cream of tartar
2 tablespoons brandy

✳ In a blender, purée the prunes with the water. Add the sugar and cinnamon and purée again. Place in a saucepan over medium heat and cook until a candy thermometer registers 230°F (110°C).
✳ Meanwhile, in a large bowl, beat the egg whites until frothy. Add the cream of tartar and beat until they form stiff peaks. Add the prune syrup in a thin stream. Continue beating until the mixture cools, about 10 minutes, then stir in the brandy.
✳ Spoon into tall glasses or a glass bowl and chill before serving.

SERVES 10

Prune Nougat (left) and Royal Eggs (right)

Bananas Flambé with Rum

TABASCO

Plátanos Flameados con Ron

Bananas Flambé with Rum

Plantains and other types of bananas are grown in many of the coastal states, but it is on the Gulf coast with its Caribbean influence that the banana shows up as an important part of the diet.

2 tablespoons (1 oz/30 g) butter, plus more for greasing
6 tablespoons (2 oz/60 g) brown sugar
6 ripe bananas, peeled
2 tablespoons dark rum
1 qt (32 fl oz/1 l) vanilla ice cream (optional)

✴ Preheat the oven to 425°F (220°C). Use the butter to grease a round or rectangular baking dish. Sprinkle with half of the brown sugar.
✴ Cut the bananas in half lengthwise and arrange cut sides down in the baking dish. Sprinkle with the remaining sugar and dot with the butter. Bake for 6–10 minutes or until the sugar melts and the bananas turn a golden brown.
✴ Remove from the oven, add the rum and ignite to flambé the bananas. Serve hot, with a scoop of vanilla ice cream if desired.

SERVES 6

COLIMA

Nieve de Mango

Mango Sorbet

Fruit ices are still prepared the old-fashioned way, by hand, in much of Mexico and are sold by vendors from small carts. They can also be made in an ice cream maker according to the manufacturer's directions. Canned mangoes may be used, but pour off the syrup and use ½ cup less sugar.

4 lb (2 kg) mangoes, peeled and pitted
3 cups (24 fl oz/750 ml) water
2½ cups (1¼ lb/625 g) sugar
8 cups (4 lb/2 kg) crushed ice
2 cups (1 lb/500 g) coarse salt

✳ Purée the mangoes in a blender, transfer to a glass bowl, cover and refrigerate for 12 hours.
✳ Make a syrup by boiling the water and sugar in a heavy saucepan, stirring constantly, for 5 minutes. Refrigerate for 30 minutes, mix into the mango purée, then refrigerate for 15 minutes.
✳ In a large bowl, mix the ice with the salt. Place the bowl with the mango mixture in the center of the ice and agitate, moving it vigorously back and forth, until the mixture partially freezes, 30–45 minutes.

SERVES 10

Mango Sorbet

GUERRERO

Niño Envuelto con Helado de Vainilla y Salsa de Cajeta

Ice Cream Cake Roll with Caramel Sauce

While this impressive dessert is not typically Mexican, it does use two very Mexican products—vanilla ice cream and cajeta.

6 tablespoons (1½ oz/45 g) all-purpose (plain) flour
1 teaspoon baking powder
⅛ teaspoon salt
6 eggs, separated
¼ teaspoon cream of tartar

6 tablespoons (3 oz/90 g) sugar
1 qt (32 fl oz/1 l) vanilla ice cream
2 oz (60 g) semisweet (cooking) chocolate, melted
1 cup (8 fl oz/250 ml) vanilla *cajeta* (page 243)
½ cup (4 fl oz/125 ml) heavy (double) cream
¾ cup (6 fl oz/180 ml) water
½ cup (2 oz/60 g) sugar
2 tablespoons brandy
½ cup (2 oz/60 g) walnuts, toasted and chopped

✴ Preheat the oven to 375°F (190°C). Sift the flour, baking powder and salt together and set aside.
✴ In a large bowl, beat the egg whites until they are frothy. Add the cream of tartar and continue beating while adding 6 tablespoons of sugar, one at a time, until the whites form stiff peaks. Then beat slowly while adding the egg yolks one at a time. Fold in the reserved flour and transfer the mixture to a greased jelly roll (Swiss roll) pan. Smooth the surface with a spatula and bake for 20–30 minutes or until the surface just starts to brown.
✴ Remove the cake from the oven, let cool for 5 minutes and unmold on a dish towel sprinkled with sugar. Set aside.
✴ Remove the ice cream from the freezer and let soften for 10 minutes. Spread the ice cream over the surface of the cake; drizzle the melted chocolate in lines over the ice cream. Roll the cake up, trim the ends, wrap in aluminum foil and freeze.
✴ Heat the *cajeta* in a double boiler over simmering water, add the cream and stir until blended. Set aside.
✴ Make a syrup by boiling the water and sugar in a heavy saucepan, stirring constantly. Remove from the heat and stir in the brandy. Set aside.
✴ Just before serving, brush the ice cream roll with the syrup. Cover with the hot *cajeta* sauce, sprinkle with the nuts and serve immediately.

SERVES 6

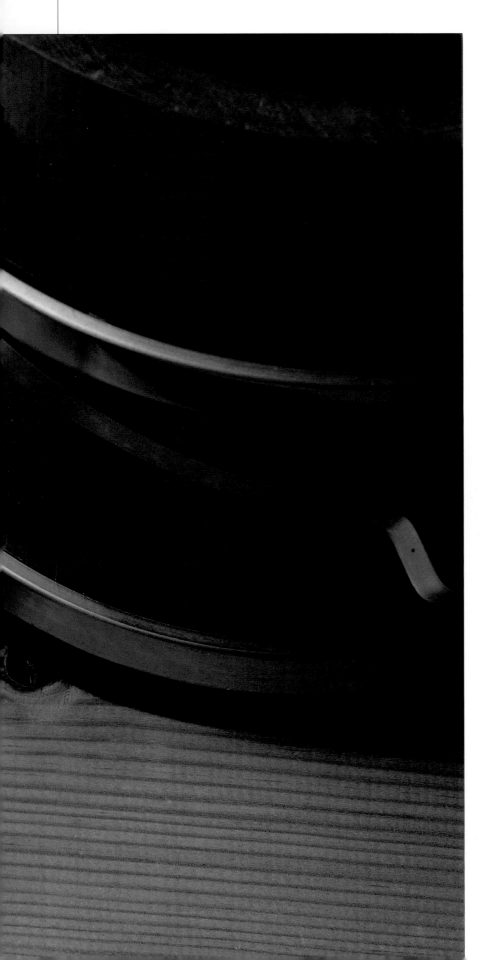

Ice Cream Cake Roll with Caramel Sauce

Glossary

It is always frustrating to find an enticing recipe and then realize that the essential ingredients may not be available. This may be true of many of the recipes in this book, so substitutes have been suggested whenever possible. The resulting dish may not have the authentic flavor of the original, but it will still retain its basic character and be a satisfying part of a Mexican meal. Just remember that these recipes were created from the plants and animals of a specific region, and so they may vary even when made in a different part of Mexico. Your substitutions are just one more variation in the evolution of these dishes.

Many of these ingredients can be found in Hispanic or Asian markets, and more and more they are being carried in ordinary supermarkets. All of the recipes in this book were tested in home kitchens throughout the United States with locally obtained ingredients.

ACHIOTE: The deep red-orange seeds of the tropical *annatto* tree are used in the Yucatán both for their distinctive flavor and their brilliant yellow color, which is used commercially to color cheese. The seeds are very hard and usually soaked before grinding into a *recado* (paste) and mixed with garlic, Seville or bitter orange juice and various spices. Both the seeds (often labeled *annatto)* and the paste are available in Latin American and specialty food shops.

ACITRÓN: The crystallized biznaga cactus is used throughout central Mexico in *picadillos* (meat stuffings), in some desserts and sweet breads, or eaten plain. Candied pineapple can be substituted, but the flavor is different. Ask for a bar of this candied cactus at any Mexico City candy store.

ALMUERZO: A hearty breakfast, usually eaten in mid- or late morning.

AMARANTH: This pseudo-grain is a native of Mexico that, with its balanced proteins, offers more nutritional value than true grain. Highly esteemed by the Indians, this nutritious plant was given by the tons to the Aztec rulers in annual tribute.

ANTOJITOS: This is a loose term for the popular snacks found on every street corner of Mexico, many taking the place of a formal meal. Most but not all are made of *masa* and are the food most foreigners ask for when they want to eat Mexican food— *tacos, tamales, burritos, enchiladas* and related dishes. If they are served before a meal as an appetizer, they are called *entremeses. Botana* is the name for a snack that is served with drinks.

AVOCADO/*AGUACATE:* A deciduous tree of the Lauracea family, which is native to Mexico, bears a fruit with a leathery skin, a large seed and soft, buttery flesh. There are many varieties of avocados—from little fingerlike ones that are eaten skin and all, to a giant pear-shaped avocado with a reddish-tinged skin. The best known outside Mexico are the almost smooth, green-skinned Fuerte, which has a bland taste, and the dark, knobby-skinned Hass, with its wonderful, nutty flavor. The other, bigger varieties that occasionally appear in grocery stores can have a stringy texture. To ripen an avocado, seal it in a paper bag at room temperature. It can then be stored in the refrigerator. The long leathery leaves are used in some dishes. Their characteristic flavor is only found in the leaves of mature trees, so ask your friends who live where they are grown to send you a supply, as dried leaves can be used in most recipes.

BANANA LEAVES: In southern Mexico, the Yucatán and the Gulf states, the large, fragrant leaves of the banana plant are used to wrap food for cooking and to impart flavor. They can be found frozen in most Latin and Asian markets. Thaw by quickly passing the leaf over a flame or steam to make it more pliable.

BITTER ORANGE or SEVILLE ORANGE/*NARANJA AGRIA:* Abundantly used in the Yucatán, the juice of bitter orange has a tart and grapefruity, lemony, orangy taste. An adequate substitute can be made with equal parts of fresh lime, orange and grapefruit juice with 1 teaspoon of finely grated orange and grapefruit peel for every cup of juice. Let sit for several hours, then strain. Outside Mexico, Seville oranges are used for marmalade and for flavoring liqueurs.

BOLILLOS: Small, crusty, French-type bread rolls with an oblong shape.

BOTANA: An appetizer usually served with drinks.

BUDÍN: This almost cakelike pudding is usually made from vegetables. It is served for a light supper or as a *sopa seca* (dry soup) during a large *comida* (main meal of the day).

CACAO: The seeds of a tropical tree (*Theobroma cacao)* that form in large pods are removed, roasted and ground to form the base for chocolate and the hot beverage cocoa. Highly prized in early Indian cultures, the beans were often used as money for trading.

CAJETA: A caramel-like sweet, traditionally made from sugar and goat's milk.

CAMOTE: This native chestnut-flavored sweet potato is eaten fried, roasted, stewed and cooked in various sweets.

CAZUELA: This traditional earthenware casserole of Mexico, glazed on the inside and rough on the outside, is used for *moles* and stews, as it heats evenly and retains heat for a long time. New ones must be cured, as should *ollas* (see entry). One prescribed way is to first rub the inside with a cut clove of garlic, fill it with cold water and slowly simmer until the pot is dry. Repeat the process several times and wash the pot with soapy water. It is wise to not store food in any glazed pots or cook very acidic foods in them because the glaze contains lead.

CAZUELITA: A small *cazuela* or ramekin, often used for egg dishes or desserts such as rice pudding or custard.

CENA: A late evening meal, often for a special occasion.

CHAYOTE: Also called vegetable pear, choko, christophene or mirliton, this pear-shaped vegetable is a member of the squash family. Three varieties are found in Mexico, the best tasting being dark green with porcupine-like spines. The pale *chayote* found in U.S. markets is rather tasteless and needs more seasoning. It stores well unwrapped in the refrigerator for up to a month. The flavor is reminiscent of its cucumber relative.

CHEESES: Following the introduction of cows and goats to Mexico in the 16th century, cheese began to play a major role in the diet, adding protein as well as distinctive tastes and textures. Some of these cheeses are hard to find even in Mexico because they are regional.

QUESO AÑEJO: A dry, salty cheese that is finely grated and used as a tasty garnish. Romano can be used as a substitute if *añejo* or *queso cotija,* as it is more authentically called, cannot be found.

QUESO ASADERO: A mild, soft, braided cheese used for dishes requiring melted cheese. Provolone, mozzarella, Monterey Jack or block Muenster can be substituted.

QUESO CHIHUAHUA: A mild, nutty-tasting cheese that was originally made in the Mennonite communities in Chihuahua but is now quite hard to find. It melts well and is used for stuffing *chiles* or to grate as a topping. Monterey Jack or a medium-sharp Cheddar is a good substitute.

QUESO FRESCO: A tangy, crumbly cheese served sliced with *salsa* as a *botana* or sprinkled on soups or *antojitos*. Feta is about the best substitute, although occasionally it can be found in Latin American markets as *queso ranchero*.

QUESO MANCHEGO: Similar to the original sheep cheeses of Spain and, like them, varies considerably in flavor and consistency. Try a young pecorino, table Parmesan or raw-milk Cheddar, depending on the recipe.

QUESO PANELA: A porous fresh cheese from central Mexico, often sold in small baskets. A fresh mozzarella is the closest substitute.

CHICHARRÓN: The outer fat or rind of the pig is scored and twice fried in boiling lard. When broken into pieces, it is used as a *botana* and is frequently served with *guacamole*. It can also be softened with sauces or ground and added to other dishes. The packaged variety found in supermarkets can be used, though it is not as tasty.

CHILES

The many *chiles* all belong to the genus *Capsicum* and vary in degree of "hotness" and in flavor, not only between species but between plants of the same species, depending on such variables as soil and climate. To confuse things even more, the same *chiles* may go by different names in the different states of Mexico. Wearing rubber gloves is a good idea when preparing *chiles*, as the pithy white placenta, or seed cluster, can burn the skin. Be careful not to touch your eyes. Remove the placenta and seeds if a less *picante* taste is desired.

CHILES FRESCOS (FRESH CHILES)

The fat, dark green *chile jalapeño*, named after the capital of Veracruz, is the most commonplace *chile* used in Mexican cooking, along with the smaller *chile serrano*. Both of these hot *chiles* are eaten pickled or fresh in uncooked *salsas* and *guacamole*. Though each has a distinctive flavor, they can substitute for each other. The *chile cuaresmeño* of the central region is the same as the *jalapeño*. The *chile poblano* is another *chile* essential in Mexican cooking. Larger and much milder than the *jalapeño*, this *chile* is best known for making *chiles rellenos*. It is also cut into *rajas* (strips) and used as a garnish, mixed with vegetables or rice, or added to sauces. The Anaheim or unnamed long green peppers in the supermarkets are marginal substitutes. The *chile güero* or blond *chile* is any very light yellow or pale green *chile*. A Fresno *chile*, the long yellow banana or Hungarian wax pepper, or even a *jalapeño* can be substituted.

TO ROAST FRESH CHILES

Chiles are roasted in order to remove the thin skin that covers them as well as to give them a unique flavor. There are several methods:

1. Over direct heat

This is the most commonly used technique. Place the *chiles* directly over a medium flame on a gas stove. Turn the *chiles* with tongs until their entire skins are "charred" (covered with black blisters). This will take 5–10 minutes, depending on the heat of the flame and the size of the *chiles*. Do not char the *chiles* too much or the flesh will burn and taste bitter. Immediately place the *chiles* in a plastic bag and close the bag. Or cover the *chiles* with a damp cloth. Leave for 10–15 minutes. This is called "letting the *chiles* sweat." This procedure has two functions: to make the thin skin easier to remove and to let the *chiles* cook slightly in their own steam.

2. On a *comal*

If you don't have a *comal*, you can use a heavy skillet (frying pan), preferably iron or nonstick. Heat the *comal* over medium heat. Place 2 or 3 *chiles* at a time on it and cook, turning, until the entire skin of each *chile* is "charred" (covered with black blisters). This will take 10–15 minutes. Be careful that the *chile* does not get too "scorched" or the flesh will burn, resulting in an unpleasant, bitter flavor. Remove the *chiles* from the *comal*, place them all together in a plastic bag and close the bag. Or cover the *chiles* with a damp cloth. Leave for 10–15 minutes.

3. In a broiler

Heat the broiler (griller) to medium-high heat. Lightly brush each *chile* with oil. Place all the *chiles* in the pan and put it in the broiler. Broil, turning the *chiles*, until their entire skins are "charred" (covered with black blisters). This will take 10–15 minutes. Do not char the *chiles* too much or they will burn and taste bitter. Remove the *chiles* from the broiler, place them in a plastic bag and close the bag. Or cover the *chiles* with a damp cloth. Leave for 10–15 minutes.

4. In oil

This method is usually used to prepare stuffed *chiles* or *chiles* with nut sauce in large quantities because it saves a lot of time and labor in peeling the *chiles*. Heat a cup of oil over medium-high heat in a skillet. Add the *chiles* 1 or 2 at a time. Use a spatula or a slotted spoon to turn the *chiles* and fry them until their skins swell and turn golden brown, 5–10 seconds. Transfer the *chiles* to a bowl containing cold water and use your fingers to peel off the thin skins.

TO PEEL CHILES

Turn on the cold water tap so that a thin stream of cold water is running out. Hold each *chile* under the running water and use your fingers to remove the charred skins. If parts of the skin stick to the *chile*, use a paring knife to remove them. Or you can dip the *chiles* in a medium-sized bowl full of water as needed to peel each *chile*. Do not let them soak or they will lose flavor.

TO REMOVE THE MEMBRANES AND SEEDS

Some sauces and other dishes use *chiles* with their seeds and membranes, but more often the seeds and membranes are removed because the heat of the *chile* is concentrated in them.

If the *chile* is to be used whole and stuffed, do not remove the stem and be careful not to break the skin while cleaning the *chile*. Use a small knife and carefully make a lateral incision in the *chile*; remove the placenta, which is the small cluster of seeds attached to the base of the stem; also remove the membranes that run the length of the *chile*. Gently rinse the *chile* to remove any seeds that are still adhering to it.

If the *chile* is to be cut into strips, cut a "lid" in the top part of the *chile*, by the stem, and remove. Make a lateral incision in the *chile*, pull open and remove the seeds and membranes. Rinse the *chile* and cut it into strips.

TO SOAK FRESH CHILES

Soaking *chiles* consists of submerging them in a mixture of 1 cup (8 fl oz/250 ml) water, 1 tablespoon white vinegar, and 2 teaspoons salt (double or triple the quantities depending on the number of *chiles*). The purpose of soaking is to remove excess piquancy. With experience, when you roast *chiles*, you will be able to tell from the odor given off how hot they are. If the *chiles* are too fiery, it may be necessary to let them soak for a little while; 40 minutes is usually long enough. After soaking, rinse the *chiles* briefly.

CHILES SECOS (DRIED CHILES)

The *chile ancho*, or "wide" *chile*, is the dried form of the *chile poblano* and is also commonly used, mainly as a base for sauces. It has a deep, reddish-brown, wrinkled skin and is about 5 inches long. It is on the mild side but does vary in hotness, with a bittersweet flavor and the definite aroma of prunes. The *chile mulato* is similar, but has a darker brownish-black color and a full, almost bitter taste. The long, narrow, wrinkled *chile pasilla* gets its name from the Spanish word for "raisin," and because of its rich very *picante* flavor it is used extensively in *moles,* sauces and as a garnish for soup. Fresh, it is the *chile chilaca*. The other commonly used dried *chile,* the *guajillo,* is long, thin and smooth-skinned, and it looks like its Spanish name, which means "old dried thing." After soaking and grinding, it is used to spice up various meals and stews. It is quite hot and has an uncomplicated *chile* taste. The tiny, very hot *chile pequín* or *piquín* is often ground. The *chile chipotle* is the light brown smoked *chile jalapeño,* which is usually canned in *adobo* sauce or in vinegar but is also found dried and smoked as is the similar *chile morita,* which is more triangular. Both have a very distinctive smoky smell and taste. The small, round *chile cascabel* sounds like a rattle when it is shaken. It adds a hot, nutty flavor to table *salsas*.

TO CLEAN DRIED CHILES
Wipe the skin of the *chile* with a damp cloth to remove any impurities. If the *chile* is going to be used whole and stuffed with a filling, leave the stem on. Make a small lateral incision in the *chile* so that you can remove the seeds and placenta, which is the cluster of seeds that adheres to the base of the stem. If you are not going to use the *chile* whole, cut a "lid" where the stem meets the base. Make a lateral incision, open the *chile* and remove the seeds and membranes.

Sometimes *chiles* are too dry, and when you try to remove the seeds and membranes, they break into small pieces. If that happens, toast and soak the *chiles* before cleaning them.

TO ROAST OR TOAST DRIED CHILES
Chiles are roasted or toasted so that they release their aroma and are easier to grind or purée in a blender. Heat a *comal* or iron skillet over medium heat. Place the *chiles* in the hot skillet, using a spatula to press them against it slightly. Turn them so that both sides begin to change color. This will take 1–2 minutes. Be careful not to burn them.

TO SOAK DRIED CHILES
Place the *chiles* in just enough lukewarm or hot water to cover for 5–10 minutes; this softens them and makes them regain body. Some recipes call for you to use the water in which the *chiles* were soaked. In other recipes you discard the soaking water and purée the *chiles* in fresh water.

TO FRY DRIED CHILES
Some recipes call for *chiles* to be fried instead of toasted. Heat a scant tablespoon of oil in a small skillet. Add the *chile* and fry lightly for a minute. If a crisper *chile* is desired, fry it over medium heat for 3–4 minutes, turning constantly so that it doesn't burn. *Chiles* fried this way are frequently used as garnishes, either whole or in pieces.

CHOCOLATE: A mixture of ground cacao, sugar, cinnamon and sometimes other flavorings pressed into various-sized tablets that are sold in Mexican grocery stores. It is made into a drink by adding liquid and whirling to a froth with a *molinillo,* a carved wooden implement twirled between the palms of the hands.

CHORIZO: This wonderfully fragrant sausage is made of sections of pig intestine stuffed with a seasoned ground pork mixture. Usually sold in links, it is more highly seasoned than Spanish *chorizo*. While quite good *chorizo* may be purchased at many meat markets, stay clear of the plastic-wrapped mixtures seen at some supermarkets. *Chorizo* must be cooked before eating. It is usually removed from its casings and crumbled. If not available, Polish kielbasa, Cajun smoked Andouille or similar spicy pork sausage could be substituted.

CILANTRO (Coriandrum sativum): Also known as coriander or Chinese parsley, this herb has a distinctive flavor that makes it indispensable in Mexican cooking. It is sold with its roots and should be stored in the refrigerator, standing in a glass of water and lightly covered with a plastic bag or wrap.

CINNAMON/*CANELA:* The light brown flaky bark of the true cinnamon tree *(Cinnamomum zeylanicum),* native to Ceylon (now Sri Lanka) and the Spice Islands, is the cinnamon found in Mexico. In the United States the darker and harder bark of *C. cassia* from Vietnam is commonly used.

COMAL: This thin unglazed clay or metal circular plate is placed over heat and used to cook or heat tortillas and other foods. A cast-iron skillet (frying pan) or griddle can be used.

COMIDA: The main meal of the day, the *comida* is usually served mid-afternoon and consists of many courses, typically soup, rice, a main dish, beans, dessert and coffee.

CORN/*MAÍZ:* The lifeblood of ancient Mexico, corn is still its basic food. Field corn is used, both dried and fresh, not the sweet corn prized in the United States.

CREAM: Sweet cream is available and usually whipped for desserts, but when recipes call for cream, it is usually a thick, slightly sour cream similar to *crème fraîche* that is wanted. To make, stir 2 tablespoons sour cream, buttermilk or plain yogurt into 1 cup heavy (double) cream, cover and let stand in a warm place until thickened (8–24 hours). Stir and refrigerate. It will keep for up to a week. The best flavor develops if allowed to age in the refrigerator for several days. Commercial sour cream is not a good substitute because of its lower butterfat content, which causes it to curdle when brought to a boil.

CUITLACOCHE: Often spelled *huitlacoche,* this fungus grows on ears of corn and is commonly used in central Mexico in soups, crêpes and other dishes. Although *cuitlacoche* has been considered a delicacy in Mexico for centuries, it is only now becoming sought after by chefs in the rest of the world. It is found wherever corn is grown but is usually destroyed. Fresh *cuitlacoche* is not generally available commercially outside Mexico, but most corn farmers will gladly give you their corn "smut." It is sometimes found canned in Latin American markets.

DESAYUNO: A light, early breakfast, usually *pan dulce* (sweet breads) with coffee or chocolate.

EPAZOTE (Chenopodium ambrosioides): This pungent annual herb, which may be indigenous to Mexico, has no substitute for its unusual flavor, which is almost a prerequisite in a pot of black beans. Although seldom available commercially outside Mexico, except in India, it is easily grown from seed and quickly self-propagates. Also known as goosefoot or wormseed, it is considered a weed in most other countries. Both seeds and plants are available from some specialty plant catalogs. It can be used dried, after the twigs are discarded, but the flavor is greatly diminished.

FLOR DE CALABAZA: The large male flower of certain varieties of hard-skinned squash or zucchini is lightly steamed for use in various dishes. They should be used the day they are picked. They can be found fresh in season at some greengrocers or canned in Latin American grocery stores.

FRIJOLES/BEANS: There are many varieties of dried beans grown in Mexico. The most common are the small black turtle beans of southeast Mexico and the Gulf coast; the fancifully named purple *flor de mayo* and the biscuit-colored *bayos* most often found in the central region; and the speckled *pinto,* the bean of choice in northern Mexico.

GUAVA/*GUAYABA:* The guava is a small, sweet, aromatic tropical fruit, usually pear shaped, with many small seeds. One variety has a large seed that looks like a prune. This fruit is often used to make *ates,* or fruit pastes.

HIERBA BUENA (Mentha spicata and other species): Also spelled *yerba buena,* this is mint, or literally "good herb."

HIERBA SANTA (Piper sanctum): Also called *hoya santa,* this large, soft-leaved herb has a strong anise flavor that is much prized in Oaxaca, Chiapas, Tabasco and Veracruz.

HOMINY/*CACAHUAZINTLE:* Dried corn kernels are cooked with powdered lime (calcium oxide) until the skins slip off and further simmered until they open up like a flower. Hominy is used in Mexico for *pozole* and some versions of *menudo* and other soups. Canned hominy can be used but does not have the same texture.

HUACHINANGO/RED SNAPPER: This magnificent Gulf coast fish is excellent cut into steaks and fillets. Those under 5 pounds are often prepared whole. On the Pacific a smaller, very red species is marketed. Both are quite plentiful and delicious.

JAMAICA: These small, dried, deep-red calyxes of the hibiscus flower *(Hibiscus sabdariffa)* are used to make a favorite drink, *agua de jamaica.* They will keep for one year if tightly covered and stored in a dry place. Outside Mexico you can find them in Latin American markets.

JÍCAMA: Indigenous to Mexico, this light brown bulbous tuber with a crisp ivory flesh (also known as a yam bean) is comparable to a water chestnut. It is usually eaten raw with a squirt of lime, a little salt and ground *chile.* It keeps a long time in the refrigerator if whole. It is generally available year-round in grocery stores.

LARD/*MANTECA DE CERDO:* The rendered fat of the pig is the traditional cooking fat of Mexico but is truly essential only in a few dishes. Lard has one-half the cholesterol of butter. It is important to use "real" lard, not the processed hydrogenated kind sold in most supermarkets. It is easy to render your own: Grind up small pieces of fat in a food processor, place in a roasting pan in a 250°F (130°C) oven until melted. Strain and store in the refrigerator.

LIME/*LIMA:* The common lime in Mexico is similar to the small Key lime, not the larger, sweeter, dark green Persian lime found in other parts of the world. The large yellow lemon is seldom found in Mexico.

LIME, SLAKE/*CAL:* White chunks of calcium oxide, sold in the markets, are moistened with water, causing them to "slake," or fizz. Dried corn kernels are then soaked in the liquid to help remove the tough outer coating before grinding to make *masa.*

MAGUEY *(Agave americana):* Commonly known as the century plant, because of the long time it takes to flower, the maguey is a very common plant in Mexico. One of the smaller species, *A. angustifolia,* is used to produce mescal, and a similar species, *A. tequilana,* is primarily cultivated in Jalisco for tequila production. *A. salmiana* is the major *pulque*-producing species. Other species are used for their fibers.

MAMEY: This large oval-shaped tropical fruit has a rich rose-peach flesh and brown leathery skin. It is usually eaten raw.

MANGO: This sweet, very flavorful and aromatic fruit from India comes in many varieties. All are a challenge to eat because not only are they extremely juicy, but they have a large flat pit that refuses to free itself from the pulp. They are best eaten peeled, with a fork or stick stuck in them like a lollipop.

MASA: This corn dough, made from treated ground field corn and water, can be purchased fresh or frozen from tortilla "factories" in major cities. It spoils quickly, so use within a day if fresh or thawed.

MASA HARINA: This dried corn flour, found in many supermarkets, can be used as an adequate alternative to fresh *masa.* It is not the same as cornmeal. The most common and reliable brand is Quaker.

MERIENDA: A light supper to tide one over the night after a full mid-day *comida.*

METATE Y MANO: These centuries-old implements made of basalt are used to grind corn, *chiles,* cacao and other ingredients. Traditional Indian cooks still kneel on the ground, rolling the cylindrical *mano* over the slanting three-legged table-like *metate.*

MOLCAJETE Y TEJOTE: A three-legged basalt mortar and pestle used to grind spices and ingredients for fresh *salsas.*

MOLINILLO: A carved wooden implement used to beat chocolate. Loose wooden rings on the top assist in making it frothy.

MOLE: A Náhuatl word describing a sauce or mixture containing *chile.* There are many variations, only a few containing chocolate.

NIXTAMAL: Dried corn boiled in lime water but not yet ground into *masa.*

NOPALES: The flat-jointed paddles of the prickly pear, or nopal cactus. They are prized for food, as are the juicy fruits. Fresh *nopales* are now found in Mexican markets, and the bottled or canned *nopalitos* are available in some specialty and Latin American stores in other parts of the world. Be careful when working with fresh whole *nopales,* as they have very sharp thorns that must be removed before cooking. It is best to wear gloves. Hold by the base and, with a very sharp knife, shave off the bumps that contain the thorns, but do not remove the entire outer skin. Cut off the thick base and trim the edges of the paddle. Rinse and cut into ½-in (1-cm) squares. Add a handful of green (spring) onion tops to a pot of boiling salted water, then add the *nopales.* Boil until tender, about 10 minutes. Drain and rinse thoroughly in cold water to remove the sticky substance that is released from the cactus.

OLLA: A large-necked clay pot with two handles used for cooking beans, stews, soups and similar dishes. It must be cured before using (see *Cazuela).*

ONION/*CEBOLLA:* The pungent white onion is most commonly used in Mexico. Small knob onions or large scallions, freshly dug with their green tops attached, are grilled and served with *tacos.* The purple onion is pickled or used as a garnish in the Yucatán and some Pacific states. Onions are usually roasted before using in *salsas* (see Roasting).

OREGANO: At least two different genera of plants are known as Mexican oregano—*Poliomentha longiflora* and *Lippia graveolens.* Neither is a true oregano, although *P. longiflora* is in the same mint family.

PAPAYA: This tropical fruit (also known as pawpaw) varies considerably in size, color and flavor, the most common being pear shaped and filled with shiny black seeds with a sweet musky taste. The milky juice of the plant has been used as a meat tenderizer since the time of the Maya civilization.

PARSLEY/*PEREJIL:* The more flavorful flat-leafed "Italian" parsley, not curly-leafed parsley, is almost always used in Mexico.

PEANUT/*CACAHUATE:* A member of the pea family, the peanut received its Mexican name from the Náhuatl language of the Aztecs. Although believed to have originated in Brazil, it has been used for centuries in Mexico as a snack, or ground and used for thickening and flavoring sauces.

PILONCILLO: Most commonly shaped into hard cones, *piloncillo* is unrefined sugar. It is grated or chopped for use. It can be found in most Latin American markets, or dark brown sugar may be substituted.

PIÑA: The pineapple, an indigenous tropical fruit, was first named by Spanish explorers who thought it looked like a pine cone (*apple* was a generic term for fruit). Mexico grows prodigious amounts of pineapple, especially in Veracruz.

PLANTAIN/*PLÁTANO:* This large, thick-skinned, three-sided banana is used extensively for cooking in the south. When green, it is cooked for a long time, but more often it is used black, sliced and fried. Raw plantains are never sweet, even when fully ripe.

RAJAS: Strips, usually of *chiles.*

RECADOS: These seasoning pastes are used primarily in the Yucatán and Central America. The best known contains a mixture of *achiote* and other herbs and spices. They are found prepared in small balls or oblong packages in Latin American markets or can be made at home (see recipe on page 121).

RICE/*ARROZ:* During the traditional main meal of the day, a dish of rice will usually be served as a *sopa seca* (dry soup) before the main course. The rice grown in Mexico is a medium-to long-grain variety that is only lightly milled and expands considerably while cooking, requiring more water than the rice of the United States, China and Australia. Unless using rice from Mexico, it is not necessary to rinse it first.

ROASTING: See *Chiles frescos* for instructions on roasting *chiles.* A similar technique (*asar*) is used to roast or grill onions, garlic and tomatoes.

    ONIONS/GARLIC: Cook on a *comal* or griddle over medium-high heat until outer layer is charred, turning as needed. The dried outer skin is usually removed first.
    TOMATOES: Place the tomatoes on a *comal* or griddle and grill until the skin is charred. Alternatively, put the tomatoes in a baking pan lined with foil and broil until skin is blackened, turning once.

*ROBALO/*SNOOK: A popular Gulf coast fish that is prepared like red snapper. A similar species is found in Pacific waters.

TAMAL: Masa mixed with lard, spread on corn husks or banana leaves, sometimes with a savory filling, then wrapped and steamed. There are a vast number of sizes, shapes and tastes of *tamales,* even sweet ones. They are usually served as a meal in themselves and usually on festive occasions. Any extras freeze very well and can be reheated by covering in foil and baking in a moderate oven (325°F/160°C) until thawed and heated through.

TAMARIND: The sweet and sour pulp of the seed pod of this magnificent tree from India is used to flavor a popular tart *agua fresca,* or fruit water.

TOMATO/*JITOMATE* or *TOMATE:* Both the common round and smaller pear-shaped tomatoes are used in Mexican cooking, but always sweet-ripe from the vine. When tomatoes are out of season, canned Italian plum tomatoes are a good substitute. For many *salsas* and dishes, the skin is charred and the flesh slightly cooked in order to enhance the flavor (see Roasting).

TOASTING: See *Chiles secos* for instructions on toasting *chiles.* A similar technique can be used for nuts, seeds and spices. Just toast them lightly on a hot *comal* or small cast-iron skillet until their fragrance is released. The seeds will pop, so be careful.

TOMATE VERDE: Also called *tomatillo* or *miltomate* in some regions, this is not a green tomato but a relative of the gooseberry, with a small fruit covered by a parchment-like calyx. An important ingredient in many Mexican dishes, it is now found in many supermarkets outside Mexico. It also is available canned.

TORTILLA: A thin round of ground dried corn made into dough (*masa*) and quickly cooked on a *comal.* It serves as the bread of Mexico—as a wrapper, an edible scoop and a plate. In Mexican villages it is common to see the tortillas "patted," or carefully shaped by hand, and cooked on an earthenware *comal.* Unfortunately, the necessities of daily life force city dwellers to eat tortillas from "tortilla factories," where the tortillas are made by machine and have a completely different flavor and texture than homemade. (To make your own tortillas, see the recipes on page 34.)
    Tortillas vary in color, from white to yellow. In the villages you can even find red or blue tortillas made from wild corn. In northern Mexico wheat-flour tortillas are common, but for most Mexicans, the word *tortilla* means a tortilla made with corn *masa.*

TORTILLA PRESS: Cast-iron tortilla presses are available in Mexican grocery stores and some specialty kitchen stores. Avoid purchasing the lighter aluminum ones. In Mexico, there are also presses made of wood.

VANILLA: This flavoring is obtained from the cured dried pods of a perennial orchid that twists and climbs its way to the tops of trees in the humid tropical forests of Veracruz. Each long, narrow, shriveled black pod contains thousands of very small seeds, the source of the flavor. Though whole pods are expensive, they can be washed off and reused many times. Because much of the liquid vanilla from Mexico contains a synthetic flavor that can be harmful in large amounts, it is banned in the United States. When bringing bottles back from Mexico, always make sure they contain pure vanilla extract.

VINEGAR: In Mexico vinegar is often made from sugar cane, pineapples, apples or bananas. Because commercial vinegars sold outside Mexico are much stronger, they may need to be diluted with up to an equal part of water.

ACKNOWLEDGMENTS

The authors and publishers would like to thank the following people and organizations for their assistance in the preparation of this book:

Alicia Gironella De' Angeli, Conchita Bajos, Ana Maria del Carmen Baca Barnard, Roberto Barnard, Sherrod Kane Blankner, Arturo Caballero, Cachis, Antonio Martinez Camacho, Familia Caraza, Martha Chapa, Susannah Clark, Juana Cruz, Landy de Figuerola, Yolanda Franco, Guadiana restaurant (Mexico City), Ruth Jacobson, Carole Jordan, Gwen Jordan, Diana Kennedy, Ed Lewis, Rosario Madero, Kay Mendieta, Alberto Miguel, Amy Morton, Sara Luisa García Sabaté de Naranjc, Adriana Bard de Palazuelos, Margot Rosenzweig de Palazuelos, Jacki Passmore, Familia Patiño, Post Art de México S.A. de C.V., Oso Proal, Rosa Ramírez, Rapid Lasergraphics (San Francisco), Carlota Rosas, Dr. Guadalupe Pérez San Vicente, Adelfa Silva, Veronica Sperling, Katherine Stimson, Fredric Tausend, La Taverna del León Restaurant (Valle de Bravo), Susanna and Elcisa Torres (Restaurant Susy, Puerto Angel, Oaxaca), Alta Gracia Aragon de Urbanek, Richard VanOosterhout, Virginia Vázquez, Therese de Veciana-Haddad, María Dolores Torres Yzábal, Socorrito Zorrilla

Recipe Testers: Janell Bartleson, Britt and Jerry Bell, Terry Brucker, Beth Calkins, Darcey Lee Clark, Virginia Lee Ellis, Doris M. Evans, Peg and Mike Fitzgerald, Mary Jo Heavey, David and Margaret Juenke, Jeanne MacDowell, Stephanie Messersmith, Lupe Ortiz, Velma J. Shearer, Theresa Taggart, Lesa von Mettenheim